CW00548296

Left Feminisms

Conversations on the Personal and Political

Praise for *Left Feminisms*

This inspiring collection of feminist voices across generations and continents reminds us that we build solidarity through, rather than in spite of, our differences.

Roshi Naidoo, Museums Association

Jo Littler's conversations over the last decade with fourteen feminist academics and activists of different generations, from Argentina to the US and the UK, collected here in *Left Feminisms*, abound with much-needed thoughts and hopes to help us live in these dark political times.

Catherine Hall, Chair of the Centre for the Study of the Legacies of British Slavery, UCL

Left Feminisms is a much-needed exploration and clarification of what a 'socialist feminist project' for the twenty-first century looks like. This is a project that looks at capitalist exploitation and sexist oppression as interrelated.

Sara R. Farris, author of *In the Name of Women's Rights: The Rise of Femonationalism*

This book not only brings together some of the most insightful 'left feminist' thinkers and activists of our time but Littler's interviews urge – and inspire – us to think beyond the destructive impasses and impulses of the present. A most timely and urgent contribution to contemporary feminist dialogues.

Catherine Rottenberg, author of *The Rise of Neoliberal Feminism*

This is a very fine collection of interviews, showcasing something of the strength and diversity of contemporary left feminisms. Littler is a particularly astute, perceptive and well-informed interlocutor, and her interviewees represent some of the most engaging and significant thinkers working on gender today. The text is a joy to read, and I highly recommend it.

Helen Hester, author of *Beyond Explicit: Pornography and the Displacement of Sex*

Alive on the page, we hear the humour and detail of entwined personal and political lives. The power of conversations draws readers into the multiple routes of feminist ideas. Layered dimensions of feminist academic lives are delivered through fine-tuned asking, listening and telling. It is a pleasure to unroll projects of enacting feminism/s differently whilst turning the pages of this collection.

Dr Nirmal Puwar, Reader in Sociology, Goldsmiths, University of London. Part of #WeAreGoldsmiths. Author of *Space Invaders: Race, Gender, and Bodies Out of Place*.

Left Feminisms

Conversations on the Personal and Political

Jo Littler

Lawrence Wishart
London 2023

Lawrence and Wishart Limited
Central Books Building
Freshwater Road
Chadwell Heath
RM8 1RX

Typesetting: e-type
Cover design: Isabel Lecaros
Printing: Imprint Digital

First published 2023
© Jo Littler 2023

This project was created in association with *Soundings: A Journal of Politics and Culture*, where the majority of these interviews were first printed.

British Library Cataloguing in Publication Data.
A catalogue record for this book is available from the British Library.

ISBN 978-1-913546-08-3
E-format ISBN: 978-1-913546-09-0

Contents

Speaking of feminism

This book brings together a series of interviews I have conducted with feminist academics on the left over the past decade. It features a spread of people, ranging from their twenties to their eighties, from political scientists to psychologists, from Bristol to Buenos Aires. All the interviewees have very different experiences, opinions and interests in relation to feminism. But they are all concerned, in some way or another, with relating gender to economic inequality; and they are all involved with political, creative or activist projects outside, as well as inside, universities.

As a project it has been a long time in the making. When I started doing interviews with academics in the mid 2000s they were not solely focused on feminism; many were about consumer culture and environmentalism.[1] But gradually it became clear to me that what I was increasingly doing was interviewing a lot of feminist academics on the left. In part this was because male academics already had enough airtime. It was also because of an obvious commonality – I was a left feminist academic! I was drawn to asking them what they did and why, to get them to summarise and contextualise their practice; to talk. Doing interviews with left feminist academics started to become a 'thing' I did.[2] I wanted to speak to people whose work, ideas and thinking I found enriching, or interesting, or important. I realised that by interviewing them I could ask questions about their work and their life beyond it – both about the text and besides the text. I could push at the areas that I wasn't sure about, ask them questions which interlinked their different work or ideas together. I could find out something of why they had written what they had and who they were; investigate what they were doing and why; contextualise their work; humanise abstract figures. I found this immensely satisfying. I have always been a bit of a frustrated journalist.

Such a mode of questioning also relates to that well-worn adage of second-wave feminism, 'the personal is political'. It is true that some of these interviews are much more 'personal' than others. But they all push towards gaining a sense of how these thinkers developed their concepts in specific historical conditions, and in a particular social and political context. I was able to do this because I was encouraged to publish the majority of these interviews in *Soundings*, a journal of politics and culture set up to act as a bridge between academic and public discussion. The journal's remit has been to interrogate the cultural and political power dynamics of the present, or the 'contemporary conjuncture'; to delve into the complexities of academic theory whilst trying to keep the prose as clear and accessible as possible.[3] This helped me to pursue a line of questioning that could focus on, first, translating academic feminist theories to a broader audience; second, to ask how these theories could be used to interpret what was going on *right now*; and third, to figure out what the personal and political context was in which they were generated.

The majority of these interviews, then, are with people who work as academics, although some are retired, and some publish academic writing whilst primarily working in institutions other than universities. The Italian theorist Antonio Gramsci once suggested there were two kinds of intellectuals: 'traditional intellectuals', those academics who produce abstract theory in universities; and 'organic intellectuals', those people whose ideas come from their own political and social contexts and which they use to shape political movements. Over the course of this project I have approached my interviewees in both senses, attempting in the process to better understand feminist theories, where they come from and how they swim in, and shape, the world. Whilst this book cannot be in any way comprehensive, and is necessarily partial in scope, it has become its own small kind of archive, and I hope it will also work to give a sense of some of the contours and complexities of feminism on the left. In what follows, I draw on the conversations in the book to sketch my own perspective on left feminism.

LEFT FEMINISMS NOW

Why do I use the term 'left feminisms' in this book? Put simply, I use it to indicate that these are all feminist discussions that come from the left: which understand capitalist exploitation and sexist oppression to be interrelated. I use it because in a time where the political right continues to entrench and extend itself, destroying the life chances of the majority, it is crucial to clearly distinguish feminism from this project. It is necessary to distinctly demarcate the vast and creative work of left feminisms from that of right-wing neoliberal feminism, which has soared into ascendancy over the past decades: which tell us we just have to lean in, and pull ourselves up the ladder, while elbowing others out of the way and trampling on them in the process.[4] I also use the term left feminisms to connect together a wide range of different strands of feminism across the left, which is necessary if we are to move, as the title of one well-known book put it back in 1979, 'beyond the fragments'. And I use it because of the rise of left feminism over the past decade, of its rebirth and re-ascendancy, even while today it is often so fractious and divided.

For after several decades of being trampled upon, pushed aside and discredited by neoliberal capitalism, left feminism is being reinvented again. These strands of reinvention can be seen in the widespread lambasting and unpopularity of neoliberal feminism; in the pivotal role of women like Ada Colau in the new municipalism; in the popular charge of Alexandria Ocasio-Cortez and 'the squad' of US democratic socialists; in the revival of interest in radical collective and left feminist histories; in the global grassroots action of the Women's Strike; in the renewed anger at gendered pay gaps; through the joint actions against violence against women and neoliberal debt in #NiUnaMenos; in the surge of women becoming involved in the trade union movement; and in the reemergence of struggles for childcare.

This resurgence of left feminism is in no small part due to a backlash against the savage effects of neoliberal capitalism, which has deepened gender inequalities, particularly at the intersections of class, 'race' and disability. As Akwugo Emejulu says in her interview, 'That's why so many activists and academics are working on feminism for the 99 per cent' (p44). For in the 1980s we saw 'the astonishing resurrection of liberal free-market ideas that everyone had assumed were in the dustbin of history forever', as Nancy Fraser puts it (p29). The strengthening of capitalism involved its rehabilitation by 'left' political parties and across the public and third sector. As Emejulu so succinctly outlines, the idea that 'somehow capitalism could be harnessed in such a way that it could be turned on its head, in a kind of jujitsu move, and then "save" the communities it immiserated, was patently ridiculous', and involved what she so accurately describes as 'a fundamental defeat of the left' (p41).

There is now widespread critique of both neoliberalism and neoliberal feminism, of its encouragement of the commodification and marketisation of all aspects of life, and its logic of hyper-individualism.[5] Such critique permeates these pages. Lynne Segal speaks of 'the ubiquitous neoliberal rationality, endorsing only endless competitiveness', arguing instead that 'we need to hold on to alternative ways of connecting with each other' (p106). Gargi Bhattacharyya talks of how in this period, capital has remade itself 'along the lines of pre-existing racial divisions, and concoct[ed] *new* racialised divisions', by 'piggy-backing on social reproduction' (p206). For instance, globalised labour chains mean new flows of migrant women working in the exploited, low-paid service and 'care' sectors, in cleaning and nursing jobs or as au pairs, draining resources of care from the global south to the global north in the process. Neoliberalism's 'wide repertoire of dividing practices', as Angela McRobbie says, involves social scapegoating and cultural castigation, marking out allegedly 'good' and 'bad' mothers and workers (p184). Nancy Fraser outlines how the 'ideal-type' gender model offered up by neoliberalism has been the dual-income household, which 'seeks to allow privileged women to lead lives that are socially male, while abandoning other women'; masking the labour of poor and migrant women that is required to sustain those 'socially male' lives (p27).

The strength of these combined analyses is indicative of how neoliberalism – the formation of capitalism which rose to power from the late 1970s, privatising as much as it could of life along the way – has now become so extensively and effectively critiqued. Since the financial crash of 2008, Nancy Fraser points out, the landscape has shifted and there is now room for more argument and mobilisation. For example, in her interview, Verónica Gago describes the eruption of massive protests and national strikes against both male violence and the social violence of neoliberal exploitation across Argentina, Chile, Uruguay and Brazil. This was a gradual building of a 'feminism of the masses', she says: we 'thought, "Well, we want ourselves alive; but we also want ourselves to be debt-free"' (p77). In the US, the #MeToo movement began with Tarana Burke in the Bronx working against male violence and racial and economic injustice. And in the UK, Sisters Uncut have spectacularly lobbied against government 'austerity' cuts to domestic violence support services and for abolitionist feminism.

Yet over the past decade there has also been a surge in right-wing populisms, disaster capitalism, financialisation, a hardening of borders and increasing xenophobia. For some theorists this marks a break with the neoliberal era of capitalism and signals its movement into a different configuration; for others it indicates its mutation into what Wendy Brown terms 'neoliberal nationalism'. Whatever we term it, this configuration of capitalism has often been accompanied by the rolling back of feminist gains, including of reproductive rights (such as the US repeal of abortion laws) and of LGBT+ rights (most notably in Poland and Hungary). As Sophia Siddiqui points out, the far right has been 'mobilising through anti-feminist measures'; and 'gender and sexual politics is absolutely key to how the far right operate' (pp249-250). This has involved 'attacks on LGBT+ rights, and trans people's rights too, and [sits] along-side an anti-migrant and Islamophobic agenda' (p250). Siddiqui's concept of 'reproductive racism' is used to explain the contempo-rary fusion of racism and right-wing politics: in which some women (mainly white Europeans) are positioned as breeders, encouraged by pro-natal anti-abortion policies, whereas others (mainly migrant women or those from the former Soviet bloc) are positioned either as threats or as a cheap labour supply for care work. The rise of the new right has also involved a shift in gendered leadership, and as Vron Ware points out, 'some of the successful far-right parties across Europe and elsewhere are actually led by white women' (p149). As I write this introduction in 2022, Italy has just elected its first truly far-right leader since the Second World War, and its first female prime minister, Georgia Meloni. It shows how, in Ware's words, 'feminism itself can be instrumentalised by the far right' (p150).[6]

Amidst these swirling political currents are other major issues, not least the intensification of extreme weather events and the Covid-19 pandemic. Climate crisis, as Gargi Bhattacharya puts it, is 'something cataclysmic that we're living through', with a key difference between the racialised, economic and gendered exploitations of capitalism in the past being that we are now in a 'world on fire' (p206). Vron Ware carefully discusses how the exploitations of land are connected to a range of sedimented histories and geographies; Verónica Gago points to how 'the question of *extractivism* is the main issue' for feminists in Latin America, rather than 'eco-feminism' (p85). Then there has been the global pandemic. Sylvia Walby talks about the 'classed, gendered and racialised' dimensions of the Covid crisis': in how Covid was gendered; what a feminist political economy of Covid would look like; and how public health interventions so often ignored the domestic relations of care (p221). Angela McRobbie shares her own experience of being hospitalised, with the people who cared for her being 'amongst the most over-looked and poorly recompensed occupations', receiving neither the recognition nor renumeration they deserved (p182). Since then we have seen more 'care gratitude', but not 'care justice' with the manipulation of the context of Covid and the language of care to inflate profits for the superrich.[7]

This section has sketched very briefly how the problematic present, the conjuncture, is gendered; even though the form this takes will depend on the particular 'gender regime' of the country as well as geographical and demographic location.[8]

LEFT FEMINIST SOLUTIONS

What solutions are provided by left feminists? There are some recurring features that are worth highlighting here. First, left feminisms of all stripes propose ending economic exploitation, and ending or at the very least vastly curtailing economic inequality, which necessarily involves large-scale redistribution. In so doing they have been concerned not only with the exploitation bound up in paid labour but also with domestic inequalities: with thinking about both those things together, through focusing on what is called 'social reproduction'. In Marxist feminist vocabulary, the free labour of housework and childrearing has been what capitalism has relied upon to reproduce itself.[9] Looking at social reproduction in its most capacious sense – in the role of housewives, nannies, maids, cleaners, grandparents, au pairs – means that left feminism necessarily should be always-already international and anti-racist, as Gargi Bhattacharyya shows.[10]

Second, left feminism often has an emphasis on prefigurative politics, on experimenting today to create the change you want to see in the world: to try to practice a more equal and decentralised politics in the present, rather than *only* putting all your eggs in the political basket of planning for future change (crucial though these different strategic horizons also are). While there are markedly different perspectives and strategies on this issue in this book, prefigurative politics remain a recurrent feature. This is, for example, manifest in the 1970s experiments in producing collective nurseries that were then scaled up to municipal and national forms of childcare, as Hilary Wainwright discusses.

Third, left feminism has always challenged narrow, sectarian identity politics through its insistence that we are collective subjects and relational beings: that it's not possible to live in isolation. As Sheila Rowbotham says, 'people are more than one category of oppression, and we all develop our ideas and attitudes in relation to others.'[11] Gender inequalities, left feminists understand, are systemic, not simply the unfortunate product of a few bad apples. This means, as Sylvia Walby memorably puts it, that 'feminism is a project', not an identity (p214). Contemporary market-oriented societies relentlessly incite us to think of ourselves as atomised individuals who should constantly brand the self and primarily compete, rather than cooperate, with each other. Left feminism works against these lonely and divisive ways of being. It is not always easy, as compulsory individualism suffuses our social and psychological landscapes – even, as adrienne maree brown's work shows so powerfully, affecting social movements through call-out cultures and the instantaneous condemnation of individuals, which brown's focus on 'transformative justice' provides a persuasive remedy to.[12]

Fourth, many new manifestations of left feminism are notably and deliberately intersectional.[13] In this they are not new: my interviews with second-wave feminists make it clear how much of their activity was always consciously internationalist and attentive to what would now be called intersectional difference (unlike many of its neoliberal, lean-in variants). But in the current conjuncture there are different forms of intersectionality, and there is a new emphasis on non-binary, queer and trans rights, and on disability, alongside a new configuration of gendered geographies in a changed global terrain. In the last interview in this book, Sophia Siddiqui discusses intersectionality's many prehistories (such as 'triple oppression') and its effectiveness in legal contexts. She emphasises the importance of pushing the theory further, to understand intersectional dynamics in relation to the particular historical moment and its capitalist dynamics.

The people I interview propose a vast array of solutions to these contemporary problems both abstract and specific, and across different scales and sectors. The interviewees vary in terms of their politics, their involvements with different movements or activity, and in type, scale or approach. As Akwugo Emejulu says in her interview,

> Not everyone wants to be a politician or engage in the bureaucratic behaviour of parliamentary politics. That's fine. But you do need people there. And you need people there to have a conversation and dialogue with, in order to move and influence them. Parliamentary politics isn't a space for everyone – just as being out on the streets isn't a space for everyone. We need people in research, we need people in policy spaces, we need people in lots of *different* kinds of spaces and places in order to take back power (p43).

Many are involved in different forms of engagement with left feminist politics, from 'gender mainstreaming' to direct action. Sylvia Walby highlights how 'unions are one of the most important organisations in the contemporary world pushing for gender equality' as part of 'a coalition of civil societal forces', even whilst a very narrow definition of feminism might ignore them as actors (p215). She argues that gender mainstreaming is about more than policy: 'It's a way of thinking about the relationship between radical politics and the mainstream' (p216). Meanwhile, Verónica Gago talks about building a protest movement in the streets and internationalising it across Latin America and beyond. Hilary Wainwright discusses the role of women in parliamentary and local politics; Akwugo Emejulu talks of the need to stop fetishizing specific forms of (young, white, social media-friendly) direct action and instead have a broader conception of activism, one which, for example, recognises everyday actions in communities or playgrounds.

A diversity of approaches to spaces for intervention appear in the book and I would argue that such diversity is necessary. Equally, running through the interviews are numerous left feminist concepts and ideas, at multiple scales, both abstract and specific. Angela McRobbie, analysing the shredding of the 'social wage' – or the provisions which lessen the cost of living, whether libraries, student fees or after-school care – envisages 'a new social imaginary which delivers universal entitlements in and out of work and for future generations': we need to 'reverse, repair, and to offer reparation to those sectors of the population that have been excluded from what were deemed "universal" provisions' (p185). Environment and climate crisis is high on the agenda.[14] Vron Ware talks about her involvement in feminism and environmentalism and the 'rapid convergence between anti-militarists and climate change activists' happening today (p148). Hilary Wainwright outlines her experience in feminist activism, local government and public procurement, and in the transition from industrial manufacturing to environmentally friendly production, discussing how they can be brought together. Verónica Gago and Sophia Siddiqui emphasise the importance of indigenous and anti-extractivist struggles.

Alongside the conversations on bread there are discussions of roses – or creativity, pleasure. Lynne Segal talks about collective joy. Sheila Rowbotham talks memorably of her relationships, noting wryly that 'each new generation thinks it has discovered sexual ecstasy for the first time' (p60). Carol Tulloch talks about the aesthetic feelings of her exhibitions about Black hair, suffragettes, Rock Against Racism and housework, displayed inside both national galleries and in small shops and suburbs. Vron Ware discusses her photography, of how 'what's important for me is the moment of taking it, or feeling joy at seeing the light on water, or naked branches against the sky' (p156).

FEMINIST FAULTLINES

Of course, not all left feminist perspectives agree – as they never will – and sometimes it can be their kaleidoscopic difference that makes them interesting. There are many 'feminist faultlines', to borrow Finn Mackay's phrase, in feminism and in left feminism, sometimes with useful and productive cultures of discussion and debate around them; sometimes not. Faultlines can be seen in the different kinds of terminology people are comfortable with or want to adopt. For instance, Carol Tulloch talks here about being more of a womanist than a feminist, following Alice Walker, who wrote about the association of mainstream feminism with white women.[15] Some of my interviewees explicitly refer to themselves as socialist feminists, but others do not, or reject that category. For instance, Finn Mackay self-locates in the tradition of radical feminism rather than socialist feminism, primarily due to radical feminism's focus on male violence against women and on liberation, yet Finn also identifies as a socialist.

The tradition of socialist feminism is obviously crucial in left feminism, and is itself broad and plural.[16] But equally and unsurprisingly there are issues there as well. In 1976 in her influential article 'What is socialist feminism?' Barbara Ehrenreich wrote that

> The problem is most socialist feminists I know are not too happy with the term 'socialist feminist' either. On the one hand it is too long (I have no hopes for a hyphenated mass movement); on the other hand it is much too short for what is, after all, really socialist internationalist anti-racist, anti-heterosexist feminism.[17]

In these terms 'socialist feminism' doesn't say enough. At other times it may say too much. In 2015 Alison Winch and I organised a seminar called 'Feminism and the S-Word' in London to debate the pasts and presents of socialist feminism.[18] The term had been used by Nira Yuval-Davis – a speaker at the seminar – which, as she had pointed out was often a subject which was there in the 1990s and beyond, but which could not be spoken aloud: the elephant in the room. After the advent of neoliberalism, the 'S-word' – like, indeed, 'class' – became decreasingly socially acceptable, increasingly politically powerless, deeply unfashionable and often marked through association with dodgy sectarian groups. Socialism, while central to the socialised forms of the welfare state – including education, pensions, libraries, childcare and the NHS – was discursively positioned as an 'ideological' term outside the centre. Whilst the S-word seminar was reassuringly packed and intergenerational, marking perhaps an early rehabilitation of the term, such coyness about 'the S-word' is today no longer necessary. The word 'socialism' is now being used with far more regularity. According to a 2018 Gallup poll[19] over half of US millennials prefer socialism to capitalism and membership of the Democratic Socialists of America is soaring. Such a shifting politics is also apparent in academic contexts. In the early 2000s, if you gave an academic paper in the UK on neoliberalism at a humanities or social science conference, you were often regarded askance, suspected of being part of an authoritarian vanguardist group.[20] Today, papers on neoliberal culture and feminism are thoroughly mainstream.

Yet as Nancy Fraser put it when I interviewed her in 2014, 'I don't feel that, for whatever reason, the word socialism absolutely *must* be at the centre of things. If we can find another term that has more capacity to mobilise people, I'm interested' (p36). Left feminism needs to appeal to a broad base of interests and support to expand and become more powerful than right-wing politics. While I am more than happy to identify as a socialist feminist, for instance, I also understand how for particular historical reasons the term 'socialist feminism' may have too much baggage for other people. In this book I therefore use the category of 'left feminisms' in a fairly broad and inclusive way.

Historically, divisions and faultlines in left feminism, like feminism more broadly, have included disagreements and battles over pornography (whether it's always patriarchal or can be non-sexist) and sex work (whether and how it should be regulated, who is being scapegoated, the role of puritanism and moral castigation). Within left feminism there are also differences of opinion over the extent of economic redistribution – from communism to social democracy – and the meanings and role of 'economic growth' (for example, from degrowth to a social democratic 'gendered growth' strategy). There are also divisions around the role of the state: ranging from an insistence on the importance or necessity of using the state to provide universal services through to, at other end, a more anarchist/grassroots bottom-up politics which bypasses the state; to stances which try to marry both perspectives (brilliantly encapsulated by the title of the book *In and Against the State)*. A wide range of these perspectives are discussed in these interviews, although inevitably much is missing, given the scope of the topic.

One key faultline that has intensified in recent years has been 'the gender wars', encompassing a rejection of gender theory and virulent debates over trans politics.

As Sophia Siddiqui points out, the anti-gender movement and the rolling back of LGBT+ rights has been very deliberately fermented by the far right and new right. Verónica Gago discusses how the #NiUnaMenos movement was deliberately built as trans inclusive; and how it attempted to construct a 'transversal' politics of shared interests across difference. Gargi Bhattacharyya discusses how this right-wing polarisation has particularly consumed British feminism, and is part of the wider culture wars, interconnected by 'the logic of a zero-sum game' (p195).

In this book, Finn Mackay discusses these issues extensively, arguing that the gender wars are part of the broader culture wars, and an attempt to 'future-proof power by elites' (p235). They also offer an extremely useful discussion of the complex histories leading to the present 'gender wars', and a nuanced sense of its present; arguing that the idea that there are simply two opposing sides adopts militaristic language. Discussing their work in the violence against women and girls sector, as well as in 'creating social spaces for butch and femme lesbians, transgender and trans-masculine identified people', Finn states that there aren't simply 'two discrete and warring camps. I know that they overlap, and I know that not least because I've been involved in both myself at the same time' (p236). They argue that we need to talk about complex and controversial issues, and areas of uncertainty, with care and nuance, otherwise the conservatives and the right will talk for us.

There are then many types of what Róisín Ryan-Flood et al term 'difficult conversations' being broached and referenced in the book.[21] There are many people engaged in the necessary labour of looking for commonalities and working with and across difference.

There are always lines of disagreement in feminism and left politics, and these take particular forms. Angela McRobbie comments on how 'as I get older I really want to walk away from this angry way of doing politics – which of course is intensified with social media, especially via Twitter. I feel the kind of mud-slinging we are exposed to obfuscates the issues, and does not allow us the time and space to rehearse what is really going on' (p186).

CRITICAL DIALOGUES

My hope is that this book will be a resource for thinking through some of the developments and difficulties, promise and potential of feminism and left politics and will be an accessible way into understanding different strands of theory and practice. What has evolved as the main purpose of these interviews is to distil the core theories and intellectual ideas of the thinkers being interviewed; to illuminate the relationship between their work and their activism (their 'praxis'); and to discuss how their life and social context has shaped what they do.

'What they do' is engage in activity both inside and outside the university; working across these domains or spheres is a recurring characteristic. (Verónica Gago, for instance, reflects on how 'struggles are always the material space where we can think better' p89). There is also a fair amount on the university and its discontents. Lynne Segal writes of how she started at Enfield College of Technology 'and stayed there for thirty years, since that job gave me time and space for my engagements as a feminist and community activist' (p120).[22] It is hard to imagine anyone saying that in today's precarious and overworked academic context. As Sheila Rowbotham puts it, 'The conditions were much nicer when I first went' (p70). Notoriously, the university Rowbotham was working in tried to get rid of her but bowed to pressure after an international campaign. Such combined ageism and sexism is not a phenomena unique to that particular university. The marketisation of higher education has caused multiple problems: widespread precarity, destructively corporate cultures, a mental health crisis, atomisation.[23] The problematic institutionalisation of feminism is also discussed here; Gargi Bhattacharyya, for instance, spoke of not organising under the banner of feminism any more, even whilst writing about it, as feminism was 'actively rushed into being institutionally incorporated in quite dodgy ways' (p199). Akwugo Emejulu has a memorable recommendation for all academics: don't be 'an asshole' (p53). We talked about the whiteness of the institutions: when I interviewed Akwugo, she was one of twenty-four Black female professors in the UK out of 19,000 professors nationwide, 14,000 of whom are men. Carol Tulloch spoke of the experience of being in 'Phenomenal Women: Portraits of UK Black Female Professors' on the Southbank, imposter syndrome and the happiness of meeting and sharing experiences with other participants.

As oral history interviews, they provide a resource for understanding what happened in different strands of the past, whether second-wave feminist consciousness-raising groups, the difficult years of so-called third-wave feminism or accounts of lived experience (like Carol Tulloch's vivid descriptions of growing up in the North of England, the role of women and the everyday, convivial multiculturalisms of mixed working-class life, and Nancy Fraser's account of growing up in racially segregated Baltimore). They indicate the marked revival of interest in radical collective and left feminist histories, from the striking women of Grunwick to the Combahee River Collective, from the legacies of Rosa Luxemburg to the Brixton Black Women's Group and second-wave consciousness-raising.[24] As Sophia Siddiqui discusses here, classic books like Amrit Wilson's 1978 work on British Asian feminism, *Finding a Voice* and Beverly Bryan, Stella Dadzie and Suzanne Scafe's 1985 *The Heart of the Race* have become 'catalysts for the following generations'.[25] These histories are being resurrected to provide resources for the present, but there is still a long way to go (I hope someone takes up Sophia Siddiqui's suggestion to make a film about the London based-group OWAAD, the Organization of Women of African and Asian Descent).

These chapters are also conversations, or as John Clarke puts it in the title of his interview book, 'critical dialogues', because 'we are all dialogic subjects, who think, reason, reflect and argue as a fundamental condition of our sociality'.[26] Over the course of the decade I have been doing this project, podcast interviews have become a lot more popular, and the technology and platform potential for producing them has rapidly developed. There were times when I wondered whether I should just be doing that instead – and I hope other people do because, despite the audio boom, there is a dearth of feminist podcasters around. But many of us still want to read words, whether on paper or screen. And so I think there is a place for the written interview form, for reading the stream of edited consciousness – more fluid than many academic books, easier to dip into, perhaps, or at least a different mode of engagement, a different 'reading-feeling'. It is conversational, and dialogic – at least I think so, and I hope you might too. I am remembering, for example, how I much I have got out of reading interview books, particularly the Virago book from three decades ago, *Once a Feminist* (1990), and more recently, the wonderful collection *Revolutionary Feminisms* (2020).[27]

FROM BACKBURNER TO LABOUR OF LOVE

This book started off as something I was putting together on the side, a slice of extremely slow academia that was my ongoing backburner project while we were incited to rush everything else into paper and digital form. At different times it has been both easy and difficult to produce. It has been a joy to talk to people – to academics, to feminists, to those on the left – about issues and difficulties and histories. It has been time-consuming; there are many different ways to present interviews, from presenting them verbatim, complete with all what linguists call 'phatic' (the ums and errs) and no punctuation. I generally spent a lot of time on editing as I wanted them to be accessible and engaging reads. I always shared the interview with the interviewee, who would typically add bits for clarification or remove parts they didn't like. Some interviews had very light editing, others extremely extensive – especially if we had gone on talking past the hour and the ten questions I had usually scheduled for (on some occasions it went to double or treble the length). Publishing some in *Soundings* and others later on in *European Journal of Cultural Studies* meant keeping them to a particular word length and so many had multiple rounds of winnowing. Sally Davison and Jilly Kay from these journals offered numerous useful suggestions along the way.

There was a stage early on when it seemed that in part what I was doing – what the book's unofficial title might have been – was, to put it very crassly, *Talking To People Before They Die*. I failed on many occasions to do even *this*, of course, given that wonderful people die all the time. (Looking back at the early plans for this book, I am reminded that I really wanted to interview bell hooks and Barbara Ehrenreich.) At one point Doreen Massey, who I was used to talking to fairly regularly, suddenly died and I wished I had asked her far more questions.[28] This galvanised me into doing more, and the left feminist academic interview project grew. Then, as the project expanded further, I found myself interviewing people of a similar age and eventually younger than myself. The interviews took place in public spaces, in hotel lobbies, in homes; then increasingly, as the pandemic hit, online. There were people I wanted to interview but couldn't. Putting the collection together generated a whole other set of issues about representativeness (and anxieties about all the friends and strangers I will inevitably have offended by not asking them to be interviewed). If I had the time I would like to carry on, interviewing across a wider range of countries, on a wider range of themes. But that is another conversation.

NOTES

1 For example, 'Consumers: agents of change? Interview with Kate Soper and Clive Barnett', *Soundings*, Issue 31, 2005, pp147-160; and 'Tackling Turbo Consumption: An Interview with Juliet Schor', *Soundings,* Issue 34, 2006. Alison Winch and I also conducted a roundtable session on childcare, published as Jo Littler and Alison Winch, 'Feminism and Childcare: A Roundtable with Sara de Benedictis, Gideon Burrows, Tracey Jensen, Jill Rutter and Victoria Showunmi', *Studies in the Maternal,* Vol. 8, No. 1, 2016, p2, available at: www.mamsie.bbk.ac.uk/article/id/4248.

2 In this book I interview women and non-binary people. Yes, male academics can be feminists too.

3 *Soundings* was set up by Doreen Massey, Stuart Hall and Michael Rustin in 1995. See www.journals.lwbooks.co.uk/soundings. I discuss the meaning of the term 'conjuncture' and its uses at length in Jo Littler, 'Consumer culture and cultural studies' in Deirdre Shaw et al

(ed), *Ethics and Morality in Consumption: Interdisciplinary Perspectives,* Routledge, 2016.

4 There is considerable debate amongst left feminists about how exactly the detrimental effects of neoliberalism on gender equality should be conceptualised. Some embrace the term 'neoliberal feminism' as a useful critical term; others think that this dynamic cannot, and should not, be called 'feminism' at all, as neoliberalism is antithetical to struggles for gender equality and liberation.

5 This was a constant theme of all bell hooks's writings; for example, bell hooks, *Feminism is for everybody,* Pluto Press, 2000. See also Catherine Rottenberg, *The Rise of Neoliberal Feminism,* Oxford University Press, 2018; Rosalind Gill, Sarah Banet-Weiser and Catherine Rottenberg, 'Postfeminism, popular feminism and neoliberal feminism? Sarah Banet-Weiser, Rosalind Gill and Catherine Rottenberg in conversation', *Feminist Theory,* Vol. 21, No. 1, pp3-24.

6 See also Sara Farris and Catherine Rottenberg, 'Righting Feminism', *New Formations,* Vol. 91, 2017, pp5-15; Alison Phipps, Chapter 1, 'Gender in a right-moving world' in *Me, Not You,* Manchester University Press, 2020; Mieke Verloo (ed), *Varieties of Opposition to Gender Equality in Europe,* Routledge, 2018.

7 See Beverley Skeggs and Helen Wood, 'Clap for Carers? From Care gratitude to care justice', *European Journal of Cultural Studies,* Vol. 23, No. 4, pp641-647; The Care Collective, *The Care Manifesto: The Politics of Interdependence,* Verso, 2020; Andreas Chatzidakis and Jo Littler, 'An anatomy of carewashing: corporate branding and the commodification of care during Covid-19', *International Journal of Cultural Studies,* Vol. 25, Nos. 3-4, 2022, pp268-286.

8 See Sylvia Walby, 'Varieties of gender regimes', *Social Politics,* Vol. 27, No. 3, 2020, pp414-431.

9 See Tithi Bhattacharya, *Social Reproduction Theory: Remapping Class, Recentering Oppression,* Pluto Press, 2017.

10 See also Angela Davis, *Women, Race and Class,* Random House, 1981; Maria Mies, *Patriarchy and Accumulation on a Global Scale: Women in the International Division of Labour,* Zed Books, 1999.

11 Sheila Rowbotham in Sheila Rowbotham, Lynne Segal and Hilary Wainwright, *Beyond the Fragments: Femininism and the Remaking of Socialism,* Merlin Press, 1979.

12 adrienne maree brown, *We Will Not Cancel Us,* AK Press, 2020.

13 Intersectionality was a term first used by Kimberlé Crenshaw in 'Demarginalizing the Intersection of Race and Sex: A Black Feminist Critique of Antidiscrimination Doctrine, Feminist Theory and Antiracist Politics', *University of Chicago Legal Forum,* Vol. 1, No. 8,

1989, pp139-167. For discussions on the term, see Patricia Hill Collins and Sirma Bilge, *Intersectionality*, Polity, 2020.

14 For an influential left feminist take on the topic, see Maria Mies and Vandana Shiva, *Ecofeminism*, Zed Books, 1993; for a recent work exploring relationships between gender, technology and environments see Helen Hester, *Xenofeminism*, Polity, 2018.

15 Alice Walker, *In Search of Our Mothers' Gardens: Womanist Prose*, Harcourt Brace, 1983. See also Françoise Vergès, *A Decolonial Feminism*, Pluto Press, 2021.

16 See for instance Chapter 3 of Lynne Segal, *Lean on Me* (Verso, forthcoming) for a summary of the histories of socialist feminism. There are many interesting transnational histories; for instance, Claudia Jones was deported from the US in 1956 because she was a communist, came to the UK and set up the first Caribbean carnival in Britain; British suffragette Sylvia Pankhurst was an anti-colonialist who moved to Ethiopia, also in 1956. See Rachel Holmes, *Sylvia Pankhurst: Natural Born Rebel*, Bloomsbury, 2020; Marika Sherwood, *Claudia Jones: A Life in Exile*, Lawrence Wishart, 2021.

17 Barbara Ehrenreich, 'What is Socialist Feminism?' *Working Papers on Socialism and Feminism*, The New American Movement, 1976.

18 Deborah Grayson, Jo Littler, Mandy Merck, Nira Yuval-Davis and Hilary Wainwright, 'Feminism and the S Word: A roundtable', *Soundings,* Issue 61, 2015, pp95-112.

19 www.news.gallup.com/poll/240725/democrats-positive-socialism-capitalism.aspx

20 Like the Socialist Workers' Party (SWP), now depopulated after multiple rape allegations and accusations of having profoundly patriarchal structures.

21 Róisín Ryan-Flood et al (eds), *Difficult Conversations: Feminist Dialogues*, Routledge: London, 2023.

22 This later became Middlesex University.

23 See for example Rosalind Gill, 'Breaking the silence: the hidden injuries of neoliberal academia' in Róisín Ryan-Flood and Rosalind Gill (eds), *Secrecy and Silence in the Research Process: Feminist Reflections*, Routledge, 2009; Sarah Burton and Benjamin Bowman, 'The academic precariat: understanding life and labour in the neoliberal academy', *British Journal of Education*, Vol. 43, No. 4, pp497-512.

24 See for instance Keeanga-Yamahtta Taylor (ed), *How We Get Free: Black Feminism and the Combahee River Collective*, Haymarket, 2017; Sundari Anitha and Ruth Pearson, *Striking Women: Struggles and Strategies of South Asian Women Workers from Grunwick to Gate Gourmet*, Lawrence Wishart, 2018; Lola Olufemi, *Feminism,*

Interrupted: Disrupting Power, Pluto, 2020.

25 Sophia Siddiqui, 'Anti-racist feminism: engaging with the past' in *Race & Class*, Vol. 61, No. 2, pp96-104. Both books were reissued in 2018. Amrit Wilson, *Finding a Voice: Asian Women in Britain*, Daraja Press, 2018; Beverly Bryan, Stella Dadzie and Suzanne Scafe, *The Heart of the Race: Black Women's Lives in Britain*, Verso, 2018.

26 John Clarke, *Critical Dialogues: Thinking Together in Turbulent Times*, Policy Press, 2019.

27 Michelene Wandor, *Once a Feminist*, Virago, 1990; Brenna Bhandar and Rafeef Ziadah (ed), *Revolutionary Feminisms*, Verso, 2020; and Fiona Jeffries (ed), *Nothing to Lose But Our Fear: Resistance in Dangerous Times*, BTS Books, 2020. Thanks to Kirsten Forkert for sharing her copy of this book with me.

28 See David Featherstone and Diarmaid Kelliher (eds), *Doreen Massey: Selected Political Writings*, Lawrence Wishart, 2022. John Clarke also writes movingly in his book of interviews, *Critical Dialogues*, about the 'missing voices' in the text.

The fortunes of
socialist feminism

Nancy Fraser is Professor of Political and Social Science at the New School, New York, US. She has written widely on political philosophy, critical theory and feminism. Her books include *Cannibal Capitalism: How our System is Destroying Democracy, Care, and the Planet – and What We Can Do about It* (Verso, 2022); *Feminism for the 99%: A Manifesto* (Verso, 2019), co-authored with Cinzia Arruzza and Tithi Bhattacharya; *Fortunes of Feminism: From State-Managed Capitalism to Neoliberal Crisis* (Verso, 2013); *Scales of Justice: Reimagining Political Space in a Globalising World* (Polity, 2008); *Mapping the Radical Imagination: Between Redistribution and Recognition* (Cambridge, 2003); *Justice Interruptus: Critical Reflections on the Postsocialist Condition* (Routledge, 1997); *Unruly Practices: Power, Discourse and Gender in Contemporary Social Theory* (University of Minnesota Press, 1989). This interview took place in June 2014.[1]

Jo Littler: Your new book *Fortunes of Feminism*, a selection of writing you've produced over the past thirty years, includes the 1994 essay 'After the Family Wage', written in 1994, in which you argued that neither the 'universal breadwinner' model (in which working mothers strive to emulate male employment patterns) nor the care-giver parity model (in which women are remunerated for being full-time stay-at-home mothers) is very satisfactory.[2] Instead, you proposed the universal care-giver model – in which both parents are structurally enabled to share the load – as a fairer solution. (As someone who campaigned in 1990s London for paid paternity leave, I'm extremely on board with that project.) What progress do you think has been made towards that model of sharing the pleasures and pains of childcare?

Nancy Fraser: In the United States, very little progress, if any. Instead we're moving towards a model that is bifurcated along class lines. There's a class of highly-educated, professional, middle/upper-class women who are in effect living the universal breadwinner model. That is, they're out there trying to compete with men, on male terms, in highly competitive professions. To the degree they manage to do it, it is because they've sloughed off their care work responsibilities onto another class of much poorer women – either in private homes, for-profit childcare centres or for-profit nursing homes. We've never had any social welfare system in the US that's treated care-giving on a par with wage earning, in terms of how pensions are calculated or entitlements to unemployment and social insurance. And in fact the universal care-giver model is part of a socialist feminist approach that would require a rethinking of the whole split between production and reproduction, which in my view is absolutely definitive of capitalist societies. So it would take a very profound structural change to begin that. Instead we have the hegemony of a liberal feminist model, which doesn't grapple with this issue at all: it simply seeks to allow privileged women to lead lives that are socially 'male', while abandoning other women. Historically, the best countries on these issues have been the Scandinavian social democracies, but they are also rapidly changing politically and becoming much more liberal and neoliberal.

JL: In your work you've often warned against trading in a truncated economism for a truncated culturalism, and stressed the importance of combining both approaches. How would you locate yourself in relation to that paradigm? How have you yourself been shaped by the politics of recognition and redistribution?

NF: That's a terrific question. I grew up in Baltimore, Maryland in the days when it was a Jim Crow segregated city. The formative experience of my life, in my early teenage years, was the struggle for racial desegregation – to dismantle Jim Crow. This was a struggle for recognition of the most compelling and obviously just kind.

And like many people of my generation, I moved in quick sequence from there to anti-Vietnam War struggles. I encountered Marxism in an unorthodox, democratic, New Left form. That gave me a way to try and think conceptually about the various battles against different forms of domination that were so intense in that period. And soon second-wave feminism erupted and came into the mix. Now, all of this was going on in a time of relative prosperity. I don't think we in the New Left and the early second-wave feminist movement worried very much about how we would support ourselves. Of course we were young, and we often didn't have children; but there was very much a sense – which proved to be an illusion, but was a felt sense nonetheless – that the first-world model of Keynesian capitalist prosperity would continue. We certainly had a perspective about class, and we understood very well that racism correlated with poverty and exploitation. But we thought, looking through a quasi-Marxian socialist-feminist analytical lens, that what seemed to be a secure social-democratic drift meant that redistribution was relatively unproblematic, and that what we had to do was to fight to introduce the importance of recognition into the forms of traditional Marxism and economistic thinking that dominated even social democracy at the time. That proved to be wrong. I soon found myself getting more and more nervous, as the 1980s wore on into the 1990s, that the critique of political economy was being lost amongst the new social movements, the successor movements to the New Left – including feminism. I felt we were getting a one-sided development of the politics of recognition. To me, recognition always only made sense when it was connected to the political economic dimension of society. Otherwise – as with feminism – you get women put on a pedestal and lots of lip service about how important care work is, but it's a sentimentalised, almost Victorian ethos unless you connect it to political economy. That's when I started saying, 'We had a great critique of economism of a vulgar sort – let's not make the same mistake and end up ourselves with some kind of a vulgar culturalism'.

Above all in the US, but also elsewhere throughout the world, there was a paradigm shift towards the dimension of recognition, and it arose exactly at the moment – it's quite ironic – when the Keynesian social-democratic formation was beginning to unravel.

We got the astonishing resurrection of liberal free-market ideas that everyone had assumed were in the dustbin of history forever. The rise of neoliberalism at the same time as left movements for emancipation that were focused on culture and recognition is a very dangerous mix: it means that the critique of political economy is dropping out at exactly the moment where it's most necessary. But the situation today is quite different. The 2008 crisis was a huge wake-up call. Today there are many examples you could cite to suggest that the critique of political economy is very much on people's minds, as in the astonishing reception of Thomas Piketty in the US, where he has become a media darling. So certainly things are changing, and that's good.

JL: You have made a very powerful diagnosis of how second-wave feminism became co-opted by neoliberalism. But exactly which feminism are you talking about? Is it activist/movement feminism, academic feminism or a more hegemonic mainstream media feminism?

NF: I mean a hegemonic form of liberal feminism, and this formation includes dominant elements of all three of those streams that you mentioned. Certainly it includes media feminism, and icons from popular culture (such as Facebook COO Sheryl Sandberg). And it also includes a strand within movement feminism, if we can still speak about 'movement' feminism? That's another question because I'd say that mainstream feminism has become something more like an interest group than a movement. If activists who work on issues such as reproductive rights or violence against women don't situate these issues in relation to a broader social critique that *includes* a critique of political economy then they too are inadvertently feeding into liberal feminism, whether they intend to or not.

Academic feminism is complicated because it takes many different forms. There are important strands of straightforward liberal feminism in the academy, certainly in the US. But then you also have culturalist strands that think of themselves as quite radical, that certainly wouldn't claim to be liberal, but also often unwittingly feed into this stream of emphasising the 'recognition' dimension at the expense of the 'redistributive' dimension. I appreciate that there are alternative currents around, including in academia and in various social movements. But I don't think these have so far *cumulated* in such a way as to present a counter-project.

JL: So this is a Gramscian reading?

NF: Yes. No domination is ever complete – there is always dissent, dissensus, opposition and so on. But in so far as this remains dispersed and marginalised and isn't able to force itself onto the agenda – into public discussion – then you don't have anything like a counter-hegemonic bloc, or project. I think there was a radical socialist feminism in an earlier period that *did* have a counter-hegemonic status. But that has been greatly weakened over the proceeding twenty-five years or so. Elements of it persist. New generations come into being and pick up and develop variants of a radical or socialist tradition, but these remain so dispersed. I don't mean to single out feminism here. I think one could make a parallel argument for many progressive elements and emancipatory social movements – LGBT struggles are also increasingly taking on a liberal, consumerist guise. Of course I completely support marriage equality and even LGBT equality in the US military, but, you know, these are not necessarily struggles at the cutting edge of socialist politics.

JL: But do you ever worry about minimising the impact of those who identified and practised as socialist feminists throughout that period and have continued to hold the flame? In Britain, for example, you might think of Sheila Rowbotham, Elizabeth Wilson, Lynne Segal or Beatrix Campbell … do you worry about minimising the impact of people who have continued not-being-neoliberal?

NF: Yes, although I'm in the same group myself – you know, these are my friends and sisters and comrades. But I think, frankly, that we have to admit that we are not particularly influential. I certainly don't feel that I am. I could give you the names of other US feminists who would also line up in that category. Britain may be slightly different: you certainly have a more continuous and weighty tradition of Marxism, trade union politics and you have a *Labour* party (which of course we've never had). In the US, we have a political culture that is deeply individualising, voluntarist, where any attempt to introduce structural thinking and criticism is pushing uphill, going against the grain. We in the US are the more extreme case, but I don't believe that we are an exception. Our extremity clarifies what is going on elsewhere in a somewhat less extreme way.

JL: Which feminism in particular inspired or shaped your thinking? What feminist theorists inspired you?

NF: I have to say that we thought of ourselves at that time as somehow having to work from ground zero. It was an astonishing time of great boldness. We had thinkers like Shulamith Firestone, Catherine McKinnon and Kate Millet, among others, and we had a sense of inventing something very new. I didn't agree with any of them fully – I often disagreed quite significantly. But nevertheless, there was something about this *boldness* – the idea that you could really change the world, you could introduce a whole new analytical perspective. And it wasn't really until later that I started studying the history of feminist thought – because it had been erased. We didn't have access to it. I went to a women's college, Bryn Mawr, with a historic legacy of 'blue-stocking feminism', where the ethos was 'we can do anything that men can do', and we were studying classics and philosophy, but we were never asked to read Simone de Beauvoir. It was not until later that I discovered de Beauvoir and Mary Wollstonecraft and feminists within the Marxist tradition such as Alexandra Kollontai. I have to say that my main experience was being part of this extraordinary generation that imagined – rightly or wrongly – that we were inventing feminist theory from scratch. Of course we made a lot of mistakes by trying to reinvent the wheel, when there were resources available that we didn't know about.

De Beauvoir still inspires me today. I've just finished teaching a seminar in feminist philosophy and rereading the new translation of *The Second Sex*, which is marvellous. I've just been impressed all over again by the power of her thinking (which is not to endorse the existentialist framework *per se*). I also taught Mill's *The Subjection of Women*. These are great, towering, inspiring works, even though they bear the marks of their own time and are not exactly what we need today. But our experience in the early days of the second wave was simply that there was *nothing* and that we had to just make it all up ourselves.

JL: Could you say something about your involvement in activism and that trajectory as well?

NF: Well as I said, I went through the sequence of struggles that is very common to the radicals of my generation: desegregation, SNCC, the civil rights movement. The John Waters film *Hairspray* is set in Baltimore, and though it is of course a highly fantasised narrative, it touches on some points of my own history, including the desegregation of the amusement park that you see near the end of the film. I was there, we were 'sitting in' – those were real events that the director is riffing on. And that TV show that had 'Negro Day' – where the kids went on to dance to the new rock music – that was *real*! It had 'Negro Day' once a week on this show because you couldn't imagine interracial dancing. Anyway, that was for me the beginning. I became very active in draft resistance to the Vietnam War and worked in Philadelphia (by that time I was already in college) organising rallies where men turned in and burned their draft cards and other things like that. Then I became active in Students for a Democratic Society (SDS) and encountered Marxism for the first time in my life.

In the US, because of McCarthyism (which was such a traumatic interruption of the radical tradition within the country), people like me, who did not come from a left-wing family, had experienced a kind of social amnesia. So it was like an illumination, suddenly you discover there is this whole other possible way of thinking, that was never part of your education or informally transmitted. The discovery of Marxism, and anti-imperialist and anti-colonialist critique, was very important to me. When I graduated from college, I really wanted to be a full-time revolutionary. I moved to New York City and worked with the Metropolitan Council on Housing, which organised tenants' rent strikes over issues like inadequate heating and rats and all kinds of very bad housing conditions. I also belonged to a small socialist, quasi-sectarian group that had come out of SDS. Then, in the early 1970s I encountered feminism. It was not until several years later that I went on to graduate school. Having at first felt a sense shared by a lot of us in those days that we actually expected some kind of real socialist revolution within a short space of time, it then became clear that that was not going to happen. You burn out, and I realised that I needed a longer-range plan for my life. It was at that point that I said 'OK, I used to love philosophy, let me see if I can stomach a PhD programme'. But I brought to my graduate studies this formation that I had from my ten years of activism. I have to say that I learned a lot in college and in graduate school, but if I had to single out one thing, my most important education was in my years of activism. And I think it's there, really, where I learned what 'critical theory' was, even if I didn't really know what that phrase meant exactly. And since then, the best I can say for myself is that I am a kind of armchair activist. I'm basically an academic and I try to be a public intellectual to a certain extent.

JL: What did you think about Occupy?

NF: What was most striking to me about Occupy was the rapidity with which it emerged, grew and won support in so many cities across the US, as with its cognate movements in Europe and elsewhere. There were polls in the US showing that, around three weeks after it began, close to 70 per cent of Americans supported the aims of the Occupy movement – higher poll results than the Tea Party! This was remarkable. But after the evictions, how quickly the air went out of the balloon, and how little has remained. In fact, what was left of the New York Occupy movement soon converted itself into a Hurricane Sandy relief operation. It almost ceased to be political. That is another striking thing – how could something so promising disappear so fast? But I believe that the sentiment remains: it's available, and could be re-activated at the proper moment in the proper way.

The story of Occupy Wall Street I know a bit from the inside, though I can't say the same for anywhere else. But I know well many of the key figures who were the backbone of that, and they are the stratum of young people who really don't have (and this, in

a way, goes back to what we were talking about earlier) any experience of Marxism at all, who were educated through one phase or
another of the cultural turn – who understand the inadequacy of
that and want a deep structural critique, who talk about capitalism
and the 1 per cent, but who actually don't have that intellectual
formation; and for them anarchism – and it is partly a kind of anti-
communism – represents the perspective of a genuine radicalism.
So these youthful activists take a principled stand against enduring
forms of organisation and structure and so on. It's a familiar idea
from the history of the New Left. From my point of view, an over-
emphasis on 'process' and consensus and direct democracy and
direct action, and the distrust of institutions, of mediation, and
so on, has been a problem. I agree that existing institutional forms
are problematic and carry a lot of baggage. But the question is how
to invent new ways of institutionalising these energies so that they
don't just dissipate: so it's not just blowing off steam.

JL: Let's return to 'culturalism'. There's one zone which yokes
together the cultural and the political into a socialist political
critique, and that's cultural studies. Work by, for example, Stuart
Hall and Angela McRobbie, has very powerfully critiqued neoliberal culture. I wondered about your relationship to cultural studies,
as there's not very much traffic in your work with that area. You
said in your 2014 talk in London that you want to 'relaunch critical
theory for the twenty-first century'; [3] but, as Ali Rattansi pointed
out to me, early critical theory was extremely concerned with the
cultural, whereas your work is far less so – it's more concerned with
the abstract socio-political. So how does your work relate to 'the
cultural' and cultural studies?

NF: There are a couple of different dimensions here. First of all I
think we have to distinguish between cultural studies in Britain and
in the US. The work of Raymond Williams, E. P. Thompson (in a
certain respect) and of course Stuart Hall, the Birmingham Centre,
all of that is a remarkable tradition. I'm sure Angela McRobbie is a
worthy continuer of that and I'm sure there are others who I may
not know. But cultural studies in the US, although it took the same
name, was really different: it was cultural*ist* in a way I don't think

this British tradition ever was. I think UK cultural studies was absolutely exemplary in linking the cultural, the social, the political, the political economic. That is the sort of thing I would very much have liked to have seen developing in the US, but alas it never did. Maybe now, again, things are changing because of the new salience of economic crisis, of financial crisis, the problem of capitalism. We may be at a moment where this kind of more integrated cultural studies will develop and expand. In the US I'm happy to see that people like Wendy Brown, who I think of as part of the cultural side of things, are developing serious critiques of neoliberalism and interesting readings of how that works on a cultural plane. So this is to me a very propitious moment for a kind of reintegration.

In terms of the early critical theory of the Frankfurt School, that's a somewhat complicated story. There was a moment in the 1930s when you had a genuinely interdisciplinary mix of stuff, including law, Pollock on monopoly capitalism – you had all kinds of things going on. But what really stamped the history of critical theory, especially Horkheimer and Adorno's work on fascism and its aftermath, was a sense of *despair*, basically. (The interesting exception is Marcuse – I'll get to him in a second.) This is a sense of despair that in *The Dialectic of Enlightenment* goes all the way back to the Greeks, the pre-Socratics and Homer. It sees the seeds of domination planted so early, and a kind of unstoppable historical train leading to total domination, the administrative society, one-dimensional man, no possibility of critique, etc. It has *absolutised culture*. That is a very problematic kind of culturalism. Habermas represents an attempt at a correction, but that too is a complicated story. A great deal of the post-Habermasian currents of critical theory have entered into a kind of disciplinary specialisation: people doing moral philosophy, philosophy of law, political theory disconnected from social theory. This is not culturalism; it's a kind of politicism, or moralism or legalism – a single-minded focus on constitutional theory. I appreciate that no-one can do everything, and that there is academic specialisation, but I think this is a sad outcome for critical theory. It has lost the attempt to think about the social totality, which Habermas, at an early stage, did try to do, for better or for worse. Honneth may be an exception, but I don't think what he does is adequate. But most other people are doing much narrower work. So I don't think we can find in critical theory today (taking critical theory in the narrow sense of work in the tradition of the Frankfurt School) a paradigm that has the kind of interdisciplinary ambition of the very early Frankfurt school. I think that Adorno/ Horkheimer led to a dead end.

But when I was putting together readings for the feminist philosophy seminar that I mentioned earlier, I stumbled upon this incredible early article by Marcuse, on 'Feminism and Marxism', which was published in the first issue of a journal called *Women's Studies* in the early 1970s. It's an extraordinary essay, in which he talks about how his women students have pushed him, and he starts exploring what he thinks is the relationship between feminism and socialism. It's so exciting – you'd never find anything like that from Horkheimer, Adorno or even Habermas. Marcuse was an amazing guy who was very responsive to the currents of his time in the US.

JL: I'm very interested in the way you continue to argue for socialist feminism – at your London lecture that sentiment got the biggest cheer of the night. Sometimes it seems that one of the few 'safe' places where it's OK to say that you're a socialist – even in academia – is in relation to feminism. In the UK mainstream over the past few decades socialism has become marginalised as a very dirty word (although I think there are signs this is changing). Could you say something about what kinds of terminology you think have the most generative or emancipatory potential?

NF: In the US, the word socialism has been so marginalised and off the agenda for so many decades that it might have actually lost some of its stigma. I'm open to other terminology – I don't feel that, for whatever reason, the word socialism absolutely *must* be at the centre of things. If we can find another term that has more capacity to mobilise people, I'm interested. I'm open. I might want to press a little bit to make sure that it's not turning out to be some kind of a whitewash. But I don't have any other term at this point.

My real interest is in connecting two strands. First, the tradi-tional labour-centred problematic of exploitation that has always been at the centre of socialism – what I call Marx's 'front story'. I want to connect that to the ecological side of capitalism, that 'back story' which is becoming so dire and so pressing that it's forcing its way into the front story. Second, the story of social reproduction. Whilst feminists historically have made such an important contribution to social reproduction theory, I don't think of it as only a feminist issue. It's the whole complex of community, of education; it's not just what goes on within the private household, but the attempt to develop a social, solidarity economy – in housing, in education, in social service delivery – in the face of crisis. It's building cooperatives, it's community-based efforts. These may not in the end be the answer, but it's where a huge amount of energy and organising is.

Then we have the issue of re-making political institutions. I think all of this has to somehow come together in ... and we are looking for a word – 'in' what? In an anti-capitalist struggle? In a socialist struggle? It would have to be not just 'socialist-feminist', but 'eco-socialist-feminist-democratic'! It'd be great to have a label for this that suggests not just the traditional labour-centred idea of socialism, which can sound somewhat parochial even though those issues remain absolutely pressing; and not just 'socialist feminism', which also has, I appreciate, a somewhat dated sound to it – it was a moment. I do think now that we're looking for something even broader but we don't know what to call it yet.

JL: The commons ...?

NF: That's a term that's certainly seeing a resurgence.

JL: Yoking together feminism and socialism has always been a concern of yours. Environmentalism seems to have surfaced in your work more recently ...

NF: Yes, it's actually something that has been in the back of my mind for quite a while but it's only quite recently become a genuine systematic concern. And this has to do with my current project, now several years old but still very much in process, which is to do with *crisis theory*. This is a kind of critique that has been very out of fashion: dismissed as deterministic, mechanistic, economistic, teleological – all those 'bad' words. And some of those words might be accurate for certain received versions of crisis theory/crisis critique. But nevertheless, we do find ourselves in a very dire and complex crisis situation. And I believe that we need to develop, to reconstruct, some form of crisis critique that does not fall prey to such objections. And clearly, the ecological dimension has to be front and centre. It is not reducible to, but it is deeply intertwined with, the dynamics of the economic, financialisation and social reproduction crises. It was when I took this objective of a crisis critique that I found that I could not any longer keep the ecological dimension in the margins. I had to bring it front and centre. So I've been doing quite a lot of reading: above all in the eco-socialist tradition, including the eco-feminist-socialist tradition. And I have to say it's a very exciting experience to try – in a systematic way – to get to grips with a discipline, in order to see what, if anything, I can contribute to this body of thought. I'm teaching it in my seminars and finding it quite a thrilling experience. I'll be writing more about this.

JL: My final question is: you write very clearly and your work is very influential. How has your sense of your audience has changed over the years? Who are you writing for?

NF: Because of the personal history I spoke about earlier, having one foot in academia and one foot in social movements is always an aspiration. And I don't want to be discipline-bound. There certainly are pieces where I am trying to work something out that's complicated and academic – I am thinking here of some early articles that I wrote about Habermas, where I was really struggling to work out what a feminist response to his thought would be. It's quite a complex body of thought and probably not a very accessible article. But even in the same period I was writing other things that *were* more accessible. My biggest regret, though, is that I don't have enough time to do much journalistic-type writing. I did publish a piece in the *Guardian* last year, and it was astonishing to me how much uptake it got, and I thought 'I really ought to do more of this!'[4] But the fact of the matter is I am still teaching full-time, with a very heavy load of thesis supervision; and my primary commitment remains to my philosophical and theoretical writing, which I feel is my strength, where I can contribute the most.

In the past I've depended on a process that was once perhaps more reliable, of flow between academic writing and extra-academic publics. Second-wave feminism, in the early period of my career, was a fantastic transmission relay. Ideas from the university flowed very easily into the movement and vice-versa: inspiration and ideas that developed outside the academy were taken up quickly and elaborated within it. I think that was a wonderful moment, where the ideas would come out – and these ideas were powerful – one way or another. Things changed. When feminism became more academicised, it was harder to make these links. Maybe now we're at another moment where this is changing again, where there's intense hunger in all arenas for new thinking. But my own situation now is one of extreme 'time poverty', and I feel I have a certain amount of time that I have to be jealously guarding for the theoretical work that I want to do.

JL: Well, thank you for spending some time here.

NF: This is a good way to spend time!

NOTES

1 This interview was first published as 'The fortunes of socialist feminism: Jo Littler interviews Nancy Fraser' in *Soundings: A Journal of Politics and Culture*, Issue 58, 2015, pp21-33.
2 Nancy Fraser, *Fortunes of Feminism: From State-Managed Capitalism to Neoliberal Crisis*, Verso, 2013.
3 This was the Barry Amiel and Norman Melburn Trust Annual Lecture, available at: www.amielandmelburn.org.uk/trustinfo/conferences.htm. A podcast of the 2013 Birkbeck talk can be found at: backdoorbroadcasting.net/2013/06/the-future-of-feminism.
4 Nancy Fraser, 'How feminism became capitalism's handmaiden – and how to reclaim it', www.theguardian.com/commentisfree/2013/oct/14/feminism-capitalist-handmaiden-neoliberal, 13 October 2013.

We do not have to be vicious, competitive, or managerial

Akwugo Emejulu is Professor of Sociology at the University of Warwick. Before entering academia she worked in a variety of grassroots roles – as a community organiser, a trade union organiser and a participatory action researcher – in both the United States and Britain. A political sociologist, she is the author of *Community Development as Micropolitics: Comparing Theories, Policies and Politics in America and Britain* (Policy, 2015); *Minority Women and Austerity: Survival and Resistance in France and Britain*, with Leah Bassel (Policy, 2017); and co-editor of *To Exist is to Resist: Black Feminism in Europe*, with Francesca Sobande (Pluto, 2019) and *Fugitive Feminism* (Silver Press, 2022). This interview took place in July 2019.[1]

Jo Littler: I love how your 2015 book *Community Development as Micropolitics* – which charts the different political histories of community development in the US and the UK since 1968 – ends with a broadside against entrepreneurialism. Instead, you champion democratic transformation and what you call 'the deeply unfashionable subject of political education'. Can you tell us more about these tendencies and their more recent development?

Akwugo Emejulu: Well, first of all, wow, hardly anyone reads that book, so thank you! It has made possible all of my future work, and I'm still reckoning with what I was thinking about at that time. What I found really interesting about mapping the ideas and practices of community development in both Britain and America was observing the emergence of the concept that somehow capitalism could be tamed, and save us. The idea that somehow capitalism could be harnessed in such a way that it could be turned on its head, in a kind of jujitsu move, and then 'save' the communities it immiserated, was patently ridiculous. But it was taken up because of a rebalancing: there was a turn away from political education by activists and practitioners, and an increasing number of technocrats became involved in the social welfare state, and the void that this left was filled by entrepreneurial behaviour and action – [it] was, frankly, colonised fully and completely by neoliberalism.

I think we can only understand that as a fundamental defeat of the left. And it's really important to talk about it in those terms. It involves the defeat of political ideas, but also the defeat of the idea that we can do anything big and meaningful any more: it must only be incremental. The way my work developed is in some ways a kind of mapping of these further defeats. This sounds a little depressing, but I don't have any other way of talking about it. In my next book that I wrote with Leah Bassel, *Minority Women's Activism in Tough Times*, which compared France and the UK, we were surprised by the rapidity with which 'the third sector' – by now we were using this term instead of 'community development' – had taken up entrepreneurial thinking in spaces and places that we had thought would be more resistant to these ideas. For instance, the idea of 'poverty' or 'inequality' has been commodified: it's seen as something that funders or the state or NGOs can use to fight for their own piece of survival. The way that's played out is truly horrifying, on all counts. We mapped how this process played out in the anti-violence-against-women sector in particular. The fact that the idea and the process of women fleeing from violence could be commodified through the local state putting services out to tender, and that NGOs themselves would *collude* in that process – their inability to take a step back and say 'is this a process we should be engaging in?' – I found frankly unconscionable. But I completely understand the pressures they are under – that they either comply to this regime or they die, and then other organisations come in and replace them, and often do a worse job. For me, at the end of that book, it was a question of 'what happens next?'

JL: Has there now been an expansion of critical political education?

AE: Yes, and we can see this especially in this contemporary moment. At the time of my first two books, of course, there were activists doing very interesting things, but mass mobilisations were absent. Now, with Extinction Rebellion, Sisters Uncut, Black Lives Matter, you see a range of groups doing very interesting things. And when you actually go and speak to activists in all these spaces, they now say, fundamentally this is about ideology. They reject the idea that there is no alternative; the activists themselves are very, very clear that they have a vision for another kind of society. And they undertake more spectacular protests as a form of education. And when I ask women of colour activists, 'What goes on in your networks?', so much of it is now about political education. This means not only saying, 'What is the role of capitalism?' but really insisting on understanding how dynamics of race and gender are encoded in capitalism and our everyday lives.

JL: Your work focuses mostly on grassroots and NGO/third sector activism, and it tends to be critical of political parties' lack of diversity – or as you pithily put it, 'the raceless discussions of the white left'. At the same time we clearly need mainstream political parties to diversify and get better and more democratic, and work in conjunction with grassroots movements, and there seems to me that there have been recent small but heartening and important moves in that direction. For example in the US Alexandria Ocasio-Cortez has worked with the wider Justice Democrats movement, and in Britain people like the prospective MP Faiza Shaheen have worked with organisations like CLASS and The World Transformed. Do you think there needs to be more engagement between diverse grassroots groups and mainstream politics?

AE: Absolutely. The idea that any group that cares about the most marginalised, or a different society, can turn away from mainstream politics is a folly and a fallacy. Because what happens is that other groups, your opponents, will take up all that space. Nature abhors a vacuum. The best example of that can be seen in the US, and the ways in which the Tea Party colonised the Republican Party by filling that space at the local level and the state level and then by colonising the national party. Part of why Trump exists is because the left at that time turned away from, and did not take seriously, local and state politics.

But everyone has to understand their role. Not everyone wants to be a politician or engage in the bureaucratic behaviour of parliamentary politics. That's fine. But you do need people there. And you need people there to have a conversation and dialogue with, in order to move and influence them. Parliamentary politics isn't a space for everyone – just as being out on the streets isn't a space for everyone. We need people in research, we need people in policy spaces, we need people in lots of *different* kinds of spaces and places in order to take back power. If we are serious we need an understanding of what power is, how to use it and how to win for the most marginalised. You have to have a multi-pronged approach in order to combat the devastation of austerity, and the devastating and now routinised experiences of misogyny and racism and transphobia and all the rest of it. I think it's so important to have people in lots of different spaces.

JL: I completely agree. When you were talking about the Democrats leaving that space at the local and grassroots level it made me think about the development of what the political theorist Peter Mair calls 'partyless democracy' under Blair in Britain – the abdication of real grassroots democratic involvement and the energetic structural work to make the Labour Party more of a managerial enterprise. You can map the same process in the UK.

AE: Yes absolutely, that's exactly right.

JL: Your work has a pronounced comparative dimension and points out how different nations operate in relation to anti-racist and feminist politics. Can you talk about why you take this approach? Presumably a key benefit of that comparative work is to indicate the international allegiances that can be made.

AE: Yes, my starting point is always about the possibilities for solidarity. I always assume until I'm shown otherwise that somehow we can find a way of working together – whether it's different kinds of activists working in different spaces, or transnational connections between people. The only way you can do that is if you have a meaningful understanding of the similarities, but also the differences, and the particular dynamics at play that foment and make possible certain kinds of activism. Because activists don't come out of nowhere. When you can understand that context, and understand what gives rise to the patterns of particular kinds of activism, it gives you the ability to *reach across*. This isn't anything new; this is the lesson that Angela Davis and Assata Shakur taught us.

I think this kind of working together is different from the old-school internationalist solidarity of the left, which denied differences and said 'capitalism above everything'. It is, but there's also so much *more* going on than that. That's why so many activists and academics are working on feminism for the 99 per cent. Because learning not only how Indigenous women in the Global South are subjected, but also how they organise and talk back, *act* back, is crucial to building a broader movement. So the starting point is saying, OK, what is it that we have in common? Institutionalised misogyny, yes; land theft, yes; all of these things, that is our starting point. It's not identical but that's the beginning of a dialogue and a conversation. That's why I think taking different nation states as cases is really interesting and important, and what's driving my later work is really taking that comparison seriously. You learn a lot; and what you learn is that things look very similar everywhere. Rather than that generating hopelessness, that should be a galvanising process, realising that, wow, women of colour and Black women in particular are at the bottom and are hated everywhere, and yet we organise in very interesting and innovative ways. So let's get to work.

JL: Can you say more about the difficulties and strengths of Black feminist solidarities?

AE: There's a difficulty organising around both the pain and pleasure of being a Black woman – and also assuming that there's an agreed idea of what it means to be a Black woman. I think there's a conversation to be had about how we define these terms and who's allowed in this space. That has its own kind of difficulty because of some very disturbing, excluding conversations about the status of trans women in Black feminist spaces.

For me, it's about a balance. It's about the very real material and discursive inequalities that Black women experience; it's the rally cry, the clarion call for Black feminism. But that always and forever has to be linked to understanding the creativity, the innovation, the *pleasure* of joining in struggle with others, which I think is really important. I don't want the pain ever to overwhelm the pleasure. adrienne maree brown has a new book out called *Pleasure Activism*. It's important to say we can't always organise around death. The reason why we join together is because there's some great injustice. But it can't always be a drag. There have to be spaces where we insist on community and enjoyment alongside the sadness and death and destruction. It's important to get that balance.

JL: In the introduction to *To Exist is to Resist*, the new book you've co-edited with Francesca Sobande, you mention that US Black feminism can overshadow European Black feminism. I was thinking about how that's part of wider forms of cultural imperialism – for instance, in the UK we have large exhibitions on Black American art, like the Tate's *Soul of a Nation*, but you don't have the equivalent on that scale on UK Black art, and we have far more prominence given to Beyoncé and Janelle Monáe than their UK equivalents. How is Black European feminism different, and what needs to be highlighted?

AE: I think what's so interesting about Black European feminism is to understand how it is firstly a diasporic feminism. It is always in conversation with the Caribbean and the African continent. The colonial legacies of empire live on through these particular kinds of feminism, where folks are here because the empire was there, and in the US case this is a very different experience, because – speaking as a Black American – we are cut off from our relationships to the continent. There are very important and crucial pan-African traditions, but in the American case those are in many ways *imagined* communities and solidarities, whereas in the European case people are travelling back and forth right at this moment. Some of the activists I talk to are second and third generation Europeans and so their parents and grandparents are from the Caribbean or from the African continent. Travelling back and forth they have those very immediate connections that matter. So the struggle is not only about recognition and redistribution in Europe, but it's also about reparations and anti-colonial activism in the Caribbean and on the continent. All of those conflicts and debates that were taking place during empire, during imperialism, live on in very real ways for folks in Europe. That's not the same as the US.

But the differences are not always clear because we're still in the middle of American empire. Many Black American feminists don't understand how they speak with authority and dominate by virtue of being at the heart of empire. It's oftentimes a very difficult conversation to have. How can you be at the bottom in one case but also be dominant in another? That's always an important lesson to learn. No one is saying that you are all powerful, but in this space, in terms of thinking about Black feminism, *you are*. You crowd out other conversations. Cultural hegemony is about the ways that American imperialism works. It's absolutely fascinating, particularly in the Black feminist case.

Linguistic distinctions are so crucial. In the case of Germany and France, for example, there are still plenty of key activists and theorists talking about all the same issues that are not translated – or their translations are hard to find. As English-only speakers, their analyses and ways of seeing the world are lost to us, or blocked from us. And that's our problem, as English speakers: if you are serious about solidarity that means you better go and learn another language. Because in the rest of Europe, they do.

JL: Why is Europe the frame that most interests you?

AE: For a number of reasons. We Americans kind of fetishize Europe – so sophisticated, so fabulous, no one's driving cars! But when I was still living in Scotland I visited Luxembourg, and I saw more Black people there than in Scotland, which is one of the whitest places on the planet. But the way Luxembourg conceives of itself is as completely and totally white. And it made me furious. Scotland, on the other hand, is such an interesting place because it's trying to change. When I was there it was 98 per cent white, but it's starting to change because of migration, and that's very interesting when I go back, especially to Glasgow. But when you go literally anywhere else, you see all these Black people everywhere, but in terms of European cinema, literature, for example, none of this is reflected. So I started asking some of my colleagues questions, you know: when you're talking about gender policies in Europe, where are the women of colour? Where are they in your theoretical conceptions? I was just getting furious. Because to see and to watch how Black women and other women of colour, especially on the continent, are written out of national stories, was fascinating and infuriating.

I was really interested in saying no, and telling a different story. It's not my place to tell someone else's story. But certainly what I can do is to try and create space to understand how these women are organising, and how that is an important counter-narrative. And this is not just about the culture industries but also about academics – especially in feminist social science in Europe, which works very hard to colonise Black women's ideas but refuses to have Black women in their spaces. Even in the European feminist imagination! I find that fascinating. I feel a keen responsibility to correct the record and not let people off the hook. To say, 'No, you're not going to use intersectionality simply as a way of talking about different kinds of white women, not on my watch. You're going to be asked some very hard questions, but also I am going to show you how you are using this term that actually centres the experiences of Black women and other women of colour.' I feel there's some urgency there – trying to understand genuine dynamics. If you could understand these experiences then the rise of the far right wouldn't be so shocking to you, you know? Or these awful border politics wouldn't be surprising to you. And then we would be much further on in actually trying to organise ourselves and others, and in having some effective influence in terms of policy-making as well.

JL: At the London book launch of *To Exist is to Resist*, you said 'No one is coming to save us, we have to do it ourselves'. Could you say a bit more about that, and about activism more broadly?

AE: This is the first lesson of activism, right? If you see something that needs to change, you have to do it yourself. The idea that someone else either understands the issue better than you or has better ideas than you seems anti-egalitarian and anti-democratic. This does not mean you are making someone take all the responsibility for their own liberation – saying, 'Well, you pointed out the issues now you must go and do it'. Rather, it's to say: 'If you want change to happen then you actually have to grab a broom and gather with others to make that happen'.

When you see other people seeking to make change, there will always be something wrong with it. But I'm of the mind that you can't just criticise from the outside: you have agency, you have the ability to act to try and make a difference. I think it's beholden on all of us to do so – but not on our own. It shouldn't be an individualised process, it always has to be a collective process, where you can have a conversation: 'Do you see this?! Isn't this madness? Maybe we should do something?'

And time and time again, when you are speaking to activists, they say the experience of collective action is the most worthwhile thing that they have. It comes at great cost, in terms of burnout, and frayed friendships, and mental health issues and all the rest of it – and I think that's something we don't talk about enough. But we have activists saying, *that moment has completely changed our experience*. I was interviewing some folks who occupied Holloway Prison, and they talked about how it was the most consequential thing they'd ever done. Everything else is like a downer since then, that's in vivid colour and everything else is a bit in black and white. That's its own issue, the highs and lows, and the risks, of activism.

'No one is coming to save us and we have to do it ourselves' should be an incredibly empowering statement, but it's also frightening. Because I don't know how much more clearly the world can show us. You have Trump crazily tweeting about sending people back to where they come from, and half the country agrees with that. Literally, *no-one is coming*. In fact the only time anyone *is* coming it's to try and deport you, or to try to do you harm. It's in our greatest self-interest to understand that lesson. But it's also the greatest expression of the idea that we have to be in charge of our own liberation.

JL: In *Minority Women and Austerity* you argue for an expansive conception of activism as a politics of survival. What does activism encompass, how far does it go, and what are its limits?

AE: Leah and I have always been very clear: if you want to understand the failures of the Women's March, Occupy, XR – all of these folks, again and again – and as women of colour activists consistently argue – you have to realise that not only have these movements not been prepared to entertain conversations about intersectional inequalities or intersecting inequalities; they also have not entertained the differing *temporalities* of crisis, nor tried to make activism reflect everyday experience.

The women of colour anti-fascist activists I work with are very clear that they don't engage in the black bloc, they don't do any frontline work, because they are hyper-visible to the police and to fascists, who will come and either kettle them, take them to prison, or inflict very real material violence against them. If what you do is spectacular activism, many women of colour will say, we're not going to put our bodies on the line for that because we have homes and children that we have to get to tonight.

You can't only look for activism in terms of spectacle. If we're honest about refocusing our attention on the most marginal-ised, then we also have to go looking for activism in other spaces and places. Activism also has to be about everyday struggles for survival, especially in and around issues of social welfare. Activism at the school gates often either gets branded as NIMBYism, or gets called something completely different from activism such as parental involvement. It actually matters if your school or commu-nity centre is going to get taken over or closed down. It's these kinds of immediate quality of life issues that are felt hardest by women of colour, who are more likely to be living in the poorest, most unsafe communities, which are also the dirtiest communities because environmental services are also unevenly cleaning the streets, and all the rest of it.

That *is* activism, but it's not 'sexy'. You're not covering your face, in the streets, or smashing windows, you're not part of an encampment sleeping in the streets for several months because you need to go to work and you have kids to look after. But sometimes that's the only kind of activism that's seen to count. This other stuff often doesn't get labelled as activism but as voluntary or community activity. The US Immigration and Customs Enforcement (ICE) raids that are happening at the moment have been made less effective because there have been women of colour running 'know your rights' campaigns so that people know not to open their door to ICE, or to say they're not going unless ICE get a warrant signed by a judge. That's not *seen* as activism, but that's actually what's going to have a real material consequence for people's lives. For me, having a broader understanding of what political behaviour looks like is crucial.

JL: So what links them all together? How would you define activism?

AE: I always think about it as a *collective public politics*. It's a 'going-together' of different kinds of people in solidarity who are seeking to make some sort of change in public space. That's what it's about. It's a public politics, whatever that looks like. I have a particular interest in people who are choosing to defend and expand the welfare state, or are involved in anti-fascist resistance and migrant justice. There are other ways of thinking about one's public politics. But for me it's collective, and it's about taking the risk, a real risk, of interacting in public space in particular ways. There are issues about what counts as public space. To me, it's about joining together to say: we're going to do something, something that has immediate material consequences and makes a difference to people's lives.

JL: Should academics be more activist?

AE: You know, I don't know about that. It's one of those things where folks got to do what they got to do. As I was saying before, we need to have different kinds of people in different spaces. Those who care about these issues and are engaged with them should be activists. I have a lot of colleagues who talk about the kind of activism that they do, but they keep it very separate from their academic work. They might be very active in their local community, doing stuff with their kids' schools, or doing really interesting undercover migrant justice work, but they don't ever talk about it because they don't want it captured by 'impact' and the Research Excellence Framework (REF) and all the rest of it. Whereas I do all this stuff and I'm very happily writing my REF impact case study about it as well, which is, I understand, a little gross. But I don't think anyone should feel compelled to do either. And I also don't think an identity as an academic should frame what you do. You should do something because you care. And not everyone will be in a position to understand their activism through their working lives.

JL: Can you outline your path from community organiser and trade unionist to academic?

AE: While I was still at university I was part of a programme called Americorps, which President Clinton set up, which was meant to be like a domestic peace corps (I know …). The university was in Washington DC, and I was working in a poor Black community in the city. That was a really interesting experience for lots of different reasons, and I thought, I want to do more of this! I was working on a youth literacy programme and I bonded with the kids and it was all lovely. Then I did some organising around migrant justice and anti-poverty in Edinburgh for a time. After that I went back to the US briefly, for two years, to Texas, where I was a trade union organiser for one of the big public sector unions – but a union that had no power because in Texas it is illegal to strike for public sector workers. So it was a union in name only, because you couldn't withdraw your labour, and that's your main union tool.

It was probably one of the worst experiences of my life, but also the most important. It brought me to political maturation. The teachers' unions were separate – they're the most powerful because they're easy to organise – so we were organising other kinds of public sector workers. We were organising a very disparate group of people: folks who worked in welfare offices and benefits agencies, in the probation service, in mental health institutions, all of them located in rural areas and spread out.

I'll never forget getting up in the morning in a place called Brenham, Texas, where Bluebell, a famous ice cream brand from the South, is headquartered, near to a massive secure unit for people with learning disabilities plus people who have committed crimes and are locked up. It's a prison but also not a prison. (In the US we still have large hospitals where we keep people in secure accommodation, which is truly barbaric and unbelievable.) We were not allowed to be in the grounds, so we had to stand at the gates at every shift change, starting at 5 a.m. So we were there at 5 a.m., 1 p.m., 6 p.m., handing out flyers, trying to get people to organise. It was one of my worst experiences ever because people were like, 'You want me to join the union? Do you *know* how many packs of cigarettes that is?' And ours was a very weird, non-ideological union. People didn't once talk about political education because it was thought that would be 'alienating' to these workers. It was only about bread and butter issues – more pension contributions and a higher wage. That was it. No talk of socialism, none of that. That seemed crazy to me because it was as if we were fighting for some vague gain in the distant future, which might one day be an extra £100 in your pocket; but in the meantime we're denying you the instant gratification of smoking your cigarettes. It was a terrible transaction. We weren't asking people to make some sort of immediate sacrifices for the sake of some kind of social change, a distant revolution to come – it wasn't even that! But what was being presented as, effectively, a simple financial transaction was still always talked about in this weird middle-class way of entailing delayed gratification for the goodness to come later. Plus it was a super insulting, top-down, hierarchical approach – working *on* people, not *with* people. It was gross, and ridiculous. But it was one of those great experiences that taught me lots of things. I thought, 'I don't want to do this anymore'. I probably always knew I was going to drift back into academia eventually. Now I guess I'm making sense of the experiences that I've had.

JL: In the UK you are one of twenty-four Black female professors out of 19,000 professors nationwide, 14,000 of whom are male. What does it feel like to be in that position? How do you negotiate it? What are the main factors that could drive progressive change?

AE: How does it feel? For me now, being at work is very interesting because when I fled my last position – and fleeing is what I did – all I wanted was to be respected and left alone. Those were the two things that I got at Warwick [University]. People are very nice and they let me get on with things without being harassed and managed. I guess you can ask others about their experience of working with me, but what's nice is to be able to model behaviours that I would have appreciated when I was a junior colleague, and then also to have the power to shape the life of a department, and to be able to actually encourage and support junior colleagues and early career researchers. I keenly feel that it is my responsibility to say, 'No, first of all, we do not have to be vicious, competitive, or managerial'. Everyone knows what their job is and that there are other ways of thinking about and being an academic, and one of the ways you can do that is not be an asshole. Many academics seem to be unable to understand that basic lesson. Do you know what I mean? I say to people all the time, academics are so weird. Because there are so few people that you meet that are actually geniuses. Everyone is just rubbing along in the middle. So everyone just needs to get a grip.

JL: Sometimes being an asshole is a criteria for promotion.

AE: Well this is it! For me one thing that's important is that apparently I am the first Black woman professor ever in the history of the University of Warwick, which is both hilarious and ridiculous. But if that is the case, then not on my watch are we going to engage in terrible behaviour. It's going to be called out publicly. And behind the scenes we are going to support those who, in other places, would have been crushed under foot. I feel as if that's my duty and responsibility.

We also need to think about this issue in larger terms. Our friend up at Durham, the educational sociologist Vikki Boliver, has done very helpful work that shows that Russell Group universities refuse to give offers to best performing Black and minority ethnic students – so we are not using the right words when we talk about 'a pipeline problem'. It's *not* a pipeline problem. It is institutionalised racism in the higher education system. It's an absolute scandal. So, first of all, the best performing Black and minority ethnic students are less likely to gain entry into the most elite universities (and Warwick is just as guilty of this as anywhere else). Then we have what is called 'the attainment gap': when they have managed to break through into these elite spaces, even though they're there with the same qualifications, or better, than their white counterparts, Black and minority ethnic students are less likely to leave with a first or a 2:1. And I am actually seeing it happen in front of my eyes. At Warwick, I teach third years on a very specialist module called 'Feminist Pedagogy, Feminist Activism'. So you're only getting a certain kind of student who wants to engage in this kind of conversation. And let me tell you, my Black women students are broken by the time they come to me. There's something that has happened to them, even in right-on Warwick Sociology: they are less willing to speak, though they have a whole lot to say. Even if their analyses are fantastic, they have to be coaxed in ways that I find surprising. Something has happened to them. We know what's happened: all the research says they're talked down to, they're disrespected, in their tutorials, in their seminars, in their lectures. They're not learning about experiences that are *meaningful* to them, but when they make suggestions they're shut down, and so it's a process of demoralisation. It's the brave few who, when they get to masters and PhDs, are able to get through it. It's truly incredible what happens.

Just two weeks ago I was at a politics and gender conference in a room where a woman was using Nancy Fraser and Iris Marion Young to defend the far right. It was insane. When I said, 'What are you *saying?*', she doubled down on it. There wasn't a session at that conference where something crazy didn't happen. And I thought, 'If I was an early career researcher, could I survive this?' At every stage of the process, BAME young people are less likely to get studentships, to get the mentoring, to gain access to those career-defining networks with the big name, to be pushed; they are not getting put on grants. We *know* what to do about this. We know exactly what needs to be done. But again it goes back to: are academics assholes? You know what I mean? We're thinking this is some huge mystery. But it's not.

NOTES

1 This interview was first published as '"We do not have to be vicious, competitive, or managerial": Jo Littler talks to Akwugo Emejulu' in *Soundings: A Journal of Politics and Culture*, Issue 73, 2019, pp73-86.

Every generation has to make
its own women's movement

Sheila Rowbotham is a historian and writer. She wrote the influential pamphlet *Women's Liberation and the New Politics* in 1969 and was involved in organising the first national UK Women's Liberation Movement (WLM) conference held at Ruskin College, Oxford, in 1970. Her many books include *Women, Resistance, and Revolution* (Pantheon, 1972); *Woman's Consciousness, Man's World* (Penguin, 1973); *Hidden from History: 300 Years of Women's Oppression and the Fight Against It* (Pluto, 1973); *Beyond the Fragments: Feminism and the Making of Socialism* (Merlin Press, 1979); *Promise of a Dream: Remembering the Sixties* (Verso, 2000); *Rebel Crossings: New Women, Free Lovers, and Radicals in Britain and America* (Verso, 2016); *Daring to Hope: My Life in the 1970s* (Verso, 2021). She is currently writing her memoir of the 1980s. This interview took place in July 2019.[1]

Jo Littler: In your 1969 pamphlet *Women's Liberation and the New Politics*, you wrote that 'women have been lying so low for so long, most of us cannot imagine how to get up'. Your work has always been what would now be called 'intersectional', in that it discusses gender in relation to multiple dimensions of class, 'race' and sexuality, as well as geography and history. But it's not about individualised identity politics or making capital out of victimhood, it's about creating solidarities. Can you say something about how you've created these kinds of solidarities in your writing, activism and feminism?

Sheila Rowbotham: In the early days, when we were first beginning to form Women's Liberation groups, many of the people like
myself who organised the first women's liberation conference,
which was held at the end of February 1970, had already become
interested in left politics through movements during the previous
decade – first around the issue of nuclear war, and then the Vietnam
War, which went on for so many years. So issues of peace and anti-
imperialism and national liberation were part of the awareness of a
lot of women who got involved. The rise of civil rights and then the
militant Black Panther movement in America influenced many of
us in Britain as well. Then in the late 1960s in Britain there were
also rebellions among working-class women. In 1968, the Ford
women were demanding equal pay – I remember wincing when I
saw the headline 'Petticoat Pickets' on newsstands. The papers also
attacked men on strike, but not by referring to their underwear! I
had friends in Hull so I responded in a personal way too when the
women from the fishing community there protested about the lack
of safety in the trawlers, and eventually got put down by some of the
men for campaigning on their behalf. And the activism of women
in national liberation movements was also important to many of us.
A delegation of women from Vietnam came to London at the end
of 1970 and the Women's Liberation groups went to support them.

Left-wing activism and ideas thus contributed to the WLM,
although it spread much further quite quickly. Reports on us in
the press were often sneering, and women who had felt some vague
dissatisfaction with what was happening picked up on that and
identified with 'women's lib'. They tracked us down and started
coming along to the groups. They arrived without any preconcep-
tions about politics but with a feeling that 'something's wrong'.
Those of us who had become involved in left politics at university
also shared a sense of discomfort. We might have read Marx, but
the kind of socialism we encountered said little about our problems. For a minority of young women, hopes of wider possibilities
in life had been raised through the development of higher education. In the early 1960s when I went to university, we women were
a tiny minority. We *knew* that we were a bit odd. Nevertheless,
we were determined not to do what we thought our mothers had
done. Yet when women had children, the options began to close

up. Expectations had risen and then been thwarted. That uneasy sense of incongruence was there at the beginning of the discontent. Ideas of resistance and rebellion on the left fused with it. But then we were exasperated because many men on the left refused to listen. Some, however, did support us – and of course social attitudes to women in conservative circles were actually far, far worse.

JL: You've said you found yourself 'uncomfortably straddled between the left and the underground, always arguing with both sides'. How did the underground and alternative culture shape your feminism and left politics? (I heard you planned to create a group called 'Magic Marxism'?)

SR: In 1967 I was active in the Young Socialists in the Hackney Labour Party. Suddenly there was all this wonderful music and beautifully vivid coloured clothes. My rebellion had begun with the beats, and I'd read medieval mystics and Blake, so the hippies going on about everybody's consciousness being infinitely expanded attracted me. But while the people I met through the hippy underground were aware of race, they didn't relate to trade unions. Plus some of the hippy types could often be worse than the left on gender, because they didn't go along with even basic notions of equal rights or equality. Indeed they could be exceedingly elitist. In 1968 I joined the International Socialists (IS) after Enoch Powell's 'rivers of blood' speech because I was concerned about racism. At that time there many disputing tendencies in IS. For example, the left psychologist Peter Sedgwick was quite anti-authoritarian and interested in anarcho-syndicalism, but the leading figure in it, Tony Cliff, decided that fascism was imminent because of Enoch Powel's popularity and that a tight, disciplined organisation was needed. So there was this Leninist move within International Socialists. I ended up leaving after about eighteen months. But before then I wrote my Magic Marxist discussion document calling on everyone to open their consciousness or something like that. I recruited only one other person to the Magic Marxist faction, a friend called Roger Huddle who is a graphic designer and still in the Socialist Workers Party, which is the descendant of IS. Not long after I left International Socialists, women started meeting as women. They faced a lot of opposition from some of the men. But they went on to produce a paper called *Women's Voice*, published by IS, which was a really good paper because like *Spare Rib* it contained a wide range of accounts of women's daily life problems. I thought it was a great pity it was closed down by the centre.

JL: Did you ever go back to the Labour Party?

SR: I rejoined the Labour Party in the 1980s. I stayed in it until Blair and the war in Iraq, and then I just couldn't bear it any longer so I left. Then I rejoined because of Jeremy Corbyn.

JL: A recurring feature of your work, like a lot of other second-wave feminism, is that you put the personal in there a lot alongside the political, obviously in your 1960s autobiography *Promise of a Dream* but also in lots of your other books. You write about Marxism and mascara throughout! Can you say more about how you came to combine that felt experience of social structures and your own history?

SR: I think it must have been talking about personal things through women's liberation groups. I was aware how socialist theorists never mentioned these, as if they thought it was a bit silly to say anything about little things. I decided it was better to risk looking silly by exposing your fears, which other women would probably recognise. I eventually had to stop wearing mascara [laughs] because I got blepharitis, so I had to face the world without it. But I really seriously used to think that I would look so terrible without mascara that I couldn't go out without it!

JL: I remember there was one line where you talked about how Simone de Beauvoir was against mascara, but she wasn't ginger ...

SR: I know! She had dark hair, but mine was ginger. Like many others I was profoundly influenced by de Beauvoir, but on this I parted company with her. When I was young in the 1960s, I did not think of myself as a 'feminist'. I thought there was a puritanical severity about the older generation of feminists. I think that may be a generational assumption – each new generation thinks it has discovered sexual ecstasy for the first time. When I later got to know some of the women who could remember the suffrage movement or had been active in campaigns for women's sexual freedom during the 1920s, I was amazed at how similar they were to us in many ways. Dora Russell – the second wife of Bertrand Russell – had defined herself as a socialist feminist in the 1920s, and she explained to me how, through the Workers' Birth Control Group, they had campaigned in the Labour Party, opposing the powerful Catholic lobby.

JL: You have said movements develop 'in the process of communicating themselves'. What different forms of communication were important to that moment of second wave feminism?

SR: I wrote my first ever article on women at the end of 1968 and it appeared in the left alternative paper Tariq Ali edited, *Black Dwarf,* in January 1969. I knew I must draw on what I'd observed and not say 'Lenin said such and such a thing on the Woman Question' or something like that. Received authority was not going to affect people. I had to find a way of rooting it in some present awareness. So I did talk personally in that piece, saying 'we', and 'we want this'. The impetus must have come from all of the emphasis on subjectivity in the May 1968 events, which in turn were linked to alternative left politics like the Situationists in France and Black writers like James Baldwin, who had been talking about how there should be other dimensions to political expression. I was also aware of discussions about linking politics to sexual psychology. So very early on I remember being certain that I had to risk talking personally, even though it made me vulnerable. And I did get attacked contemptuously by a left trade union man, who said he supposed it was good for me to get my *own* feelings out. Then the most wonderful moment came when Ann Scott, who was about seventeen – ten years younger than I was then – said: 'It's not just *Sheila* who thinks those things'. And I was rescued. That was so important to me.

Before there was a movement we were made to feel we were hysterical, that there was something the matter with us. But even two women saying the same thing made for strength. We quickly came to realise that by trusting and depending on other women we could do all kinds of things that we couldn't do on our own. I remember reacting very early on against something a man said that was very insulting about women at a socialist student meeting. A little group of about three of us happened to be in the Ladies afterwards. I had no idea whether any of the others shared my response, and then we all started to say, 'Wasn't that terrible!'

It was simply by talking to one another like this that we started to form little groups. Women brought friends so these would increase in numbers and then we'd divide and form new ones. I remember a woman I knew in Leeds laughing because a man who was in the International Socialists was saying, 'How *did* you recruit these members?' And of course she hadn't *recruited* anyone – she'd just started talking! That was how it felt – as if it was just developing spontaneously. We talked and then followed our thoughts up collectively in an open manner and that enabled us to grow.

We also became aware something similar was happening in other countries. I learned about Holland, France and Germany by going there and interviewing women and I remember devouring every pamphlet that came from America. We'd circulate them – everything was so precious because we had so little. We really didn't want to have leaders. Some of the young men in small revolutionary groups saw themselves as the vanguard and this encouraged them to be irritatingly bossy, while in America some of the women whose names became known as individuals had suffered by being extracted out by the media, so we consciously avoided hierarchies and media exposure. In Britain we were so wary of communicating with the media, even with women journalists. To our annoyance the media then started to invent people who they called the leaders of 'women's lib'. After the 'Women in Media Group' began it was easier to get a fairer hearing.

JL: Were you part of a consistent group of women? Like a consciousness-raising group that continued, or was it more ad hoc?

SR: The first group I joined was in 1969 in Islington. The meetings had to move and ended up gathering in my room in Hackney.

So many women started turning up we split into three smaller groups and I went to Arsenal Women's Liberation Group, which was at Hermione Harris's house near the football stadium and the tube. We wanted to read Engels and Simone de Beauvoir, and we also supported campaigns as well as talking personally. We'd heard about consciousness raising from America. Some people in the group used to worry whether we were doing it right because though we liked to talk about our own experiences, we also did do other things. For instance, in 1970 a cleaner, May Hobbs, asked for help in organising contract cleaners, and so, along with another Arsenal member, Liz Waugh, for three years I used to leaflet them about joining a union. Arsenal was also involved in leafleting and campaigning in defence of family allowances and against attempts to curb abortion. We carried on until 1978, when Hermione left Britain to work in Honduras.

These women's liberation meetings differed very much from going to listen to a speaker who gave you a talk on a topic, which was the only kind of political meeting I'd been to. I think the openness to personal experience was not only more interesting than many formal meetings; it could bring you close to women, even ones that you weren't necessarily personally that friendly with. Because once you've heard people talking about themselves, their childhood and what happened to them when they were young, you feel an understanding of them which is really deep.

More generally though, the emphasis on personal experience and expression *did* contain problems that later became apparent. I think gradually we came to realise that consciousness raising wasn't an alternative politics, it was a different organisational form which contained snags as well as good things. An obvious one was that people could reiterate 'I feel, I feel, I feel', and then it became impossible to have an argument because you couldn't really lay ideas out on the table and say, 'Well what about this or that?' It would simply be, well 'I *feel* I don't want to have men on the march', so you hit an impasse. The other problem with our structure in women's liberation was that people kept coming to the groups and going away; so the ones who'd survived in the groups the longest tended to get seen as somehow 'in the know', and therefore became sort of covert leaders. We became worried quite early on in the

1970s that we were getting some kind of hidden hierarchy without intending to. We really wanted it to be open to everybody and for everybody to be making the ideas together. But then how did you go into something in more depth?

JL: It's interesting about the connections with the States. Doesn't the term consciousness-raising come in part from the US Black Power movement?

SR: It is fascinating and there are different sources. The oldest forms were religious, the Quakers devised those open kinds of groups. And the Methodists had witnessing in their meetings (I used to go to a Methodist youth group when I was still at school). In America, a Catholic-backed mothers' group called La Leche encouraged small group personal discussions, and the US Communist Party, in the time of the Cold War, held one-to-one sessions because people were under such psychological stress; not only were they losing their jobs, they lived under surveillance, were forced to meet with the curtains drawn and treated as pariahs. In the 1960s, Civil Rights groups in the South started to adopt a form of consciousness raising because they were under such complicated pressures confronting white racism externally, while facing conflicts around race and gender internally. So there are several possible influences, but within the American women's liberation movement it seems to have been Kathie Amatniek (later Kathie Sarachild) who devised and pushed for consciousness raising within the radical feminist groups in New York. Some people say Kathie Amatniek invented it, others say it developed in the South.

JL: You've said that you think that socialist feminism was dominant within second-wave feminism in Britain.

SR: Initially we didn't have any such definitions. When we formed the first British Women's Liberation groups over the course of 1969 we simply agreed that we wanted to assert our oppression as women because that was what was always ignored on the left. Early in 1969 when we held a large meeting at a Revolutionary Festival at Essex University, some idiot guy disrupted it by arriving carrying a woman in on his back, then another very severe Maoist held forth to us at great length. It was very difficult to talk. So we were adamant when we met afterwards in London that we did want to talk *as women*. We needed to be on our own in order to work out what it was that we were trying to think about. That desire for autonomy was the first break with the normal way of having left meetings. But it was not a separatist politics. Men supported us on demonstrations and we used to go around speaking on Women's Liberation to all kinds of meetings of women and men. Quite often we went in twos, even threes, to help build up the confidence of everyone to become speakers.

There was so much going on in the early 1970s, so many strikes and workers' occupations, and violent conflict in Northern Ireland. A real intensity of struggle, you couldn't really disregard it. It was around you all the time. So many of us would also go on marches against the Industrial Relations Bill, Edward Heath's effort to curb unions, or against the war in Vietnam or apartheid in South Africa, as well as doing things that were explicitly about women. Around 1973 some women started to define themselves as radical feminists. They didn't necessarily think that you had to be absolutely separate from men personally, but they felt that you had to put women's issues first and not go on about the other things. Whereas those of us who then started to call ourselves socialist feminists thought you couldn't really solve all the problems, even the ones that affect women most especially, by simply focusing on the relationship between men and women, and that class and race also interconnected and affected women's lives. The two wings of the movement could still co-exist, nevertheless.

Several years later when separatism emerged as a *politics*, many of us argued there was a difference between wanting organisational *autonomy* and not wanting to separate our politics from men totally. So socialist feminists argued for instance that men should come and support our demonstrations. By the mid 1970s, at meetings in London to prepare the International Women's Day march, conflict developed because other feminists said, 'No, we don't want to have anything to do with men.' And from the late 1970s the Yorkshire Ripper murders had a profoundly upsetting impact. Women were being attacked and killed in such horrific ways, and the police persisted in making distinctions between 'prostitutes', as they called them, and 'respectable women'. It was not only outrageous – their prejudices impeded them finding the culprit. There were a lot of demonstrations around violence in the late 1970s and these were important. But unfortunately a minority of women began to castigate *all* men as 'potential rapists' and, what many of us found even worse, were hostile to boy babies and small boys. I saw this version of separatist feminism as extremely reactionary in its deterministic implications. It generated a destructive atmosphere of denunciation, guilt and fear. The women who were the bravest in challenging it were lesbian feminists.

JL: Turning to masculinity, you have written about how men need to be pressured to change whilst simultaneously warning of the dangers of them closing up. You argue that 'we must keep this dialectic open' around masculinity. I was thinking about the expansion of new types of misogyny today and wondering to what extent you think that project of reinventing masculinity ever went far enough – if that dialectic is in urgent need of resuscitation?

SR: Men started forming men's groups in the 1970s to think consciously about masculinity. Both women and men also made really determined attempts to get men involved in caring for small children. This meant the generation of boys and girls brought up in this way came to take it for granted as normal. More broadly too, despite the intensification in how work is now organised, there have been marked changes in my lifetime. It is much more common to see men of all classes and ethnicities pushing small children around or carrying them. But on the other hand, as the decades have gone by there's been such a venomous reaction by other sections of men in physical and verbal attacks on women. So there are men who really have shifted quite a lot, and then men who feel that they're not going anywhere – that they're humiliated and treated with contempt. There's a kind of suppressed rage, isn't there, that has turned into hostility towards women, but also towards anybody that can be turned into an outsider group.

JL: And scapegoated.

SR: Yes. That's a really distressing thing. But I don't think it's something that you can solve by simply berating people. When you accentuate competition and dominance over cooperation and caring for others, which our kind of capitalism revels in, it is not so surprising. You have to dig down to what is causing it and use several strategies to undermine and oppose what is happening. But as a basic starting point I've noticed that people's attitudes tend to begin to move when they *like* people – even if they disagree with them. And over time when they have fairly regular contact with people they like, despite the arguments, attitudes can change.

JL: Yes, you talk in one of your books about the East End skinhead boys you taught in a Further Education College during the 1960s, and how they changed their mind on issues about class and 'race' eventually through prolonged discussion and exposure to ideas …

SR: Yes, I did really like them. And I think they were fond of me too. And because, for the first time in their lives, they were taught in groups of about ten instead of thirty or forty, or even fifty, as they had been at school, they gradually opened up to more radical ways of seeing. Some of them were aware of unions through being skilled apprentices and so they felt a consciousness of class in a traditional way. Then others were being affected by music and the hippie counterculture. Even the ones who were saying they were *against* the hippies were attuned to some of the things that were going on. So I used to try and encourage them to question and think their attitudes through. I gained some allies who would argue alongside me. I remember one of the students, an engineering apprentice, who was sixteen and had joined the Maoist group led by a trade unionist called Reg Birch. He had started questioning cultural and political attitudes because the only neighbour who would report the cruel treatment of a local child was a prostitute. He was furious when people spoke disrespectfully about her because she was the moral person to him.

JL: In London, at the re-issue of *Promise of a Dream*, you said that 'every generation has to make its own women's movement'. What do you find depressing and hopeful about contemporary feminism and politics?

SR: I'm not that well-informed really so I'm a bit hesitant to make comments. But as an observer reading the news I thought it was great when all the Me Too stuff came up against Trump. I have never myself encountered men like some of those powerful rich men in the American entertainment business behaving in such horrible ways, but the collective courage generated by the women who protested was moving. When I was young I was so desperate to escape from all the restrictions on our freedom I wanted liberty most of all, rather than protection. But the absence of sexual restraints seems to have resulted in some men treating women as prey. So I think it's a good thing that there is this rebellious *awareness* among young women. I just hope it can extend to women who are totally trapped, stuck in really low paid jobs, and have difficulty combining these with looking after children, and who suffer from the accentuated forms of inequality which this long period of austerity has imposed on people who are really poor. I know there are smaller groups of women who have a renewed interest in socialist feminism and have been campaigning and organising on these issues so I hope that this resistance will expand.

JL: You've had a really varied set of experiences as an educator. You've been a teacher in schools and adult education, your work is on the A-Level syllabus, and you've worked at universities. How has this breadth of educational experience shaped what you're interested in and write about?

SR: I went to work in a Further Education college by chance. Around 1964 I lived in a flat in Hackney and there was no phone in our flat. We would go outside to the Hackney Downs station where there were public phones, and I was ringing around to try to get part-time teaching from the public call box. And this weird person answered the phone and asked me if I'd heard of a French revolutionary called Blanqui. I said I had! I was really interested in Blanqui because I'd had this tutor, Richard Cobb, at university who'd specialised in French revolutionary history. So I was given my first job because I'd heard of Blanqui. The voice on the phone was Bill Fishman, who had grown up in the East End, had been involved in the Labour League of Youth and later became a historian of Jewish anarchism. When I first met him he was a very eccentric principal of Tower Hamlets Further Education College. That was how I started to teach the day release students 'liberal studies'. Then, from the late 1960s, I taught in the Workers' Educational Association (WEA), through a man called Jim Fyrth, who was a very nice man. Jim had stayed in the Communist Party after 1956 but was very non-sectarian. He recruited a lot of young people, including my then partner Paul Atkinson, as well as Sally Alexander and Barbara Taylor, to the WEA. I was employed as a part-timer doing three lectures on separate topics each week all over London. During the 1970s I also taught part-time in comprehensive schools. One was a very gruesome boys' comprehensive, and another, called Starcross, was an enlightened school with a truly liberal head who was very concerned about all of the girls in the school.

JL: I was interested in your work with the GLC because some of the feminist suggestions you make are municipal in character: you write about how you might imagine more nurseries, launderettes, municipal restaurants, imaginative architecture, cheap council flats for teens (when I read that, the latter was the most jarring one now!). As there's a renewed interest in municipalism now, what lessons can we take from what the GLC did between 1981 and its abolition by the Conservative government in 1986?

SR: After abolition the memory of the extraordinarily far-sighted and creative things that had been done just got completely pushed aside. The GLC's radical scope was so much wider than previous left councils had been in the past. Ken Livingstone had been influenced by Harvey Milk in San Francisco and was aware of gay liberation and feminist politics in a way that was unusual among left Labour Party politicians. I worked in Industry and Employment, the area for which Mike Ward was responsible. Mike had been inspired by the visionary measures adopted by the Communist council in Bologna, but he also knew in detail about the history of local government in London. Robin Murray, the chief economic adviser, had experience as a development economist as well as in community politics in Brighton where he lived. My immediate boss was Hilary Wainwright, then in her early thirties. She never ever stopped you doing things and always defended you to the teeth. Although rather chaotic in her ways of behaving, Hilary was a very good boss. She contrived to link the creation of forms of democratic planning with economic policies that served human needs, transplanting the Lucas Aerospace Workers' Alternative Plan into local government.

JL: What did you do at the GLC?

SR: I initiated the policies on childcare, domestic labour and contract cleaning for the London Industrial Strategy. I also co-edited a newspaper with John Hoyland called *Jobs For Change*, which reported on what Industry and Employment was doing, including creating jobs by funding women's workplace co-ops and nurseries. We also funded a launderette run by older women under the Westway. About 20 per cent of people in London at that time didn't have their own washing machine. Many were pensioners. There had been municipal washing places that were being closed. The women who used one had campaigned for a replacement, a community launderette. Westway was funded by Industry and Employment and the nursery by the Women's Committee, headed by Val Wise. So the women who used the launderette had contact with the little children, and they also used to do the washing of all the nappies for the nursery.

When I went to visit Westway I noticed they still had wooden washboards, and they used to scrub all the stuff with soap, just like women used to do when I was a little girl. We had this technology group in the Greater London Enterprise Board, and I kept saying, 'Well there's this nursery, and there's this laundrette. They've all got these very backward sort of methods of washing and drying and things'. And these technology guys came in and they developed something called combined heat and power so that you could use the heat that came from the dryers to go into the washing machines to save energy. That was a very neat way in which activities and resources could come together.

At the same time as providing practical help to groups of Londoners who had previously lacked access to public resources, there was also an openness to fun and music in the GLC. There were all these festivals that we had, and music and dancing in the parks for pensioners. It was very inspirational and creative. It was a great pity that so much of it got lost and abandoned. It was an act of real Tory desecration. They even captured County Hall. Though Hilary and Maureen Mackintosh edited a book called *A Taste of Power* (Verso, 1987) which contains accounts we wrote based on interviews with people who had been affected by the GLC's economic and social innovations, I fear so much of the memory of what was done has been subsequently buried. So I am really heartened there is interest. The more people who start looking at it the better.

JL: Later on you wrote about homeworking, didn't you?

SR: Homeworking was part of the London Industrial Strategy, but I became involved later on through contact with Jane Tate, who set up networks from her base in West Yorkshire, and I also met Renana Jhabvala and Ela Bhatt, who organised the Self Employed Women's Association in India. Along with the economist Swasti Mitter, I helped to get a group together internationally on women's low paid work, including homework, through the World Institute for Development Economics Research (WIDER) in the early 1990s. We edited a book called *Dignity and Daily Bread* (1994).

JL: What was your university teaching experience like?

SR: Well, it changed over the time. The conditions were much nicer when I first went. There were quite a lot of radical people in the sociology department and a sharing of work and ideas. Gradually it became more and more formal, with all the increased pressures that were put on academics.

JL: And what was happening to socialist feminism when you worked at Manchester University?

SR: I was there from the mid 1990s to 2010, and initially the kind of feminism the students encountered came mainly through women's studies rather than through political activism. Then I observed from the late 1990s and into the early 2000s another generation coming along who didn't really see feminism as an issue, but were extremely active on the environment and world trade and those kinds of global politics. Some were also interested in the global oppression of women and in poor countries. And while I was working at Manchester, with the help of the socialist feminist economist Diane Elson, we held several international meetings on home work.

JL: Reading *Women, Resistance and Revolution* now, one of the things that's so striking is how it ranges over such vast historical as well as geographical periods – over so much time and space. And you were twenty-nine when it came out, is that right?

SR: Yeah, I was very ignorant really. But that first book really got me reading a lot. I started to write *Women, Resistance and Revolution* in 1969. I was trying to look at different ways in which women had resisted and been part of revolutionary movements more or less everywhere, and then I wanted to talk about the modern women's movement as well. So in the end it got divided into two, and the stuff relating to Women's Liberation became *Women's Consciousness, Man's World*.

I had originally thought, in a very arrogant way – like quite a lot of us in 1969 – that we'd more or less invented all this from our own heads. But then we discovered that actually the women's movements in the past, both the suffrage movement and women's movements around livelihood and economic survival, had characteristics which we could recognise. And women in revolutionary movements in France, and then later in the Soviet Union and China, had also expressed the need to connect the personal and the political, which we had regarded as our discovery!

I was very enthusiastic too, and excited, and that probably comes over in *Women, Resistance and Revolution*. Although I mainly brought a lot of secondary sources together, I was able to read French women' s revolutionary newspapers in the library at Colindale. I was amazed by how they voiced personal feelings along with political demands for the rights of women and of workers. I

later learned how a key figure, the seamstress who'd been part of
the 1848 uprising, Jeanne Deroin, had come to Britain in exile
after being released from prison. She was later in contact with
William Morris's Socialist League, and knew the socialist feminist, Isabella Ford, who was active in suffrage and the Independent
Labour Party. These personal connections in how ideas get passed
on intrigue me.

The crucial historical influences upon me had been my tutor
Richard Cobb, who was part of a movements of 'history from
below' in France, and also Dorothy and Edward Thompson, who
wrote on Chartism and the early working-class radical movement. They made me aware of the need to look at history in *depth*,
but also to ask questions from your own knowledge or particular
understanding. I have kept on trying to put both aspects together,
though the questions that have preoccupied me have varied. My
earlier books focused on interconnections between personal experience and public politics. However, throughout the 1970s both
the left and women's liberation were debating how to relate to the
state. We needed it, but in its present form it could be coercive and
convey oppressive values.

In the 1980s Margaret Thatcher, privatisation and municipal
socialism at the GLC combined, combined to make me look more
closely at the state. I had done a play about a socialist feminist in
Derby called Alice Wheeldon, who was wrongly accused of plot-
ting to assassinate the prime minister, Lloyd George, during the
First World War, and when it was published I did an exceedingly
long introduction to it, documenting her supporters in suffrage and
the shop stewards movement as well as her prosecutors in the police
and the embryonic secret services.

The gay socialist Edward Carpenter has fascinated me since I
first went to read his papers in Sheffield when I was doing my PhD
thesis on the nineteenth-century adult education movement. In
1977 I wrote about him in a book I did with Jeff Weeks, *Socialism
and the New Life*. I was interested because he wrote on same-sex
desire so early on, and also on green politics, art and culture, the
transformation of daily life and living, as well as on socialism in its
more conventional forms. Eventually I did a big, fat biography of
Carpenter called *A Life of Liberty and Love*. It was originally fatter

even than the one that was published – the very fat version lives in manuscript form in the Sheffield archives.

JL: But *A Century of Women* is bigger!

SR: Yes, *A Century of Women* came about at a time when I was very broke in the early 1990s and I was encouraged by my agent Faith Evans to put this proposal forward. No sooner had the proposal been accepted by Penguin than I developed a bad repetitive strain injury and couldn't write anything for about two years. So it had a bit of a chequered career. When it was published I don't think it really had the impact that we'd hoped because by the time a new century arrived, people were interested in the new century and not really in the one that had just gone! But it was an education for me. I learnt a lot of stuff about all kinds of things, including women and sport, which had never been my strong point. And it was nice to be able to write about women who were artists and musicians. It was fun doing that.

JL: I think you've easily written more than anyone else I've interviewed. The sheer volume of volumes!

SR: Oh dear, it's a bit alarming.

JL: It's great!

SR: It's also alarming in terms of archives. When I moved from Hackney to Manchester in 1995 I gave away many papers, mainly on women's liberation in the 1970s, as well as my ephemeral writings. These eventually got catalogued and now live in the LSE in the Women's Library. Then I gave away a whole lot more in 2010 when I moved from Manchester to Bristol. I think there were about thirty boxes! And they're still uncatalogued. I am currently working on a memoir remembering the 1970s. It follows on from *Promise of a Dream*, which ended in 1969. Before the Covid lockdown I visited the Women's Library many times to go through the boxes and took notes, and fortunately I also still have some stuff here [gestures around her home]; it's been a very weird experience, researching this stuff from my own life, not only books but pamphlets, letters and diaries. It's partly because, being an historian, I always wanted to make sure records survived, so whenever I went to Women's Liberation conferences I used to buy every local newsletter because I knew those are the things that disappear. Everything that might disappear I kept buying, and adding to this archive …

JL: It could be some archivist's dream.

SR: Or horror!

JL: Can you say something about your attitude to writing and how it's evolved? Your writing has got a levity and comedy to it as well as breadth and is very quotable.

SR: I wanted to write from being quite young and started a journal when I was in my early teens. I always loved trying to craft words. I was seen as a peculiar swot. I didn't come from a family that used a vast amount of unusual words, but I was always trying to discover words. I literally used to sit and read a dictionary when I was about fourteen! It was a feeling of great power to get your hands on some new word that would be *just right*. I thought probably I would do English at university. But I had a wonderful history teacher who told me, 'You should be a historian', which I think was right, and I'm glad.

I still love words and ways of saying things that might jog people's attention without showing off. I try to write as clearly as I can and have often worried when I found socialist and feminist writing was not that clear. I know that it's not always possible to be clear and it could be rather repressive to insist that people must be clear. But on the other hand, I do think you can be *more* clear than often people are. And I don't see why people aren't. I have always wanted people to be able to easily read things that I write. On the other hand, I have to admit that I did hear once someone saying that they'd read *Hidden From History* with a dictionary [laughs]. So it shows that you're not always necessarily that clear. And I think if you're referring to a body of ideas, it's very difficult to be completely accessible. A friend said to me that her daughter had read *Promise of a Dream* and not understood some things in it. I had thought that was pretty straightforward, but of course there was a lot of references to the politics of that time, which to a younger person wouldn't be obvious.

JL: You can never be completely transparent.

SR: No. Sometimes there are words that give me a sort of physically ecstatic feeling. I read something that someone's written and I think, 'Ah!' So it's also an aesthetic yearning as well as a practical one. I have a bit of a secret life writing poems, and I do quite like reading them, but nobody ever asks me to do that [laughs].

JL: Are they out there in the world?

SR: Not too much out in the world. Some of them went into *Dreams and Dilemmas*. And I do enjoy reading them. Occasionally I've been asked.

JL: Do you have a plan for a volume of poetry?

SR: No, no! [laughs]. But I still keep them.

JL: I think you should publish them! And thank you.

NOTES

1 This interview was first published as "'Every generation has to make its own women's movement'": Jo Littler talks to Sheila Rowbotham' in *Soundings: A Journal of Politics and Culture*, Issue 77, 2021, pp37-54.

We want ourselves alive and debt free!

Verónica Gago is Professor of Social Sciences at the University of Buenos Aires, Argentina, and author of *Neoliberalism From Below* (Duke University Press, 2017); *Feminist International: How to Change Everything* (Verso, 2020); and *A Feminist Theory of Debt*, with Lucí Cavallero (Pluto, 2021). She is an active member of the grassroots feminist movement Ni Una Menos, founded by a group of artists, activists and academics in Argentina. Ni Una Menos has described itself as a 'collective scream against machista violence'. It has regularly held protests against femicides, and has connected femicide to a range of other issues, including sexual harassment, abortion and reproductive rights, transgender and sex worker rights, the gender pay gap, gender roles, neoliberalism and debt.[1] Its first demonstration of 200,000 people was organised in the wake of a fourteen-year-old pregnant girl, Chiara Paez, being beaten to death by her boyfriend, in Buenos Aires in 2015. In 2016 the movement came to wider attention on social media through the hashtag #NiUnaMenos, and protests spread throughout Latin America, particularly in Chile, Uruguay and Peru, where it prompted what has been described as the largest demonstration in Peruvian history. In 2016 Ni Una Menos launched a national women's strike. This interview was conducted in July 2021.[2]

Jo Littler: In your book *Feminist International* you discuss being inspired by Rosa Luxemburg's words, 'Every strike takes on its own character'. You use this idea to theorise the women's strike and the Ni Una Menos movement more broadly. Could you outline their 'character' for us here?

Verónica Gago: The first demonstrations in 2015 were saying 'stop the femicide'. That was the main characteristic of the first major mobilisation. Then after that first year the movement became more complex. It started to think about how to connect together different *kinds* of violence against women, to try to get a more complex idea of this web of violence. It started to think about what constituencies and subjects were involved – lesbian, trans people, and *travestis* – or what the movements were within the movement.[3] So, after that first year we were becoming engaged with more complex ways to conceptualise violence. And then by 2016 I think we were realising how to *connect* different kinds of violence, especially through the tool of the feminist strike. I think the movement was becoming a way to make sense of the connection between violence against women and *travestis* and police violence, and economic and financial violence. The movement has been building a common sense about what this kind of *machista* violence means for certain bodies and certain territories. We have been creating a very slow, but at the same time very large, movement which was connecting these different sorts of violence. It was a sort of pedagogical exercise, one which would discuss, but also produce, assemblies and organise transnational forms of coordination which would go beyond the idea of 'ni una menos'. It was like we stopped and thought, 'Well, we want ourselves alive; but we also want ourselves to be debt-free'. So we started to go beyond a very narrow narrative of gender violence.

I think what has also been very important for us is how this movement has built so many Latin American and global connections. Over the last five years, I have increasingly been talking about it as a 'massive' feminism, a feminism of the masses. This is a new cycle of feminism. Of course, we have different lines and genealogies of feminism, but I think that the very novelty of this feminist movement is its *massive* feature. We are, all the time, producing these significant events but also conducting forms of political work which organise feminism as an everyday practice. And we are also continually doing political work to connect different organisations and different conflicts. I think it is very impressive how in the last two years feminism has become a very important term in the different political struggles in Latin America. For example in Chile, in Ecuador, in Colombia, where you have different uprisings, strikes and popular demonstrations, feminism has had a very important role in terms of organisation and vocabulary; in terms of doing and practising politics in other ways.

JL: Both the movement and your writings emphasise the relationship between gendered violence, disenfranchisement and neoliberal financialisation, and break new ground in drawing these themes together. 'The debt is owed to us' is a hugely powerful slogan used by Ni Una Menos. Can you summarise what it means, how it evolved and has been used?

VG: I think that the question of debt and financialisation is, for us, the key issue which connects a reading of neoliberalism to the feminist movement. It's not just an analytical framework that we are using; it's a very concrete comprehension of how these different forms of violence are entangled and embedded in our everyday life. Debt is especially important because on the one hand it's a more abstract form of violence, but at the same time it's become so much more widely extended today through massive impoverishment. So we started work with this slogan – *we want ourselves alive and debt free* – and started considering different debates and ways of connecting domestic or household debt with different aspects of violence.

A key question for us was: how can we organise a demonstration against debt? By the time of the strike in 2020 the common slogan we were using was, 'The debt is owed to us' ('La deuda es con nosotres'). It was a way to change or to shift the sense of what debt is. We conducted different kinds of demonstrations in front of the Central Bank, and in a variety of different political spaces, to connect the issue of the public debt with domestic debt. We were campaigning to reclaim public services, and also to reclaim public budgets – to reclaim them against the corporate exploitation of, for example, food and medicine during the pandemic. Over the last year or so we have also been reconnecting the issue of debt with the question of housing, especially against eviction.

The slogan 'The debt is owed to us' has been a device to rethink economic and especially financial violence, and to show how this violence is practised against certain bodies and particular territories. Another key aspect of this political and conceptual work is to show how these forms of environmental extraction against common resources and territories are also bound up with what I call financial extractivism. The household debt is a political device, as are new forms of labour exploitation. The slogan enables all these things, which are not always obvious, to be shown as issues that are on the feminist agenda, and translates these problems into a demand of the movement: the debt is owed to us.

JL: Ni Una Menos's movement against gendered violence is very inclusive (of women, lesbians, trans people and *travestis*) and radical; and in discussing this you have written that it is a hackneyed argument that to be inclusive 'it must moderate and soften its demands'. How important is this combination in the movement's success? And to what extent do you think the success of this double move – inclusive solidarity and bold demands – is an effective general recipe, or particularly conducive in Latin America?

VG: Well, I don't know, but I think that here in Latin America, and in Argentina in particular, this building of transversality - the inclusion of different political actors and different political conflicts within the movement – has been very important in building its size, its massiveness. Because, of course, there are the very important, traditional feminist organisations, and there are historical feminist dynamics, but we also need to go beyond this 'sectorial' definition of feminism and start to think of feminism as a political praxis in each different space: for example, in unions, in political organisations, in social movements, in schools and universities, in communitarian spaces. It was very interesting to see how, in those different spaces, people began to ask, 'What kind of feminism are we developing?' or, 'What kind of feminism are we trying to develop?' or, 'What are the features of feminism that we have to develop in our own organisations?'

Thinking in terms of feminism as a zone of conflict was very important for this kind of politics of inclusion, as it was trying to go beyond a merely formal idea of alliances between different forces or organisations. I think that its scale, its massiveness, shapes its political capacity to produce proximity between very different organisations and very different struggles; which also – and I think this is a question that you are interested in, how to build solidarity – involves going beyond formal mechanisms of solidarity, to try to produce this more dense idea of coordination, transversality and massiveness.

JL: Was it ever easy?!

VG: No, no, no, all the time it involves very complicated articulations and a *lot* of political work. And it does not always function, or function well. But I think we felt feminism as a common force – a force that you can translate into your own space and your own experience, and can have internal battles around in your organisation – was key in producing this idea of inclusion, of being part. And it is the movement that gives you force or strength in your own organisation, but also means that you can be part of a movement *beyond* your own organisation. I think this double move has been both very amazing and very important for a new generation of feminist leaders in popular and community organisations, unions, social movements, student networks, migrant collectives. And it is also a political experience of subjectivity for a very new generation which is outside traditional political organisations. They are building new collectives and developing a new sense of what organisation means, which has to do with, to quote Sara Ahmed, the question of how to live a feminist life in a collective dimension.[4] That, of course, is not easy; but it is an exercise which is a new articulation, and which goes beyond the idea of coalition, as it is not so formal as a coalition – it is a *movement*. And so it's trying to rethink the idea of radical inclusion, in the sense of enlarging definitions of feminism in a very practical way.

JL: I love the geographical scope of *Feminist International*, and I wondered if you could say something about the potential and the challenges in this regard? So, how international is it at the moment? What are the possibilities, what are the challenges?

VG: I think that if we have to name the salient features of this cycle of this movement, its *internationalism* is one of its most distinctive features. Massiveness and internationalism are both very important forces of this movement and both are related. In terms of ridding ourselves of neoliberalism, and ridding ourselves of financial capitalism, one question is: how can we confront this globalisation of capital from our concrete and situated struggles? At the same time, we can also think about how, for example, in one year the movement is very strong in Argentina and in Italy; and in the next year, the movement is especially strong in Spain; and in another two months, a movement arises in Mexico, and then Chile is in the front line. So we can also connect, and *feel*, that we are part of this movement that has different rhythms and forms of accumulation. And I think this idea of being part of a movement that is not always in your country, or in your geographical space, but that you feel that you are *in*, is very important. In other words it has been important to rethink the idea of concrete internationalism: it's not an abstract structure that we are, or are not, part of. And the ubiquity of feminism nowadays is an effect of these struggles.

Its strength also has to do with a capacity to reorganise our political agenda in terms of the conjuncture. For example, during the pandemic, all the dimensions of feminism [that work] against the precariousness of life, and all the vocabulary about care and reproductive labour was a part of international exchanges which could produce a diagnosis. But it was also connecting different struggles – from domestic work to migrant collectives, from struggles against evictions to struggles against neoextractivism – in order to reframe the idea of crisis. So, I think that this dimension of internationalism is also the plane where a common diagnosis is elaborated that is all the time expanding its vocabularies, and its comprehensions of violence, and also its political force, in order to organise different measures that translate this diagnosis into concrete action.

JL: So, Latin America was one of the early neoliberal test-beds or starting grounds. Do you think it will be one of the places where it ends? That is my very hopeful question.

VG: Well, we are very confident with our comrades in Chile especially, where effectively neoliberalism started with the Augusto Pinochet's dictatorship.[5] I think that here in Latin America we have a very strong archive of the origins of neoliberalism as a fascist regime because the different dictatorships – especially, but not only, the forms of state terrorism in Chile and Argentina – have been intimately linked to neoliberalism. We do not have the experience of a 'liberal' neoliberalism or a 'progressive' neoliberalism. We intimately understand what violence, conservatism and fascism has to do with neoliberalism because, from the beginning, our experience in the region has been an experience of neoliberalism combined with state terrorism. Neoliberal violence is not something that comes later, as a sort of deviation from 'original' neoliberalism. And I think we also can read neoliberalism itself in these forty years as a different reaction to different types of struggles. We are now seeing an alliance between neoliberalism and conservatism as a reaction to this massive feminism movement. We can see the impact of feminism in connecting migration, anti-extractivism, different popular indigenous struggles, against a very conservative and racist management of the crisis. We are now witnessing very important struggles in our region against neoliberalism, against tax reforms, against the police, against different types of extractivism against populations. And we are also trying to discuss how neoliberalism is also a battleground of different subjectivities – subjectivities that feminism, and especially transfeminism, are developing.

So I think this double movement for and against neoliberalism is very much at the frontline of different struggles in Latin America or, more accurately, to go beyond the colonial name, Abya Yala. We are in a very dramatic moment in terms of impoverishment, in terms of repression, in terms of the militarisation of regions. But, at the same time, *it is not pacified*. The different conservative and neoliberal powers cannot pacify this region. It is not easy to establish a government authority that can establish austerity and can establish fear. All the time, different movements, mobilisations and different uprisings are emerging. There is no pacification at all.

JL: You follow Rosa Luxemburg's complication of reform or revolution and her notion of 'revolutionary realpolitik' – a left political pragmatics from below. How does it move beyond the strike? Can you talk about the relationship between the strike, the state, and political party politics?

VG: In Argentina this is a very important issue because here the feminist movement has always historically had a very complex ideological composition. There are different comrades in the feminist movement who are also within a very wide range of political parties, from the left wing all the way to Peronism.[6] I think it was easier when the strike was developed against the previous government – the [right-wing] Macri government – because that regime was very clearly neoliberal.[7] He took on the biggest external debt in national history, as well as the biggest debt created by the IMF in its own history. It was easier for us to create this coalition, and to generate a very big movement that included political parties from the left alongside Peronist parties, when the confrontation was with this very neoliberal government. Nowadays the composition of the movement is very different to two years ago. In the first place this is because of the change of the government [Argentina has had a centre-left government since 2019] and secondly it is because of the pandemic. The last strike was in 2020, just a few days before the pandemic started, and now all the different organisations within our popular feminist network are focused on dealing with that crisis. So I think the relationship between political parties and the feminist movement is also now in a very difficult and dynamic position in terms of the conjunctural conditions. That also has to do with other elements: the composition of forces between political parties and social movements and the scenario where some social movements are also part of political fronts.

JL: Could you say a bit more about what has happened since the advent of Covid?

VG: In Argentina, in the first year of the pandemic, a lot of different popular and feminist networks and organisations were co-ordinating campaigns to reclaim and improve the wages of care workers. Plus, in the first year of the pandemic there was a very important campaign for abortion rights. Last December a law was passed that made abortion legal on demand for the first time ever in Argentina.[8] It was a very important victory after the 'green tide' and all the militant efforts over so many years. We carried out different kinds of actions, trying to make issues visible, and to organise in different spaces and different networks. Last year we created a slogan, 'Nos sostienen las redes feministas', or 'feminist networks sustain us'. It was a common slogan across the movement, including the unions. We were trying to visualise and *make visible* how the feminist movement was at the frontline of the crisis.

Over the past few months the feminist movement in Argentina has campaigned for employment rights for *travestis* and trans people. That was achieved: the law was passed two weeks ago. We've also been campaigning to reclaim vaccines for the community, and wages for care workers; and we've been campaigning against the corporate control of food, especially, and against housing evictions. This has been our agenda over the last month. In the midst of the pandemic we have tried all the time to continue organising through assemblies, to connect different conflicts and to *produce* the political agenda. But it is not the same, of course, because up to now our main space was the street.

JL: And it's now moved from the street to online?

VG: Yes, although it's neither completely 'virtual' nor completely 'real' because the networks and the activist initiatives are criss-crossing different territories all the time. It has not been easy to converge and to be together in our massive mobilisation, but we are trying to maintain different assemblies and different networks, and try to organise different kinds of meetings.

JL: The theme of environmentalism is present in both your work and the movement. For instance, in *A Feminist Reading Of Debt* your interviewees talk about how the purchase of expensive seeds and agrotoxins becomes a cause of debt, unlike in organic farming. You've also discussed the Bolivian dam construction; extractivism; and the mystification of woman as an exploitable natural resource. So, I wanted to ask you: as the environmental crisis becomes more pressing, how should those demands be extended?

VG: I think in Latin America the vocabulary of environmen-talism has more to do with anti-extractivist struggles than with 'environmentalism'. This vocabulary is changing fast with younger generations. Whilst comrades in other areas talk about eco-feminism, I think that here, in Latin America, the struggles, the vocabulary, the imagery, have to do more with strategies of anti-extractivism and indigenous movements. There are a lot of very young activists who are making links between environmentalism and feminism, but still I think the question of *extractivism* is the main issue for us in rethinking the exploitation of land, the exploitations of corporations and the distribution of common resources. In Latin America the question of how we can reframe imperialism in terms of a discussion of eco-feminism, which also goes beyond the idea of green capitalism or some sort of 'ecology-light' for consumerism, is a very important issue and debate. The agro-business model is now exploding in terms of environmental problems, both with the basic issues of food and water, and with the dispossession of indigenous people through the expropriation of plants. There is also a very long discussion about the colonial frame of developmentalism in 'the Third World' and the dilemmas related to the international division of labour for our countries. So this genealogy, in terms of indigenous, community and anti-colonial struggles, is very important for us in working out how feminism and ecological demands and struggles are entangled nowadays. Today these different vocabularies are being connected to the crisis of the pandemic.

JL: I particularly like how your work emphasises interdependence rather than individualism; for example, you wrote 'the body never depends solely on itself' (which resonates a bit with what we tried to do in *The Care Manifesto*, I think, and with Judith Butler's recent work on interdependence and violence).[9] Related to this, you also write about the importance of avoiding cultivating a ranking of suffering, and the frozen categories of '"pure victims" (that place where the patriarchy loves to situate us)', and the need to 'politicise violence against women by displacing the status of victimhood'. Can you say more about the dangers of this narrow, individualist, anti-contextual presentation of victims – and how to avoid it?

VG: Yes. I think that going beyond a narrow understanding of victimisation and the 'necropolitical' counting of femicide as our legitimate place of enunciation was very important for the move-ment.[10] It involves problematising the idea of permanent pain and sorrow; moving beyond that necrological narrative about ourselves. This is in part because we have had the experience of a human rights movement that went beyond the idea of victimisa-tion – in order to reclaim 'disappeared' people, and in order to reclaim political and activist and militant trajectories. For us, for the feminist movement in Argentina, as in other parts of Latin America, connecting these trajectories and genealogies of Madres y Abuelas de Plaza de Mayo and different political organisations related to human rights (but not a liberal definition of human rights!) was very important.[11] It was fundamental to reclaim other subjective frames for pain and violence.

It was also very important to connect the different genealogies of social movements to the feminist movement. We were trying to think: 'Well, we are dispossessed, we are under attack, we are experiencing different kinds of violence, but how do we produce ourselves as a subject of struggle?' I think this is an open question. We are, all the time, in different situations, trying to rethink how this conflict can be named or narrated as a *political* conflict – not just an individual or interpersonal conflict. I think that making this practice a collective practice is crucial. It's also the case when we talk about, for example, movements like #MeToo. How do we go beyond the idea of personal problematic or interpersonal matters? How do we produce a collective, and also a *political*, diagnosis of this collective matter?

So it was key for us to produce feminism as a political movement and not just as a narrative of victimhood. And in that sense, what you talk about, interdependence, is very important. It's what we do all the time; and it's not visible, it's not recognised, and it's not named as a part of political praxis. So, I think this idea of inter-dependence as political praxis is also very important, although it's not interdependence in biological terms, it's in terms of its political dimension.

JL: Yes, absolutely! My next question is about the relationship between your political activism and your academic work. Your work is very theoretical but also full of very barricade-worthy slogans.

It's also a good mix in terms of showing overlapping contexts and connections, and in thinking about intersectional gendered inequalities.

VG: I worked for many years as a journalist and so I think that I developed a practice of writing in ways other than that of a purely academic style. I'm also a member of the independent publisher Tinta Limón, which has produced a range of books and materials from, and for, the social movements.[12] I think what I do is bound up with this experience; but also, in Latin America, there is also a long and expansive tradition that enables the public university to get very close to different popular social movements. The connection between public universities and social movements is very common here. There's a very strong tradition of autonomy in terms of public universities, and of a connection with social movements, with political practice. Not everybody is interested in that, but it's a strong tradition, and nowadays it's important. So I think of writing in terms of political intervention, but also I am very interested in research taking into account political commitment.

JL: Is journalism something you do alongside academia or were you a journalist before?

VG: I started when I was a student, as a job, to pay for … my life! I was very young, I was twenty-two; but also at twenty I started to collaborate with a magazine published by a union and then in different activist publications at the university. So for me it's a practice of writing which has always been a form of political writing. That is, I think, part of my style. But there is also a sense of urgency when you are doing that kind of writing; it's a different temporality than if you are only producing for the academy, for the university. I do like writing in that register too, very much. It's more free, and for a wider public.

JL: Yes and I think it's healthy to work in different registers and not just to write books.

VG: Yes!

JL: How has your background shaped your current concerns?

VG: My family was always politically engaged. My father and my mother were both militants in the 1970s, so in my home all the time political discussion and political engagement was an ethos. I started to be an activist at university when I was very young. The political tradition of activism is very important in Argentinian history, and for my generation, especially the relationship with the struggles of the 1970s. We are the generation of the sons and daughters of the 1970s militants, and so being interested in political action and political debates is a sort of common sense.

At university I was very interested in debates but I was also a very engaged militant. For our generation the Zapatista uprising was very important. It was decisive in terms of rethinking what politics *is*, and what kind of balance we might create in terms of the politics of emancipation; and in terms of reworking the political tradition from the 1970s in Latin America. I think that it was part of … yes, a war. It was a form of political pedagogy. And after the Zapatista movement, the crisis in 2001 was crucial, as was the Seattle movement, the Genoa movement, Argentina 2001; and all the different revolts and uprisings in Latin America in 2002 and 2003. I also mentioned earlier the different forms of activism and struggle around human rights in Argentina; for our generation it was very important to denounce the military dictatorship, and to follow this debate and try to understand how democratic transition has to be rethought in terms of the struggles in the 1970s and so on. So, I think that this is what is behind what I do.

JL: And finally, I have an academic question. Your work draws simultaneously from theory found in international socialist feminist traditions and also post-structuralism, like Deleuze and Guattari, so could you say what this mixture provides and enables?

VG: What a difficult question! Well, I have been part of different collectives, and I have experience of militant research in Colectivo Situaciones, so I always have this question of how to relate conceptual and theoretical work with praxis, with political engagement. I try all the time to connect my reading with my work as an independent publisher, and my work as a teacher with my political practice. I think that this mixture is what is always, for me, producing a kind of entanglement between concepts. For me it's very important to produce theory within struggle. I feel more comfortable producing within collectives and movements because I think that struggles are always the material space where we can think better. It's also very important to fight against the anti-intellectualism that sometimes surfaces in struggles, in terms of the classical division between who thinks and who acts. I think that is also a very pronounced division here in Latin America; that idea of, 'Well, here it is, you have the intense experience, you don't need the words, or concepts, because you have the *experience*'. In those terms, 'the theoretical' is always a kind of intrusion against 'real' practice or the intensity of practice. My work is all the time trying to confront this anti-intellectual tradition and at the same time to work against the idea of having a theoretical perspective that is completely disembedded from the struggles.

NOTES

1 For a discussion, see Sara Motta. 'Feminising our revolutions' in *Soundings* 71, 2019.

2 This interview was first published as "We want ourselves alive and debt free!": Jo Littler talks to Verónica Gago' in *Soundings: A Journal of Politics and Culture*, Issue 80, 2022, pp9-20.

3 In *Feminist International*, Gago and her translator Liz Mason-Deese write that 'the formulation "women, lesbians, travestis, and trans people" is the result of years of debate within the feminist movement, and is meant to demonstrate the diverse political subjectivities and collectives involved in the movement and to highlight its inclusive character, beyond a limited category of "woman". In this translation, we keep the term "travesti" to recognise it as a political strategy built through years of struggle against marginalisation and violence, often related to struggles for recognition of sex work.' Verónica Gago, *Feminist International: How to Change Everything*, Verso, 2020, p251.

4 Sara Ahmed, *Living a Feminist Life*, Duke University Press, 2017.

5 A few months after this interview took place, the left-wing Social Convergence party won the general election in Chile, and Gabriel Boric became President.

6 Perónism refers to an Argentinian political tradition based on the ideas and legacy of Juan Perón – president in the 1940s and 1970s. Perónism involves a blend of populist politics combined with free market policies, the nationalisation of private industries and union control.

7 Mauricio Macri is a businessman and politician who was President of Argentina between 2015 and 2019 as Leader of the right-wing Republican Proposal Party (PRO), which was founded in 2005. The current President is the centre-left Alberto Fernández from the Justicialist Party (also a Perónist party).

8 Under fourteen weeks.

9 The Care Collective, *The Care Manifesto: The Politics of Interdependence*, Verso, 2020; Judith Butler, *The Force of Nonviolence: An Ethico-Political Bind*, Verso, 2020.

10 Necropolitics is the use of political and social power to determine how people live and die, and in particular to rule in such a way that condemns people to terrible lives near that of the living dead, or in 'death worlds'. It is a phrase coined by Achille Mbembe in his article 'Necropolitics', *Public Culture*, Vol. 15, No. 1, 2013, pp11-40.

11 Mothers and grandmothers of people who were 'disappeared' under Argentina's military dictatorship, which ruled between 1976 and 1983, protested in the Plaza de Mayo in the capital, Buenos Aires. They also formed an NGO campaigning for the children to be found and restored to their families. See www.abuelas.org.ar/idiomas/english/history.htm.

12 www.tintalimon.com.ar.

Where the fires are

Wendy Brown is Emeritus Professor in the Department of Political Science at the University of California, Berkeley. Her books include *In the Ruins of Neoliberalism: The Rise of Anti-Democratic Politics in the West* (Columbia University Press, 2019); *Undoing the Demos: Neoliberalism's Stealth Revolution* (Zone Books, 2015); *Walled States, Waning Sovereignty* (Zone Books, 2010); *Regulating Aversion: Tolerance in the Age of Empire and Identity* (Princeton University Press, 2006); *Edgework: Essays on Knowledge and Politics* (Princeton University Press, 2005); *Politics Out of History,* (Princeton University Press, 2001) and *States of Injury: Power and Freedom in Late Modernity* (Princeton University Press, 1995). This interview was conducted in 2018.[1]

Jo Littler: In *Undoing the Demos*, you examine how neoliberalism's rationalities 'disembowel active citizenship', or the rule of the people by the people.[2] How have these rationalities extended and mutated since you wrote the book, in the era of Trump?

Wendy Brown: One of the things I paid too little attention to in *Undoing the Demos* was the disintegration of the social, something Britons have been very familiar with ever since Thatcher declared that 'there's no such thing as society'. In the American case that disintegration has had two important effects. First, this process literally takes apart social bonds and social welfare – not simply by promoting a libertarian notion of freedom and dismantling the welfare state, but also by reducing legitimate political claims only to those advanced by and for families and individuals, not social groups generated by social powers. Second, something I didn't emphasise adequately in

2015 but would now stress, is the extent to which neoliberalism could generate a political formation that combined libertarianism with a very strong *statism* that works to secure, essentially, the deregulated public sphere that neoliberalism itself generated.

As a libertarian order of freedom is unleashed and legitimated, it attacks social bonds and obligations, social conscience and social welfare. It disintegrates society and disinhibits individuals. This in turn produces the need for strong authority to secure order, to secure boundaries, to secure against what a declining middle and working-class experiences as ravaged ways of life for which it blames 'others': immigrants, minority races, 'external' predators and attackers ranging from terrorists to refugees.

Despite some resonances with 1930s fascism, this libertarian authoritarianism is a novel political formation, one, as I've suggested, that is an inadvertent effect of neoliberal rationality. It's a formation that I think should not just be reduced to the idea of fascism or populism. Its sensibility is: 'I can say anything, do anything, be anything I want, I can call for a certain restoration of my former entitlements (among whites), insist on my liber-tarian rights and at the same time demand statist protection of my country, property, and racial and sexual entitlement.' But in addi-tion to what this formation features, it's important to note what it omits. What's missing is any reference to, or care for, democ-racy. It's quite striking that you don't get from Le Pen or Farage or Trump any talk of democracy *at all*. You get law and order, you get statism, you get nationalism, you get restoration of white entitlement through nativism from extreme right politicians. But reference to democracy (other than to make it a stand-in for nation-alism or patriotism) is very, very rare. What brings someone like Trump to power was the combined emphasis on (non-democratic) liberty and authority; on both statism and the right to say, feel and do whatever one wants. Again, this is a peculiar political forma-tion that we've not had before and that we should not reduce to or equate with older forms of authoritarianism, populism or fascism.

JL: You've argued recently that 'Trump's rise is nothing but neolib-eralism's effects'. Can we also understand Trump as a kind of neoliberal nationalism?

WB: Yes. Many people think: well, how can this be neoliberalism if it involves calling for markets that are regulated or protected by nation states? How can the renegotiation of trade and tariff agreements like NAFTA, Brexit and other forms of economic protectionism be neoliberalism? Here we need to recognise that neoliberalism has never been one cogent, coherent doctrine. It's had many iterations, including the difference between its theoretical founding formulations in Hayek and Friedman and the Ordoliberals, and the way it was actually rolled out in practice by Reagan and Thatcher in the Global North, and Pinochet and others in the Global South. There's also a difference between the iteration of neoliberalism in the 1980s and its quite dramatic shifts through financialisation when it gains financial semiotics, coordinates, imperatives and vicissitudes. It's perfectly possible to continue the basic planks of neoliberalism – privatisation, dismantling whatever is left of the welfare state, slashing away at taxes for the rich and for corporations, keeping capital the centre of state concerns – while, at the same time, producing new regional domains of protectionism or rebellions against the EU or NAFTA. We are not 'over' neoliberalism just because we are 'over' a certain kind of right-wing alliance with globally de-regulated trade. There's a reconfiguration going on and it's important to see the extent to which the right has not rebelled against neoliberal reason or doctrine but only certain effects. Neoliberalism is being retitrated … again.

JL: When Trump was elected, Cornel West said that 'the neoliberal era in the United States [has] ended with a neofascist bang'.[3] But as you've just argued, neoliberal rationality hasn't ended. Can you can say more about the parallels, connections and disconnections between neoliberal rationality and twentieth-century fascism?

WB: First, I appreciate why Cornel is saying what he is saying. He is marking the extent to which rising white nationalism, white supremacism, masculinism – all kinds of values that have been brewing and boiling for decades but got put on steroids during the Obama years – have exploded onto the mainstream political stage. Not only in the form of Trump and a plethora of European white nationalist leaders, but also in the form of emboldened and empowered social movements.

The reason I am arguing that this is a development of neoliberalism is: the *legitimation* of those white supremacist energies itself comes from the neoliberal attack on the social, which includes an attack on equality, social belonging and mutual social obligation, and also an attack on the replacement of traditional morality and traditional hierarchies (including racial hierarchies) by social justice and social reform. This strand of neoliberalism, this attack on equality and social justice, shapes and enables a white supremacist reaction to the 'dethroning' of whites that itself is a neoliberal economic effect (the result of globally unleashed capital, the outsourcing and de-industrialisation of the north, etc). If that white supremacist reaction is labeled fascism, it's easy to think we're just having a sudden eruption of hatefulness and activation of people with already existing fascist sensibilities. In fact, most of these people, these white supremacists, are using the word 'freedom' in the beginning, the middle and the end of their sentences. In their mind, a liberal or social democratic agenda that promotes equality means promoting the interests of refugees, of Black people, of women, of others, *above* them because equality and worse, affirmative action, have replaced individual freedom.

'Fascism' is a shorthand that's perhaps not quite in our service, as liberal and left intellectuals trying to understand where we are and what to do next. I think it makes more sense to understand the energies that have been unleashed as, in part, products of neoliberal deracination, displacement and disintegration. So too is white male rage an energy intensified by neoliberal reason, and the ways it has been disseminated in law and culture, not only the economy. This rage takes shape as 'freedom' to be a racist, a sexist, a homophobe or Muslim hater, and to push back against the 'tyranny' of the left that tries to outlaw this. I'm not saying that neoliberal governmentality or rationality created the rage, though neoliberal economic policy certainly orchestrates a lot of the economic suffering and cauterized futures experienced as social castration by whites that is fueling it. Rather, I'm saying that this rage erupts in the form of libertarian freedom to speak and enact the power of white male supremacy against principles of equality and policies of social justice that neoliberalism itself cast as illegitimate and worse, totalitarian.

JL: Let's talk about gender. How is this conjuncture gendered?

WB: I think that many people were shocked not just by the election of Trump, but by the surprising number of white women who voted for him. Just over half of white female voters supported Trump. That's a lot of women voting for an openly sexist, misogynist man in 2017. And not only sexist and misogynist but noxious, narcissist, infantile and boorish – really the kind of dude that hardly any woman likes. So we do not just have a problem with misogynist, masculinist, angry, socially castrated male voters; we have a problem with all kinds of white men *and* women bringing someone to power who speaks and conducts himself in a way that no other configuration of human could. If any Black person, if any Muslim, if any queer person, if any woman, spoke just one or two of the utterances that Trump has spoken by the hundreds of thousands, that person's political career would be *over*. We know that. So the boorishness, the misogyny, masculinism, and old fashioned chauvinism that Trump represents is not just 'his': it's also something that is obviously still *ours*, that of white people. It is on white people as a whole because he survives in politics as an unrestrained figure of white male entitlement to do and say whatever it wants when no one else can. And that white male supremacy was underwritten by white women, not just white men.

So we have two problems. We have both women and men supporting this, and presumably finding the particulars of his speech and conduct towards women maybe not desirable, yet recognisable and tolerable. It's what they live with, what they know, how boys are. And then we have the problem of a national political culture, in our case, that also tolerates this, but only in this one kind of being – only in white men.

How do we find our way out of this? I disagree with those who feel that the problem with Clinton was that she was too ardent a feminist and too affirmative of identity politics. What we've learnt over the last year and a half, from the Trump campaign and the presidency, is that we have both a *white* identity politics that's quite fierce, and a *male* identity politics that's quite fierce. It's quite silly to say that Clinton was boosting the wrong things because that rage built on white male identity was already there, ready to destroy her. Of course there were many things wrong with the Clinton candidacy – she was a terrible candidate for the times. Not because of her identity politics, but because of her Washingtonian and Davos politics, her establishment credentials at an anti-establishment political moment.

JL: How can we shift out of these regressive gendered dynamics?

WB: I think the extent to which women in positions of power – positions of political, economic, and social power – have in the past year been speaking out about what it is like to *be* women is really important. It's probably just as important as what we have all been doing for ages, which is teaching gender studies in schools and building social movements from the bottom. It's also of course very different from the 'go along to get along' approach of many women aspiring to positions of power, and the suggestion that the only ones that complain are the radicals. What has happened in the Silicon Valley and Hollywood exposés of rampant sexual harassment and assault, and rampant second-class treatment, promotion and remuneration, and in the exposés of political life and even sports – all this is important because it develops consciousness of gender power in places and in ways that people weren't looking at, or looking for.

On the other hand, I think we have to recognise once again that it's not simply a matter of social progress. This is a battle. This is a war. 'Time's Up!' (coming out of the #MeToo movement) is a great political slogan but isn't true unless the fighters are out every day and everywhere to make it become true. People don't give up powerful and privileged positions with ease or grace. We're learning that about whiteness, and we're learning that about maleness, anew. I mean, yes, there are some men in Hollywood and Washington who have hung their heads in public shame about what they've done or what they failed to do in stopping harassment or assault. But they were basically cornered into this by their milieu. And how many white cops have been publicly brought to heel by Black Lives Matter? How many men has #MeToo suddenly transformed from gropers and harassers into feminist freedom fighters? Count them on your fingers. And how many more has it sent into rage at the wrong and unfairness of it all?

We also face the problem of an increasingly sectoralised media, and an increasingly sectoralised population attached to different medias. I don't know how we are going to get across these divides. I really don't. I mean if you watch Fox News, or read Breitbart, let alone the Daily Stormer, or go back to Gamergate, or go into the blogs and the twitter feeds of the right, where misogyny, racism, homophobia, anti-Semitism and hatred of Muslims are regular fare, you're left with this question: how can we affect social, cultural, political change in relationship to gender, among other things, when we are not reaching those places and when those places are reaching so many? I do think that remains a very open question.

JL: That leads us to hope and despair, and how we navigate them. You've talked about how within neoliberalism, nihilism is made into a commodity; and you've emphasised that we shouldn't abandon democratic projects and actions just because they're not yet realised. You've also talked about how you think there's a distinction between hope and the construction of progressive alternatives. This is really interesting given how important and fragile hope often is to the left, and how we talk so much about it (e.g. Raymond Williams, *Resources of Hope* [1989], David Harvey, *Spaces of Hope* [2000]). Can you say something about these entanglements between hope and despair?

WB: We live in such nihilistic times. By which I mean, drawing from Nietzsche, not that there are no values circulating, but that our values are commercialised, trivialised, fungible; they're traded, trafficked in, used for branding and profit. How, in this context, can we mobilise for a different world? How little do right and left stand for more than hating each other at this point? I think that's one reason you get so much bellicosity these days from the right, as opposed to old-fashioned conservatism, which was rooted in a world-view and a set of foundational justifications. Instead you get bellicosity, aggression, rage ... and there's plenty of that coming from the left too. I'm not equating them. But I do think we need to take the measure of what nihilism has done to political worldviews animated by deep conviction and desire for the good.

Now, hope. Look, I don't have a lot of hope for this world. In the face of the climate change emergency, the kinds of people that are in the major power positions in our universe – Putin, Trump, and so forth — the rise of right-wing forces, the miserable corruption and deprivation that neoliberalism's contributed to much of the postcolonial world, the massive pile up of humanity in global slums, and the seeming endurance of capitalism beyond, beyond, so far beyond when it should have given way to something else, it's hard to have hope. I think we need grit, responsibility and determination instead of hope. We need to clean up the messes humans have made – socially, ecologically, politically. We have no choice but to try to redeem our species and make a better world than we have to date. It's not about hope but something more like responsibility and maybe even curiosity: with our extraordinary brains and imaginations, our technologies and spirits, can't we do better?

I think efforts at alternatives feel most possible and promising when they are very local, even small. When we work at the level of co-operatives, local ordinances, developments within our towns, or neighbourhoods, or schools. When we are able to produce differences at this level – producing renewable energy for a whole town, or converting a region from toxic to organic farming, or solving a housing crisis – we feel our capacity to live differently through collaborative efforts. I think it is most difficult to feel hopeful when one is trying to enact global transformations, for all the obvious reasons. So probably ideas and practices for transforming an order that is not sustainable for humans, the planet or all the species on it will come from local levels. I don't think there's some great giant, global revolution to be had. I think it's a question of transformations that connect to one another at local levels.

One more thing on this topic: it is important to ask ourselves what we can do to *produce* more prospects for hope, rather than trying to *find* hope in order to act. I think sometimes that means, for example, transforming the lives of two or three teenagers; cleaning up a strip of coastline and gazing on its beauty; scouring the racism from a police department; working to alter ordinances that are highly punitive or cruel; or stopping (in the case of the

US) the deportation of undocumented people. Those kinds of activities I think are often called 'resistance', which they are; but they also help generate a sense of collective human power against our routine feelings of powerlessness and isolation. These kinds of things re-enfranchise us politically and socially in a time when most people feel quite disenfranchised in both ways. So that experience of acting together in order to produce a difference in a certain political or economic setting is itself generative of hope. We can't go looking for hope in the sky. We have to make on earth. That's the difference between a religious and a political attitude.

JL: Could you describe or sketch your own intellectual formation? You produce political theory with a very pronounced cultural and psycho-social dimension; how did it emerge that way, and why?

WB: As an undergraduate I was an economics major before I turned to political theory. I thought economics held the truth! I had the fortune of studying with a number of Marxist economists, and through Marx went to Hegel, and through Hegel to Plato, and – whoops! – fell in love with political theory. Really, it was a love affair, and that part of intellectual life is not to be under-estimated. However, by the time I started this love affair, I had already been steeped in the importance of capitalism, including capitalism's capacity to produce *ways of life* – what we call culture, society, social forms. So as I took up with political theory, I wasn't drawn to it as a conceptual or analytic practice. I was drawn to its enormous power in illuminating the elements and predicaments of collective human existence. I was drawn to its promise to see the world differently from how the world saw itself without ever leaving the world.

At the same time I was also becoming a fierce feminist and anti-racist activist. Those two dimensions of my young intellectual-political formation also meant that political theory for me was never simply going to be about generic 'man'. And my first book was an attempt to take apart the idea that Man in the history of Western political theory really did refer to all of us – a radical claim at the time, now stupidly obvious. The book was concerned with the co-constitutive nature of Western political theoretical notions of manhood and of politics.

In the 1980s, I read Foucault and Stuart Hall and a number of other poststructuralists, but also continued reading in Marxist and feminist and cultural theory more broadly. And I read a fair amount of Freud and also turned back to political economy. This mix meant that I was beginning to take myself out of the proper world of political theory – I was supplementing it more and more with things outside of its usual boundaries. So I suppose what I am saying in response to your question is that by virtue of having studied economics first, and political theory second, and at the same time always being interested in gender and race and psychoanalysis, I never went down the narrow tunnel of political theory. Still, I have never ceased to love teaching courses in the history of political thought, and it remains a distinctive genre for capturing human existence, writ large, in the form of associations, collectivities, powers, identities, citizenship, and institutions.

JL: What's the relationship between theory and praxis in your work, and your connection to activisms in the wider world?

WB: Most recently my main 'activist' focus has been on the problem of privatising public universities and the tremendous chain of effects that privatisation has had, not just on higher education, but on what we teach, how we research, how we relate to one another, what gets valued and who gets access. It's also been focused on the broader effects of privatising higher education on citizenship: on what it means to convert education into job training as opposed to education for democracy. A lot of my work as an activist has been both to speak about the privatisation process and also to try to contain it. I would say that's largely been a losing battle. But many of my activist endeavours have been losing battles, and that's not a reason to stop.

My activism as a feminist has often been rather issue-specific. Since I was very young I've been engaged with reproductive rights. We're still struggling to keep abortion legal in the US, but also to make it broadly available, and accessible, to those who can't travel long distances or pay a lot of money for it. Other kinds of feminism that have called my name for activism have been everything from questions of status and equal pay and work, to concerns with sexual harassment and sexual assault. Affordable housing has also been an issue I've cared about forever – I worked as a young person in campaigns for rent control and affordable housing – and I am currently trying to figure out how to be useful to addressing the extreme housing crisis that we have in the Bay Area of California where I live. Rents are unaffordable even for the middle class and homelessness is skyrocketing.

As I think is true of many of us on the left, I go where the fires are – either where they need putting out because there are fires that threaten to burn us down, or where they need stoking because there are fires we need to ignite sometimes. Since the Trump campaign I have tried to lend my voice to concerns that range from protecting the undocumented, to hanging on to what remains of our wildernesses and protected coastlines, to protesting against white nationalist rallies.

JL: Is your culturally, ideologically attuned analysis unusual in political theory? Is there enough traffic between political theory and cultural studies?

WB: I don't think there is adequate traffic. And I will put the challenge to both sides. I think that most political theory hunkers down with its own audiences and its own reference points. When it speaks of culture, it often does so rather ignorantly. By ignorant I mean it neither reads cultural studies, nor does it read a field that has done nothing *but* study culture: namely, cultural anthropology. You see this disturbing ignorance in much (not all) of political theory's treatment of the so-called 'multiculturalism' debates, where it often reifies culture, making it a thing or an object and something only non-white people have. Of course there are exceptions to this, and the feminists contributing to these debates tend to be the most thoughtful and careful here. Still, it was a feminist, Susan Okin, who consecrated the idea that white western liberalism was cultureless, hence free and equal, while peoples heavy with culture were patriarchal and oppressive. Ye gods! Anyway, political theory has much more to learn not just from cultural studies but also from other disciplines – anthropology, religion, sociology, political economy, and so forth. I wrote about this some years ago in a screed entitled 'At the Edge'.

On the other hand, some cultural studies – though not all – has, I think, ignored some of the analytic contributions that political theory could make to it. It tends to do theory without apprenticing itself to some of the rigours and the reach of imagination that political theory might lend it. Stuart Hall was an exception, and remains a model for doing social, cultural and political theory that draws on the literatures of those fields as well as psychoanalysis, political economy, semiotics and an attention to discourse. This range wasn't just the result of being so damned smart and well-read. Rather, he was *open*. Every time I go back and read him, I am struck by his intellectual *openness* to the disciplines and sources that could shape and inform his work without ever claiming it. Of course, this is difficult – it's the demeanor of a rare and mature thinker. I also happen to have studied with a political theorist, Sheldon Wolin, who read across history and political economy, literature, philosophy, political science and theories of language. This palette allowed him to think in bigger ways about the problems of democracy – and what he called 'the political' – than our discipline normally affords. Hall and Wolin are giants. But for this very reason, it behooves us all to go back and read them again and again. Not just for what they said, but for how they *do* it. That's how we learn to be big thinkers, by reading and studying big thinkers.

JL: Could you also say something about the traffic between your writing, its dissemination though journalism, and activism? Are you, for instance, doing more journalism than you used to?

WB: I'm writing differently than I used to. I used to write for academics. I think I do that less and less. It's not that I am not interested in having conversations with scholars, and certainly I still understand myself as a scholar, but I am more interested in being pedagogical with an interested, educated public. By educated I don't mean elite; I just mean 'educated' in the sense that they want to *learn* something – they know enough to know what they want to learn. So *Undoing the Demos* was written to a wider world than simply academics. And in fact, I mostly hear from non-academics who are reading it. Some of the other things

I am writing right now have that same quality. It's always a bit of a tension for me because I am still very drawn by going deep down into a text and having all of the excitement and pleasures that come from a close reading or a careful genealogy or an exceptionally complex formulation or a question that is unanswerable. *And*, I think understanding this world requires reading it closely, tracing its genealogies, appreciating its complexities and standing mute before its confusing predicaments. However, that doesn't go down so well in a journalistic sound-bite, or even an interview like this, let alone Twitter. And while some people still read books, one cannot count on books as a medium for ideas and political criticism today.

So engaging as an intellectual with the world and also being a scholar is not neat, seamless or easy. And sometimes I'll do one and sometimes the other, which strikes me as fine. I think it's important to not expect intellectual life to go easily towards a public when we also are trained in the intricacies of certain kinds of academic research and brought up on certain kinds of conversations and engagements. I also think that this is not unique to academics. Musicians understand that there are certain kinds of music that are composed for other musicians – it features intricacies and theory and complexity that you have to have an incredibly well-trained ear to hear and appreciate. But that's not necessarily what moves another kind of musical audience, one that also matters. I think we need to let ourselves off the hook about this. Sometimes we will have purely academic conversations, writings or debates, and sometimes we will be speaking outside the academy in a different voice. And I think we (and by 'we', I am speaking to a community of scholars now) need to be careful not to fault each other for either. There shouldn't be disdain for popularising what we do, or, to put it less tendentiously, for translating it into a non-academic idiom. But there also shouldn't be reproach against scholarly worlds of discourse and engagement. Of course, the real danger today lies in neither of these, but in the profoundly anti-intellectual and anti-democratic pressure for all academic knowledge to be commercialisable. That pressure bodes the end of critical theory, but also the end of a democratically educated public.

NOTES

1 This interview was first published as '"Where the fires are": Jo Littler talks to Wendy Brown' in *Soundings: A Journal of Politics and Culture,* Issue 68, 2018, pp14-25.

2 Wendy Brown, *Undoing the Demos: Neoliberalism's Stealth Revolution,* Zone Books, 2015.

3 Many thanks to Catherine Rottenberg for this question and for her generous help with this interview.

Democracy in the making

Lynne Segal is an activist and academic. She was born in 1944 in Australia and came to Britain in 1970, where she was very active in feminist and anti-racist politics, helping set up and run a women's centre and an alternative newspaper, the *Islington Gutter Press*. She worked as an academic in psychosocial studies, first at Middlesex Polytechnic and University, and later as Anniversary Professor at Birkbeck, University of London. In 1979 the influential book *Beyond the Fragments* she co-wrote with Hilary Wainwright and Sheila Rowbotham was published, which argued for more alliances between trade unions, feminists and diverse left political groups.

Other books include *What is to be done about the family?* (Penguin Books, in association with the Socialist Society, 1983), *Is the Future Female?* (Virago, 1987), *Straight Sex: Rethinking the Politics of Pleasure* (Verso, 1994), *Why Feminism? Gender, Psychology, Politics* (Polity, 1999), *Slow Motion: Changing Masculinities, Changing Men* (Virago, 2007), *Making Trouble* (Serpent's Tail, 2007), *Out of Time: The Pleasures and Perils of Ageing* (Verso, 2013), *Radical Happiness: Moments of Collective Joy* (Verso, 2017), and, with the Care Collective, *The Care Manifesto* (Verso, 2020). She is currently working on a new book, *Lean on Me: What We Owe Each Other*, for Verso. This interview took place in February 2018, shortly after the publication of *Radical Happiness*.

Jo Littler: Why did you write *Radical Happiness*?

Lynne Segal: Good question, I've wondered myself! Speaking about my last book, *Out of Time: The Pleasures & Perils of Ageing*, I was often asked what I'd write about next. 'Death?', one person grinned.

'No', I said, 'perhaps the opposite.' That's when I started thinking that what I'm always trying to address, for myself as much as anyone else, are our attachments to *life*. What promotes this and creates our well-being, I thought, is not really individual pursuits, such as pumping muscles at the gym, nor other forms of self-improvement we are endlessly urged to pursue, it's having friends and contacts; it's making life meaningful, together with others. Confronting the ubiquitous neoliberal rationality, endorsing only endless competitiveness – individual or corporate – we need to hold on to alternative ways of connecting with each other. Surely it is mainly our ties to others that make life worth living. This makes the work some people are doing around the notion of 'the commons' so important – the idea that we need shared spaces, quite outside the commercial arena, for us to *be together*, if only to ponder what life is about.

Radical Happiness was written against what is known as 'the happiness industry'. It connects with what became the interest of our national governments in measuring 'happiness': an interest which in my view stemmed from and served to obscure their covert worry about the high, and increasing, levels of personal stress, anxiety and depression. All the statistics indicate that it is actually misery that's really on the rise. Our government's solution to this has been to put money into CBT (cognitive behavioural therapy) in order to get people back to work as fast as possible. But what is this thing called happiness anyway? We'd hardly agree on its definition. I suggest, like all emotions, happiness is not best seen as an individual, quantifiable trait, but has a social or public dimension as well. Personal happiness is not separable from our relations with others, which is why I am interested in exploring those obviously shared moments of pleasure or delight, occasions of collective joy.

JL: The dominant idea of happiness today rotates around an idea of the individualised self: that we are responsible for our own happiness, and for our own care, or 'self-care'. Which brings us to your next book, which is on care; and to how, there, you're continuing to write against neoliberal individualism.

LS: I usually say that all my books have a common thread, I just get a new peg to weave them around! The mantra promoting notions of the autonomous, individualised self is indeed so strong today, although it has little connection to what it is to be human. This is especially pernicious when we enter the world of care, one where public support is crucial for so many. For instance, spaces for mothers with young children are being demolished before our eyes. According to the Sutton trust, there was a 50 per cent cut in early years day care provision between 2010 and 2017, and at the very same time there was almost the exact same rise in referrals for children in crisis, creating an explosion in demand for child protection services; it's all so short sighted. State endorsed neoliberal market fetishism has involved the commercial outsourcing of welfare and public resources, but this goes along with an underlying contempt for dependency, indeed for anything that is not about 'productivity' in terms of money-making.

The extraordinary crisis of care we're now facing is one of the most important issues at the moment. The North American feminist historian Laura Briggs argues that today all politics would be better seen as reproductive politics;[1] we can't get our basic needs for survival met properly, and that's just not factored into what we are talking about when we reduce politics to economics and GDP (Gross Domestic Product). Even those of us who have young children or other dependents in need of our care are so often not in the position to provide it. Instead, we must often rely upon what is called 'the global care chain'. This involves women travelling from the 'third' world to care for those in the 'first' world who don't have the time to do our own caring work, even when wanting to. This includes both women and men, but of course it is women who are still deemed mainly responsible for either providing or arranging for the care of children and other dependents. Moreover, the appalling combinations of enduring sexism and racism mean care work remains, for the most part, extremely poorly paid and precarious. We can observe people, mostly women, having to abandon those who need them in their own communities to traverse the globe to meet caring needs elsewhere. It is surely a crazy situation.

JL: Your book *Slow Motion: Changing Masculinities, Changing Men* has been through three editions since it was first published in 1990. How would you update it today?

LS: There's one question I was always asked about that book: have men changed? And of course men are changing all the time, along with the very different situations men face. I wrote *Slow Motion* as part of my attempt to hold onto a socialist feminist agenda, as distinct from an increasingly popular radical feminist one, which endorsed the Manichean view of women as the 'solution' for everything, and men as always the 'problem'. In our socialist-feminist vision, we began by thinking that gender issues would recede more into the background as we struggled to create a more egalitarian world for all. We hoped that men and women together would be sharing both the world of caring and commitment in domestic intimacies, at the same time as women would be out there with men in the workforce and the cultural and political arena. We started from wanting shorter working hours in paid employment, hence making caring work and intimacies more compatible with the workplace. This was the feminist agenda that faced most defeat, being completely at odds with the ongoing rise of a neoliberal agenda exclusively focused on productivity and profit.

Second-wave feminism was interested not just in changing the world to facilitate women's entry into the workforce and public life, with some having equal power alongside men; we wanted more fundamental social change, rethinking how we conceive of life itself, placing economic production and social reproduction on an equal footing. In the harsher economic and ideological climate from the 1980s, this more utopian thinking was side-lined. A greater feminist focus on shifting subjectivities and men's violence overshadowed the question of how we transform domestic, social and working lives to enable men and women to be equally engaged in them all. My concern with masculinity came from that project of transforming family and working lives, suggesting that there was intrinsically no reason why we had the public/private split lined up with gendered or sexual difference.

So I was concerned with the construction and maintenance of gender hierarchy. Masculinities and femininities are performative categories in which differences become socially embodied. But when the book was published some feminists criticised me for not beginning and ending with the issue of men's violence against women. These critics suggested that the relationship between men and violence parallels the correlation between smoking and lung cancer. I rejected this for ignoring both the huge diversity within genders, as well as the complex dynamics underlying existing gender contrasts.

The main thing that has changed since I completed that book at the close of the 1980s is women's ever more entrenched role in the labour market. More women, including mothers of young children, are working very long hours, with some professional women acquiring significant managerial authority alongside men. Indeed, women's lives have been transformed more than men's, although men's lives have often become more precarious, their position in the workforce more vulnerable. This can at times increase the pathological manifestations of manhood, at least for those men trying to cling to the *difference* manhood supposedly promised, with violence against women used to shore up a fragile sense of masculinity, or assuage personal failure.

JL: Would you still push for a four-day week, and shorter working day?

LS: Definitely! Don't we need it?! It's almost ninety years since John Maynard Keynes predicted that technological advances would enable us to work a fifteen-hour week. Yet, we have all been pushed in the opposite direction, and are now working longer hours than ever, if often in pointless pursuits. As Keynes forecast, we probably do now only need the equivalent of two or three days in paid work from each of us – or else four-hour days – especially once we have automatons doing even more of the work that they could be doing! Instead, paid work is absurdly unevenly distributed, as working days lengthen. The question should be, what work is *significant*, consequential and useful? As David Graeber writes, so many jobs are 'bullshit jobs' – they are not producing anything of any worth, and the world might be a better place without them.[2]

JL: There was a real groundswell of interest in studying masculinity in the 1990s, which perhaps isn't being quite as vigorously pursued by academics at the moment, even though we have so many regressive masculinities occurring in public life. I'm thinking about Trump, Breitbart, *Top Gear*, Jordan Peterson ...

LS: Yes. Going back to the 1970s: with the emergence of women's liberation, you did find a significant minority of men wanting to support women and be involved in caring. There were Men Against Sexism groups which produced magazines such as *Achilles Heel* and organised creches at conferences. There's a lovely photo of Stuart Hall doing the creche at the very first Women's Liberation conference in Ruskin College in February 1970. Then, when gay liberation blooms alongside feminism, you have a lot of gay men re-thinking and theorising 'masculinity'. They reveal that there have always been hierarchical groupings amongst men themselves, which are usually racialised and sexualised. Men falling in love with other men, or enjoying gazing at men's bodies as well as women's bodies, was seen as a terrible threat to hegemonic masculinity. This is something Alan Sinfield wrote about in *The Wilde Century*, where he noted that 'the feminine boy' was deemed 'despicable' simply because he was 'girlish' rather than because he was homosexual.[3] We see this particularly at the close of the nineteenth century, when gender contrasts are seen as bedrock – and imperial Britain is trying to maintain the colonial status it's about to lose in the world – that the archetype of the tough, manly man is being vigorously policed. Sinfield's work was part of the broader flourishing of queer scholarship, which often had a particular interest in hegemonic masculinity, alongside the growth of men's studies, with writers such as R. W. Connell and Michael Kimmel key figures, both of whom supported feminist goals.

However, masculinity is still policed today, as you say, despite being so visibly more diverse. I think it is very much in keeping with these harsh economic times that we have the return of the most absurdly domineering representatives of the supposedly tough, independent, autonomous man – recalling the idiocy of George Bush junior in flak jacket, launching the second tragic invasion of Iraq – despite all the ways in which this sham phallic persona has been critiqued by feminism, by gay men and by queer, non-binary and trans people. So in terms of transforming society, we still have far to go in undoing the gender binary – tough man/gentle woman.

Most women aren't gentle, most men aren't tough: they are not so very different from each other. But somehow the binary lives on, in almost every Hollywood movie, in cartoons, in magazines, in children's games. Insofar as it's challenged, it is usually by creating the tough girl rather than the gentle man, which is rather sad.

JL: How do those gender dynamics relate to contemporary feminism?

LS: I think we are now in a strange place in relation to feminism. Whilst some people say there hasn't been any change in men's violence against women, there *has* been an enormous change insofar as women everywhere are talking about it. When women's liberation was still brand new in the 1970s we had to think up new words for sexual harassment, rape in marriage, and so on, because they didn't exist. Now sexism, and violence against women, and the demeaning of women's bodies, is on the tip of everyone's tongue. That's a huge difference. I absolutely welcome all these campaigns, whether it's #MeToo or global marches against femicide, rape and violence against women. These have grown into a wonderful 'green wave' of feminists movements in Latin America, birthing the global Women's Strike movement, also focusing on recognition of women's crucial caring work. I also welcome women's slightly more playful and provocative engagement with sexism – such as the SlutWalks, which became a very big movement only a few years ago, and which said, 'We will present ourselves however we want in the world and we are still in charge of our own bodies'. I noticed that a lot of gay men and trans folk, together with women, were very much involved with dancing and singing in the streets in SlutWalks, all around the globe. I would add that violence against women needs also to be seen in relation to underlying structural inequalities, in the home and workplace, *enabling* gender violence, and impeding women's escape from it.

As I've said, I came into British politics at the start of second-wave feminism, when we were going to transform the world so that both men and women could together find our place in the sun. Third-wave feminism was more focused on the differences *between* women; the voices of Black women, lesbians and disabled women came more to the fore, and difference of all kinds became a more important issue. And it is very important that they did – though, for me, a problem with thinking about subjectivities and distinct belongings is that we always *also* need some broader transformative, indeed anti-capitalist, politics to unite us in solidarity to improve the lives of all. This means that building coalitions across all our differences will always be central.

In the 1990s we didn't just hear about the proliferation of differences; there was also a questioning of whether there is *anything* fixed at all underpinning those differences. In the footsteps of Judith Butler, Eve Sedgwick, and all, the whole point of 'queer' was to challenge the idea of there being any serious underpinning unity between women, or within gender, that wasn't performative, imposed through diverse linguistic reiterations. That led to a plethora of symbolic and performative subversions suggesting 'we can display ourselves however we like'. Important as that is, there is the slight problem of too neat a fit with neoliberal seductions promising (though never delivering) choice for everybody. We do want people to have some sense of autonomy and choice in their lives; but this is problematic if we don't begin from noting how appallingly uneven and unequal are the choices people can make. Nowadays most people have less, not more, choice over their lives. There was also a slight tension over how to keep queer theory really radical. As soon as you have the category, queer, it tends (like any label) to become an identification in itself, and we surely know how quickly anti-normative identities can themselves become normative …

Another debate surrounding gender that's dividing feminists now is all the discussions and arguments about transgender politics. Trans people are absolutely right to say that they have been amongst the most ignored, as well as some of the main targets of violence (sometimes deadly), for not slotting into the normative gender binary. And it's only been in the last ten years that trans issues and the assertion of *their* rights have come to the fore. But here we immediately face a problem over what we are talking about when we talk about the category 'trans'. For some people, trans is a gender category: individuals can see themselves as being born into 'the wrong gender' ('I am really a woman – or a man – so I need to transition in order to become my true self'). Indeed, trans people used to have to assert, almost rigidly, a distinct, even exaggerated, gender identity in order to be allowed the hormones or surgical interventions they desired to change gender from the one they found it too painful to inhabit. But other trans identifications vigorously reject gender binarism, taking us back to the ebullient transsexual lesbian, Kate Bornstein, who wrote *Gender Outlaw: On Men, Women, and the Rest of Us*, later saying that 'I'm *probably* the only lesbian to have successfully castrated a man and gone on to laugh about it on stage, in print and on national television'.[4] So these issues are immensely complex.

Those who are focused on rejecting transphobic discourses within feminism are in conflict with other feminists who oppose legislation allowing people, in this case those who were assigned male at birth, to 'choose' to change genders and thereby enter 'women-only' spaces or shortlists reserved for women. Given the history of trans oppression, I support the diversity of trans rights, whatever the complexities we may sometimes have to deal with. After all, Norway has had gender choice legislation for years, without any subsequent serious problems. Moreover, feminism has always been full of paradoxes. These connect with Joan Scott's classic description of gender as at once 'empty and overflowing'. There is nothing that ultimately defines all women or all men, without stifling 'alternative, denied or suppressed definitions'.[5] But at the same time, gender categories remain invested with deep psychic and erotic meanings, alongside enduring, if nowadays somewhat more open, social structures shaping our sense of what men and women ought to be doing – especially in relation to reproduction and childcare. Symbolically, power remains aligned with men, on the side of the phallus, that *thing* men are supposed to possess, which forever escapes them.

Thus, feminism remains a contested domain. The socialist feminist wish that gender might in itself become a less significant issue has yet to happen. But it is why I feel sympathetic to a trans politics wanting to transcend gender binarism. I doubt we will ever completely obliterate sexual difference, as some hope. I think we are always likely to create stories about our embodied selves that elaborate upon anatomical contrasts, however loosely. These are always, as Butler would say, regulatory fictions. But we *need* social fictions, however diverse, for identifying ourselves and acquiring some sense of belonging. At birth it is hard to distinguish between infants when all they are doing is wailing and feeding, but it is usually possible to observe genital difference. So, I suspect some acknowledgement of that difference will remain, though its elaborations will hopefully become ever more fluid.

JL: In *Why Feminism?* you discuss the necessity of not reducing biology to culture or culture to biology. How do you think gender studies is progressing in that regard?

LS: It's interesting how discourse around 'trans' highlights that strange paradox. Biology and culture, biology and environment, are never in any way separable. Donna Haraway has so much to say about how *complicated* this relationship is, seeing biology as an 'endless resource' of 'multiple possibilities'. Similarly, the neuroscientist Steven Rose points out how even the environment of chromosomes is unstable, making patterns of genetic transmission entirely unpredictable. Genetic outcomes not only depend upon endless external physical, social and cultural factors, but also on unstable internal cellular features. So, when we are trying to explain something as complex as how we become women, or men – if indeed we do identify with these gender positions we're seen as born into – the complexity is quite phenomenal! The idea that we could separate out the intricacies of the biological from the convolutions of culture is foolish. And yet we have evolutionary speculators, such as Richard Dworkin, providing 'biological' explanations for why women wear high heels and tight dresses. However laughable, the media presents these biological musings as the gold standard of science. Thus, popularisers of scientific folk tales come to be *seen* as leading scientists.

There have been more serious attempts by artists and scientists to work together, engaging with the nuance and richness each can offer the other in their tales of life, today with added input from cybertechnology – and the Wellcome Trust in London encourages such initiatives. They have done some interesting work around gender. On the one hand, we exist within mortal, material bodies, and in that sense are never outside of the biological. That was one of the criticisms some theorists, such as R. W. Connell, made of what they saw as some of the excesses of social constructionism, or of Foucauldian thinking and the theoretical turn to language. The corporeality of the body disappeared into discussion about the metaphors and language through which it is mapped and spoken. On the other hand, it's also true that the body *is* only mapped and spoken through language, so there's no teasing the two completely apart: there's only possible exploration of the very interesting ways in which body and language fit together, or remain, perhaps, at times unmarked or repudiated in discourse.

JL: Jeremy Corbyn is your MP in Islington. What is your relationship to the Labour Party?

LS: In the 1970s I was not in the Labour Party, but attached to community activists who saw ourselves, rightly, as far more radical than reformist social democracy! For a while I joined Big Flame, which described itself as a revolutionary socialist feminist movement, trying to unite grassroots community and industrial struggles. But then when Margaret Thatcher loomed on the parliamentary horizon, with her brand of right-wing populism, the political landscape became more ominous. It led to the very first book I was involved in writing, *Beyond the Fragments: Feminism and the Making of Socialism*, in which Sheila Rowbotham (the lead author), Hilary Wainwright and I argued that the organised left overall needed to abandon its sectarian vanguardism or bureaucratic complacencies and start listening to, and learning from, the diversity of feminist, anti-racist and other forms of movement politics. We had achieved a lot through local movement coalitions, extending community resources and working against the cuts (already beginning under Callaghan). Now was the time for broader left coalitions across all our differences in order to defeat Thatcher and the march of corporate capital. We needed the most progressive government in power if we were not to lose the ground we had gained.

So I joined the Labour Party. That was the end of Big Flame because half of us went off and joined the Labour Party and the others didn't. The Labour Party in the early 1980s was an exciting place to be, at least in Islington. Jeremy Corbyn was put forward and elected to stand as Labour's candidate, and my house served as the ward committee room for the general election in 1983. Many non-party activists came along to help us get Jeremy elected. Suddenly, as today, there were complaints about radicals coming into the Labour Party and 'taking over'! I so vividly recall the night and day of that election, when we just worked, literally non-stop, from 10 a.m. to 10 p.m., racing around the streets, in the end pulling people out of bed to get them to vote ... (I remember an old Irish neighbour putting his hands up just before 10 p.m.: 'I give up! I give up! I'm going!'). Jeremy was duly elected and we were so excited. Yet I also recall him warning us, 'You know there is not going to be a lot I can do!' He was right when of course Thatcher was re-elected, so the night was somewhat catastrophic, despite our cheering that we had got Jeremy elected. It had all been quite a struggle, because the SDP/Liberal Alliance was strong in Islington, which had previously been represented by a right-wing Labour candidate, Michael O'Halloran. He had been working hand-in-glove with the rather notorious Murphy Construction Firm, which refused to allow workers to unionise, and I don't think O'Halloran had ever opened his mouth in parliament. So from the beginning it was a huge battle to get a left Labour person elected; quite how this Labour outsider got into the position he's in now (as leader of the Labour Party) is one of the amazing stories of our time.

JL: How has your relationship to the Labour Party changed over the years?

LS: We stayed in the Labour Party – me and my left friends, feminists and socialists alike – until the end of the 1980s. We started leaving under Kinnock. This was not so much because of his attack on Militant (we shared little with that form of sectarian Trotskyist entryism), but simply because not much seemed possible in relation to advancing a progressive agenda. Of course, it got worse under Blair. I would not say that I was right to leave, for just as I think everyone should be in a trade union, however limited their vision of change, it also makes sense to join whatever we see as the most progressive party of the moment – although one can of course always try and influence party politics from the outside.

I've never been a member of the Green Party, although I support much of their agenda, and have sometimes voted for them. In fact, I've swapped votes tactically, so I've sometimes had a Green *and* a Labour poster up – knowing that nowadays Corbyn would always get elected here. I've voted Green as a swap, to get someone in Hampstead or somewhere else to vote Labour, where Labour is more marginal. Since we don't have proportional representation, it's an attempt to try and create it. My politics has not shifted far from my outlook at the close of the 1970s: I still see it as very important for movement politics to flourish, which of course has become ever more difficult with everybody working longer hours and there being so few public spaces to congregate. This is such a contrast with the era of Livingstone's GLC in the early to mid 1980s, when Ken was determined to open the council grounds as a sort of commons. There were open air concerts and endless other projects sponsored by the GLC during that period, which, while it lasted, were all so significant in supporting trade union resistance as well as a rainbow coalition of creative, political aspirations.

Thus, despite leaving the Labour Party, I remained committed to ideas of movement solidarity and coalition building, as well as the formation of regional and global alliances of the left, all working to oppose much of what has happened over the last thirty years: the deregulation of finance, the privatisation of state resources and the outsourcing of care, largely to the same few corporate companies. Almost all relevant research has highlighted the wretched misery created by these policies. Studies commissioned by trade unions and charities have for years been highlighting the drastic deterioration of service provision, which has not only led to greater job insecurity and worsening conditions for workers, but has inevitably resulted in an altogether more fragmented and poorer quality of care at almost every level for those in most need. All this Alan White, among others, covers in book, *Shadow State.*[6] So for me an anti-state position remains extremely problematic, despite the enduring need to democratise state resources.

JL: For a long time you've been, simultaneously, an activist and an academic. How have these different roles worked together for you?

LS: I've often joked that throughout the 1970s I was an underground academic, and an out revolutionary! Many people I knew thought I worked at the Islington Community Press, which operated from a squatted building and produced an alternative community paper, the *Islington Gutter Press*. As a radical resource centre, it facilitated the campaigns of progressive groups working around almost anything at all, globally, nationally and locally. It was a hub of activity: there were people active in support of Eritrean liberation, the anti-apartheid movement, peace in Cyprus, as well as all the diverse feminist and anti-racist work of the 1970s. I was also active in Essex Road Women's Centre, and a local Islington socialist centre which we began at the close of the 1970s in the upstairs of a pub, the Hemingford Arms. There were also festivals on Highbury Fields organised for community activists, all contributing to a collective spirit that continued from the 1970s into the 1980s. We had a vague sense of ourselves as revolutionaries; although as feminists we always had a more complex relation to the state, calling for increased resources, and the democratic sharing of its resources.

At the same time, I was also teaching in the Psychology department at Enfield College of Technology, later Middlesex Polytechnic and finally Middlesex University. It's where I got my first job, and where I stayed for thirty years, until I was asked to apply for a position at Birkbeck, University of London, in 1999. They were at the time appointing a few 'anniversary' professors to celebrate Birkbeck College having existed for 175 years, originally having been founded to give working men – and quite early on also working women – access to higher education. I was lucky enough to be chosen as a cross-disciplinary scholar because I had started writing about contemporary feminist and left politics at the close of the 1980s, when political activism was dying down. I was influenced by and remained very close to Sheila Rowbotham, who had worked at the GLC, producing the magazine *Jobs for a Change* in the first half of the 1980s.

However, by the second half of the 1980s, without a doubt, much that we had been fighting for was facing defeat, and the GLC itself had been abolished. Community resource centres could hardly survive. The 1990s loomed as, and became, a decade of mourning for many former radicals. The only exciting politics was queer activism – with the challenges of HIV and Aids generating a culture of resistance and politics of care to deal with the disease – and the fight back against rising homophobic abuse or neglect. Certainly, Thatcher's anti-union legislation meant that trade unions were declining rapidly; they had lost nearly half their membership by the close of the 1990s. Meanwhile, deep divisions had arisen in movement politics, with socialist feminism, for instance, practically disappearing, as the emphasis shifted to the protection of women from men's violence. So I began writing more, and completed *Is the Future Female? Troubled Thoughts on Contemporary Feminism* in the late 1980s, as a defence of socialist feminism. I think all my books practically end with the very same sentence, whether it is that first one, *Why Feminism?*, my political memoir, *Making Trouble*, tackling ageing in *Out of Time*, or the most recent, *Radical Happiness*: they all reflect upon my generation, with its high hopes for a transformative politics, and end up wondering what hopes remain today. Each book is about that question really – *how we keep hope alive.*

By the late 1990s I had managed to become a senior academic, because I had been writing these political books. And by then I had also come to see higher education itself – now under significant attack, especially in my own field of the humanities – as an important political terrain in a way I didn't fully appreciate in my younger academic life. I saw that we teachers had the enormous privilege of being able to be pedagogic activists. This was definitely the case with my very dear friend Alan Sinfield – mentioned earlier – who died recently and whose obituary I have just written for *History Workshop*. A charismatic gay theorist and literary scholar, Alan was always concerned with pedagogy: how to prevent the cultural clout of the elite from undermining the educational possibilities of those who don't possess similar cultural authority. He addressed, for instance, how you could teach Shakespeare, overturning patrician readings that had served to justify colonialism and imperialism, racism and sexism. And I also realised that I had always had mentors – Stuart Hall was another – for whom radical teaching, radical pedagogy, was so very important. That became clear to me eventually in my middle age.

JL: Your work is marked by interdisciplinarity. How do you work through and around different academic disciplines? What have been some of the challenges of transdisciplinarity, and why do we need it?

LS: My work always *had* to be interdisciplinary, first of all because I was trained as a psychologist at Sydney University in the 1960s. The main thing psychologists did then was to run rats through mazes and imagine that they were learning something about universal learning patterns via their observations of rodents in restricted, artificial situations. It had next to nothing to do with human behaviour, which is meaningful and rule-bound (or rule resistant!). When I did my PhD in the 1960s, *Conceptual Confusions in Experimental Psychology*, that's what I pointed out: it was written as a critique of behavouristic psychology. Pure psychology was then, and often remains, a science of experimental methods and conceptual confusion, because the descriptive categories it uses to encompass human behaviour are inadequate for the task, lacking any historical, cultural or political focus on the accounts we give of human behaviour, with their distinct specificity at any moment in time. Is that man, for instance, expressing his love for a woman, or harassing her, when stroking her body? Making that critique of mainstream psychology in my PhD meant that I was not going to get a job in Australia, especially as there were only a few universities in Sydney back then. So I slunk off to London (bringing along my baby son, born soon after I completed my doctorate) – where R.D. Laing was popular at the time, with his views about the madness underlying our perceptions of sanity, and sanity underlying certain 'mad' behaviour – not myself then quite knowing who I was, or what I would be able to do. However, this was exactly when universities were expanding in the UK, so I snuck into Enfield College of Technology by the back door (someone was on maternity leave), and stayed there for thirty years, since that job gave me time and space for my engagements as a feminist and community activist.

I was in the psychology department as a licensed educator, although I certainly wasn't going to teach any mainstream psychology, except to critique it. But again, fortunately for me, under the shelter of 'social psychology', I could address issues of gender, class, race, sexuality, and more. I was often in slight trouble because external examiners would say 'this is not social psychology! this is all about political issues!' So I changed the title to 'Psychology and Social Issues'. Then there would be one or two progressive psychologists, alongside the young women who were now entering the discipline as feminists. Michael Billig was the external examiner one year, and he said: 'The only course where student responses were really interesting was Lynne Segal's. I want everybody who did her exam paper to be raised up a degree mark!' (I recall this happening, even though it seems rather like a dream today.) So, my teaching had to be interdisciplinary because otherwise I could not have incorporated the social issues my courses covered, relating them to the politics of the day. That type of inter-disciplinarity became easier as feminist scholarship was gradually more accepted in the academy.

JL: In *Radical Happiness* you say that 'even trying to envisage how we might help create a more equitable, peaceful and fairer world brings a certain audacity and energy to life, at least in the process of sharing such imaginings'. 'Audacity and energy' seem like appropriate keywords for you and your work …

LS: It's so easy to feel bored and enervated today. One just has to have mentors, friends and other people who can help to guide you, even if you feel you are living in the ruin of past hopes, or with the rubble of words, when surveying the devastation of neoliberal 'reforms' or the national disdain for the plight of the vulnerable and displaced. For instance, as a person of Jewish descent, I've been involved in ongoing peace work in relation to justice for Palestinians. There we have only seen conditions deteriorate for the Palestinians – I mean we have *really* got nowhere, as yet – but at the same time, one keeps going, one has to keep going, in solidarity with all those other people still involved in that struggle, saying 'we are just not going to accept this'. It is always possible to envisage something different, and to be supportive of each other in a range of ways. The audacity is to dare to hope when there seems so little reason to hope.

That's also why green politics is so important now. To talk about genuine sustainability and to think about a feminist, green economics, for instance, is where we have to begin nowadays. It is the absolute *opposite* of neoliberal rationality, concerned only with the production of profit. How do we create a better, more sustainable lives for all? How do we stop devastating the environment? We have to begin from those questions. This involves rethinking the state, locally and nationally; building coalitions and global ties that have to be continuously knitted together anew. We begin in different places, whilst working for greater equality, peace, care and environmental sustainability.

JL: So if 'the one long book' you are writing, which you mentioned earlier, is about hope, then it is also about how the personal is political and the political is personal?

LS: Yes, yes, it is about how to keep hope alive, dare I say, how to keep affirming love and solidarity. How do we relate to the world? How and where can we find the most imaginative, interesting and progressive thought and action? There are identifications that we make quite early on, and the identifications that I made, where I belong, is with the radical egalitarianism of 1960s politics, as it morphed into 1970s socialist-feminism. Of course, we will stay blind to so many issues, and fail to hear the most fragile of collective voices – we know some people will remain excluded, smeared, or mocked, as the diversity of trans people were until very recently, and often continue to be. Yet there is as well always the potential for greater openness, for *democracy in the making*. This is what I am hoping for. A type of political uncertainty is inevitable, even necessary, yet at the same time we can keep arguing, as passionately as we can, for politics to remain as inclusive as possible: knowing that we could, together, achieve something far better than the world as it is. We have to.

NOTES

1 Laura Briggs, *How All Politics Became Reproductive Politics*, University of California Press, 2017.

2 David Graeber, *Bullshit Jobs: A Theory*, Penguin, 2018.

3 Alan Sinfield, *The Wilde Century*, Cassell, 1994, p25.

4 Kate Bornstein, 'Transsexual Lesbian Playwright Tells All!', in Amy Scholder and Ira Silverberg (eds), *High Risk*, Serpent's Tail, 1991, p261.

5 Joan Wallach Scott, *Gender and the Politics of History*, Columbia University Press, 1988.

6 Alan White, *Shadow State: Inside The Secret Companies That Run Britain*, Oneworld Publications, 2016.

Municipalism and feminism
then and now

Hilary Wainwright is a sociologist, political activist and socialist feminist. She is co-editor of *Red Pepper* magazine and a fellow of the international think tank for progressive politics, the Transnational Institute, in Amsterdam. She was an Economic Advisor in the Greater London Council (GLC) in the 1980s and has worked as both a sociologist and visiting researcher in the London School of Economics, University of Wisconsin-Madison, University of California, LA and Todai University, Tokyo. Her books include *Beyond the Fragments: Feminism and the Making of Socialism,* with Sheila Rowbotham and Lynne Segal (Merlin Press, 1979); *The Lucas Plan: A New Trade Unionism in the Making?,* with Dave Elliot (Allison & Busby, 1981); *A Taste of Power: The Politics of Local Economics* (Verso, 1987); *Reclaim the State: Experiments in Popular Democracy* (Verso, 2003); and *A New Politics From the Left* (Polity, 2018). This interview was held in December 2019, shortly after the UK General Election.[1]

Jo Littler: Can you outline how you came to be interested in and involved with prefigurative politics, or as you put it, 'making the path by walking'?

Hilary Wainwright: It was really the women's movement. Before that, I was involved in the 1968 student movement and before that, the Young Liberals, when they were very radical in the mid 1960s. The student movement's emphasis on participatory democracy established the idea of creating change here and now as we protested, in order to illustrate the kind of society we aimed to create, as we created it. This emphasis broke from the methodology of the old left, for whom the ends justified the means. The student movement's emphasis on participatory democracy rejected both hierarchical and authoritarian models of organisation and an instrumental approach to strategy. These were distinguishing features of the 'new left' that emerged in the 1960s (with strong continuities and associations with the 'new left' that was organised with and around those who had left the Communist Party in 1956, but remained on the left and created new plural, open and democratic forms of collaborative action and principled, exploratory debate). But the most powerful and personal sense of creating the future in the present – rather than thinking in terms of only campaigning for demands on government, or on employers, or making a revolution after which everything would be sorted out – came with the women's liberation movement.

Not only did the women's movement affect me and hundreds of other women personally, enabling us to change our existing lives and the relationships that shaped our lives in a way that was both self-emancipating and a basis for future change, but we created a social movement which both sustained these personal transformations and also enabled them to spread. And it was not just changing us personally and psychologically. Through the women's liberation movement we created material changes in relationships and in conditions of daily life. The most obvious example is childcare: the recognition and the importance – indeed the necessity – of childcare, for any possibility of even building the women's liberation movement. There was also a strong feeling of collective self-confidence that, well, 'we can do it', we can ourselves – and involving men too – create collective childcare in the here and now, which then opens up the possibilities of women being more active, and building the movement whilst alliances were being made with sympathetic and democratic men.

Somehow that very visible, material experience through the women's liberation movement did illustrate very powerfully – because it became part of our everyday lives – a different kind of politics. This experience enabled many of us to see what was wrong with different forms of instrumental politics where 'the ends justify the means', as for example in the Leninism of the SWP, which emphasised the overriding importance of 'building the organisation' as the means to change, rather than understanding the organisation as being about supporting people to bring about change in their own lives, collectively, here and now, as well as to build sources of transformational capacity for the future.

That insight in my own thinking and development was reinforced by working with the shop stewards' movement, particularly the shop stewards' movement in the arms industry on Tyneside. The shop stewards there were wanting to fight for their jobs by developing alternatives as a central part of their struggle for jobs. The Lucas Aerospace workers did the same thing on a more ambitious scale and in a more coherent way. They too were trying to achieve very radical change in the present, and they were doing so by literally designing and proto-typing alternative products. So, while prefigurative politics was particularly central to the women's movement, its essential principles and the break it entailed from both the Leninist, party-building left and the parliamentarist left of electoral parties involved more than the women's movement. It was a shared feature of the principles and the practice of many movements that were emerging on the left, independent of party politics. A varied experience of this prefigurative politics was one of the factors which led Sheila Rowbotham, Lynne Segal and I to come together to write *Beyond the Fragments*. All three of us were witnessing possibilities similar in basic methodology to those that we'd seen in the women's movement and arising from a similar emphasis on organising now on the basis of the values and principles of the society we were working for.

JL: Municipalism fits in well with what you describe in your book, *A New Politics from the Left*, as 'power to, or power as transformative capacity' (as distinct from 'power over').[2] What do you think are particularly inspiring examples of the new municipalism?

HW: Well, the first example that inspired me and others at the GLC was a book called *Red Bologna*. I think Robin Murray probably recommended we read it. With hindsight, it was a rather over-optimistic description of what was being achieved at that time in Bologna, but the one thing it did describe that illustrated this idea of 'power as transformative capacity' was the enabling kind of support from the local council for a very imaginative and transformative kind of childcare. We're back to childcare. The book described a big nursery that had originally been created by the women's movement, and a commune movement; then the council supported and helped to consolidate it. This, plus our own experiences in the UK, led us to build support for popular movements into the economic policy of the GLC. Here was the idea that it wasn't the state alone that was going to bring about change, but that rather the creativity that was transformative, both in its energy and in its practical initiatives, was produced outside of the political process by community, women's organisations, and workplace organisations. There were many very dramatic and vivid examples of this. The community initiative in the inner-city neighbourhood of Coin Street struck me as exemplary.

For readers who don't live in London, or weren't around in the 1980s, Coin Street, by the Thames, near Waterloo station, was seen by City developers as a very valuable inner-city, Central London site, ideal for speculative office building. But a community lived there in very good, low-rise housing; there was also a good potential for small business – co-ops and so on. Property developers had plans to buy the land and, on a speculative basis, to build office blocks. Local people were so angry about this that they came together and organised a campaign around an alternative community plan. This was before the Livingstone GLC. As a result of the campaign, they managed to achieve a public inquiry; and then for the public inquiry they elaborated their community plan. They were very resourceful; they had a real sense of the social value of their own community. They created their plan, then some of them or some of their allies became GLC councillors. That was an important part of the radical GLC administration led by Ken Livingstone from 1981 to 1986. The Labour Group included councillors who had been involved in these struggles and had become councillors in order primarily to support these local struggles rather than to pursue a political career. They thought that to advance these community-based campaigns it was necessary to win the support of a political authority. There were a number of such local activists, including George Nicolson, who became chair of the planning committee, and also Mike Ward, who was chair of the Industry and Employment Committee, who became leading councillors.

The experience of these councillors influenced the thinking and the political leadership of the GLC, which acted almost sponta- neously to say, as in the case of Coin Street: 'OK, we'll support the plan of Coin Street community organisations'. This was thus an interesting combination of using the power of the state, in this case, the local state, with the transformative capacity of the people. (Local councils had considerably more power then than now – the power of compulsory purchase, for example.) The GLC took over the land with its compulsory purchase powers and blocked the private developer. But then, instead of presuming that now the land was theirs and they, the GLC, would plan it because it had the planners and the expertise, they insisted that the land be shared with local people and given to the community trust. And then the GLC told them it would make its resources available for the Coin Street Community Trust to develop the plan. If the trust needed any technical help, or it needed grants for local businesses and so on, the GLC was ready to provide it. That was a case of a really transformative municipalism. We tried to follow through Popular Planning with the campaign against City Airport and the People's Plan for the Royal Docks.

JL: What do you think are the key differences between munici- palism then and the new municipalism now? By municipalism I'm thinking of examples like Preston Council, their support for co-operatives, contracting locally and planning a mutual people's bank for the region, and Barcelona. What do you think are the major differences between newer municipal projects and those at the GLC?

HW: There are several differences. Obviously in the UK, the powers of local government have been considerably weakened. Preston is using the powers of procurement in a way which we began to use it at GLC to a degree, but they've taken it a bit further by using it to give direct support for co-operatives. We were supporting co-operatives more through investment funds, and then, generally, as part of our wider public procurement strategy. We called our strategy towards procurement 'contract compliance'. This required the companies that we'd contracted to provide supplies – whether it was pencils or school furniture for the Inner London Education Authority, or food and office furniture for the GLC – to adopt equal pay, provide good apprenticeships, pay decent wages, and respect trade union rights. So that idea was present in both the GLC and Preston's approach, and in both cases it meant that the council was setting the terms of contracts with the private sector, from the perspective of meeting public goals.

I also think that the same principle of the municipal state being a support for initiatives and transformative capacity in the community or in the workplace applies both in the GLC and in Preston, and maybe even more so in Barcelona, in its early phase. What must be remembered about the GLC, of course, is that it was very big, in terms of both its budget and the number of people it employed. The GLC had a budget equivalent to many countries and it had considerable power – which was exactly why Margaret Thatcher considered it such a threat.

So there was a difference in scope and, to some degree, bargaining power. Not just bargaining power in terms of our resources vis-a-vis contracted companies or our investment resources vis-a-vis companies that were threatening closure. But also our political platform as the elected political authority of a major capital city. The clout of our political stage meant that we could name and shame multinationals like Ford or at least subject them to public scrutiny. For example, we challenged Ford when it closed the forge in Dagenham. We had a big public inquiry into Ford and organised it on a large and very public scale with the workers, with the international Ford combine committee, and we did a similar project with Kodak. We had the confidence both to take on multinationals and also to attempt to change the basis of international trade – for example through what became [the fair-trade organisation] Twin Trading.

With the abolition of the big strategic authorities like the GLC, the Greater Manchester Authority and so on, there were no longer local authority bodies in the UK, or at least in England, with those kinds of capacities. A further difference with Preston is, I think, that we put more emphasis on a systematic strategy of transforming the state itself. I don't think that's a very explicit feature of the Preston model, but they have, in a way, *had* to begin to transform the state, because they've faced opposition to what they want to do from local government officials and have therefore had to think about how to transform the civil service there. In Barcelona, the mayor, Ada Colau, made a lot of political appointments so that she didn't depend on career public servants. Barcelona municipality has a different political system; Ada Colau has never had a majority in the legislative council. Whereas under the GLC, it wasn't a mayoral system, so councillors had much more direct control over actual implementation of policy. This is less easy under the mayoral system because the mayor cannot necessarily get all their policies through the legislative assembly which can be dominated by a different, sometimes opposing, political party.

JL: At a time just after the general election when left government suddenly seems quite far away again, do you think municipalism will become more important as a source of collective power? I'm thinking about how there's a history of projects emerging out of the wreckage of capitalism, like the Tredegar Medical Aid Society (the forerunner of the NHS) and co-operatives.

HW: Well I think it has to, but it's not going to be easy because that requires a change in the political leadership of councils, and at a time when government attacks on local services are likely to get worse. And I think that one of the reasons why we lost, say in the North East, and to some degree, Wakefield, some of the north-western towns, and certainly in Stoke, is because in fact people's political alienation, their experience of having no control over the decisions shaping their daily lives, was not actually a result of their experience of Europe, but rather their daily life experience, especially of Labour Councils that took their voters completely for granted, treating them more or less with contempt. Even on the interviews of the election night, you heard working-class people who voted Tory explain their decision by saying 'Labour's done nothing for us round here' as much as they talked about Brexit. I think the lesson of that is that the transformation of the Labour Party that Corbyn initiated, and the democratising movement that led him to take leadership, really needed to reach out more effectively and shake up those complacent local parties and local councils that had lost the trust of their voters. But the Corbyn-stimulated dynamic of change rarely succeeded in reaching most local councils outside the cities. I don't know if 'rotten boroughs' is the right word, but some of them definitely were endemically corrupt in a low level but routine manner. In Durham and Blyth for example, two towns where Labour lost seats, councillors had for decades had a monopoly of working-class representation and were unaccountable and untransparent, often dominated by families and making contracts with their friends and relations in private business.

JL: This leads very well to my next question: that one argument would be that a Labour Party that just saw its 'red wall' crumble in the general election should get more involved in progressive municipalism. Which I guess is what you're saying.

HW: Yes! That's one part of it. And even from an electoral point of view, a transformation of Labour councils is absolutely necessary. In Preston, for example, where Labour introduced significant reforms in the working of the council – reforms that improved the lives of many Preston residents – Labour held on to its vote. But this reforming, improving dynamic in a Labour Council is also important from the point of view of strengthening a sense, and reality, of popular agency, overcoming the political alienation that so damaged Labour in December 2019. To expand on this: consider why Labour did relatively well in Liverpool. I think it has a lot to do with working-class agency. In Liverpool the council was constantly changing hands and Labour had to fight for its votes over the years and had to deliver improvements in council services. It's not a brilliant council, but it's had to do things for the city because no party can take its voters for granted. Moreover, there are the specific traditions of Merseyside because of being a port and also having a large immigrant, especially Irish, population. There's a pluralistic culture, but on the other hand, there is also a great unity and pride in the city and its people. When Liverpudlians were under attack, like over the tragic disaster at the Hillsborough football stadium (which *The Sun* blamed on drunken Liverpool supporters), there was a real coming together to struggle for justice for the families and memory of those who died – a struggle consistently supported by Jeremy Corbyn. There was a real sense of agency and power which, among other victories, led to the successful 'eclipse of the *Sun*' throughout Merseyside. And so a majority of working-class voters in Liverpool voted 'Remain', partly because for a long time people had *already* been 'taking back control', and also because they are more internationalist and less parochial than in the North East.

JL: What are the possibilities of different municipal projects connecting together internationally and learning from each other?

HW: Well there have been attempts at it, haven't there, such as Fearless Cities.[3] I'm not an expert here, but I've been to numerous left seminars on municipalism where there's usually somebody from Madrid or Barcelona. So there's a modest international network already between the more radical municipalities. Obviously the possibilities of an international network are affected by what's going at a national level. In many of the countries where there used to be quite a radical municipal tradition, like Italy, they've faced political setbacks because of hostile national governments. Though, again, the municipalities have often been exceptions to the rule. Naples, for example, has a radical Mayor who is taking and supporting some interesting co-operative initiatives. Often these exceptions are beleaguered cities as well as fearless cities. Networks of solidarity and collaboration between them is important. Sometimes those networks have developed around particular sectors like water and energy, or themes like bringing services back in house. There's a lot of very practical work going on in terms of learning lessons. The Transnational Institute – of which I'm a fellow – has been very important in all that, doing work and writing and summarising all the efforts to take resources back into control.[4]

JL: I like how in your updated section of the new edition of *Beyond the Fragments* you emphasise the importance of institutional power and social relationships. You talk about the importance of understanding institutions not as hermetic things but as spaces with hidden forms of power; and of paying attention to the quality (and equality) of the relationships we create when we might try to develop forms of collective power. Can you say more about that?

HW: I suppose our experiences at the GLC were important for giving us an insight into this. My early radical politics was shaped by movements like the student movement and the women's movement, and an early disillusion with electoral politics – seeing parliament as insubstantial and powerless in the face of financial flows, transnational corporations and the civil service. Then I got very interested in movements addressing the power relations of everyday life, like in the family, and personal relations, in schools and in universities and in workplaces generally. But after some time, I also saw that a transformative politics of everyday life was not on its own sufficient. Take the case of the women's movement; we demanded legislation on equal pay and on abortion and we campaigned for local government support to extend services for women. Also in the example of the Lucas Aerospace shop stewards: they campaigned for government action to keep their factories open, and to implement an alternative investment strategy for socially useful purposes.

When the GLC moved to the left and became interested in all these issues, in the women's movement and alternative industrial planning, I decided to be part of it and applied to get a job there, with Robin Murray and Mike Cooley. I took the plunge (without quite knowing the implications). Then suddenly I was in this vast building, part of a complex institution, which was very opaque and immensely hierarchical – for instance, we were all called 'officers' based on a military model. Even the building reflected this hierarchy. There was one floor that was carpeted and oak-panelled, and this was where 'the members' had their offices, and ordinary officers like me were not allowed up there, unless we were accompanied by, or on a mission of, our senior officer – our 'commander'. I would sometimes find myself up there going to see Mike Ward, our councillor, because it just seemed the natural thing to do. But I never power-dressed and probably looked decidedly too scruffy to be a senior officer. So I would often be picked up by some traditional official, acting as a self-appointed custodian, who would say, 'What are you doing here, have you got the permission of your senior officer?' There was a group of us who would share our experiences and reflections, and we just thought 'this is completely impossible', so we had to get to work to change those relationships and we just did so in practice, supported by Mike Ward and of course Robin Murray, the head of the Industry and Employment 'Branch'. They were very much part of the change.

From the start we knew that if we were to create this support for popular movements, we had to change the relationships of the GLC itself, both those within the GLC and the relation of the GLC to the people of London and their needs, desires and struggles. And, partly from my experience in the women's movement, I had a strong sense of how existing oppressive relationships depended on people being complicit and reproducing them, even those who suffered under them. I knew from the women's movement that if you refused to reproduce them you could say, 'Hang on a minute! We *can* do things differently and we will'. So you could be a modest force for change, simply by your own action and the relationships that you create. Over time and through sustained collective action, we began to create a new institutional framework 'in and against' the GLC.

JL: And can you outline what you did when you directed the GLC's Popular Planning Unit?

HW: 'Director' sounds a lot more hierarchical than it was. We worked as a collective. We cascaded appointments, so I appointed two or three people, including Sheila Rowbotham, and then we in turn all together appointed another group ... people who'd been shop stewards, who'd been community campaigners, that is, whose previous experience had been organising popular power in some way or other, independently of the local state. These weren't people who could be 'directed'! And I had no desire to do so. I was more of a co-ordinator and facilitator. We became a kind of collective – well, as much of a collective as was possible in the context of an essentially hierarchical institution (we had considerable salary differences, which I once tried to change, but without success).

How did we understand what we were doing? We saw our work as being to unlock the resources of the GLC to support community or workplace organisations that were developing alternative strategies, or to then encourage them to do so. We worked very experimentally and tried several different approaches to finding and working with such organisations. The first experiment was based on the idea that where there is resistance, people are resisting because they are dissatisfied and have an idea of how it could be different. The first resistance that somehow came to my attention was the resistance to what is now City Airport. I would go down to Docklands, to these desperately beleaguered communities in North Woolwich, and sit in on their meetings. I would introduce myself, and explain that the GLC supported their resistance because our manifesto, which was our guiding mandate and source of democratic legitimacy, viewed the future of the Royal Docks as an integrated transport hub – a small dock facility plus rail and road servicing local businesses and communities in the East End – not as a site for an airport to service the City of London, the capital's financial centre. I asked how we could best support their campaign: 'What's your thinking about alternatives?'. They then brainstormed about alternatives and then we'd discuss them ... 'OK, how do you want to put this together and how do you want to involve other people'. Then they'd say things like, 'Well, what about having a place?'. I clearly remember the voice of Connie Hunt, an inspiring local campaigner who has since died. 'We need a place where we can gather people's ideas', she'd say. 'We could call it a people's plan centre. It would be somewhere people could just drop in when they were doing their shopping or their laundry.' Then I'd help them with a budget, working out how much this would cost, and so on, on the assumption that I could then get back to the GLC to get the Industry and Employment Committee to agree to their budget and grant them funds. They went on to say that they were all very busy and what about employing some staff, local people who would be accountable to the local campaign. And so it would develop. We would again put this into a proposal to the GLC's Industry and Employment Committee. And I joined their committee as they set up the People's Plan Centre and appointed four local people with different skills and experiences.

I don't know exactly how to put it ... I was more or less a messenger. I was finding out how we could best support local people who didn't have direct access to the GLC. Increasingly, though, they could just come and present their arguments directly to us at County Hall. Though it was us, as 'officers', who presented it to the Industry and Employment Committee. Once we got the Industry and Employment committee to come and meet in Docklands instead of County Hall. All these councillors – Conservative as well as Labour – had their official meeting in Docklands in a community centre, and local people came to observe it. So we were gradually shifting the balance of power. At one point we tried to do what they did in Coin Street, which in this instance would have been to buy the Royal Docks, to take them over to enable the People's Plan for the Royal Docks to be implemented. But by that time, Thatcher had abolished all the planning powers of the elected GLC and the local borough (Newham) in Docklands and had created the unelected, government-appointed London Docklands Development Corporation. Consequently, we had no power – or at least no statutory power – other than the power that the people were developing through their own self-organisation. With our support, the local campaign developed the plan and they presented it at the public inquiry, and it did lead the inspector to impose some limits on the size and capacity of the airport. The developers didn't get their own way completely.

So that was one thing we did. The other thing we did was that we recognised that to develop plans, people need time. Big corporations employ whole departments of staff whose only job is to think and to develop plans. So we thought, 'OK, how do we support workers, particularly, to have the time off to develop their own plans?'. And we developed a whole programme – I think we called it economic literacy or popular education – where we would work with work-place trade union reps and they would get time off which we would pay for, and then we would pay a tutor and then we would use research developed by the research unit of our branch, our Industry and Employment Branch, as an educational resource. We had these workshops with, for example, furniture shop stewards, who would analyse what was going on in their companies, and then we'd get somebody who had done research into the industry to come and share what they knew about the international markets. The shop stewards then would begin to develop alternatives. Together, we produced a little pamphlet called *Beneath the Veneer*. Other people in the unit did similar things. One member, Paul Soto, did a lot of workshops making plans for GLC workers themselves. GLC workers on the Woolwich Ferry, and GLC workers employed in County Hall, developed ideas about their workplace and what they wanted to change. Another member of the Popular Planning Unit, Dave Walsh, did the same kind of work with transport workers in the underground ... so, that was the idea. We wrote about some of this in *A Taste of Power*.[5]

JL: Can you say some more about the relationship between the women's movement and left movements, like the Institute for Workers Control?

HW: Well, it's difficult to be precise, although a new book by Sheila Rowbotham due out this year or next will shed a more detailed light on this question. It was partly about context and origins. An important impetus for the women's liberation movement came from women students who had been active in or influenced by the events of 1968; the student movement; the war in Vietnam; the protests in Czechoslovakia and their suppression by the Soviet army; and the movements of workers in France for self-management. The women influenced directly by these events generally saw themselves as socialist feminists and we quite consciously reached out to working-class women and with them campaigned for the trade unions to widen their bargaining and their campaigning agendas. This led us to be interested in idea about workers' control and going beyond the conventional limits of defensive trade unionism.

Furthermore, we were socialists in spite of, and in opposition to, Soviet-style command economy socialism, without having any precise definition of what we meant by socialism. We were exploring and experimenting as we rebelled and worked on alternatives that met our egalitarian, collaborative and democratic values. So we were open and curious about other socialists, like those involved in the Institute for Workers' Control, who shared a similar experimental and open-minded approach.

Finally, a principle we had in common with many of those who were involved in the workers' control movement and the libertarian left was a recognition of the knowledge and capacity of people who were oppressed or exploited and marginalised. The idea of them as agents of change was not fully recognised by the Labour Party, which included both workers and women! A lot of us, and Sheila [Rowbotham] and I particularly – without implying we were some sort of vanguard – shared the view, being socialists too, that socialist change is going to come from below, and that means conscious change, creative change – supporting workers' knowledge, women's knowledge, and the knowledge of people who would otherwise be marginalised. In a way, feminism, I think maybe more than any other movement, gave us that emphasis. And so we would always be thinking about what makes it possible for workers to exert their possible powers of control. Socialism was always seen as not some ready-made formula, but as something that had to be worked on, and where the process was as important as the goal ... and also, within that, there was a shared belief in the need always to create space for voices that were otherwise being silenced, whether in trade unions, community groups, the women's movement or political parties.

JL: Have you got any examples of that?

HW: In the Lucas Combine Committee they had a methodology which was very much encouraging everybody to speak, because they had to make sure that every factory was behind what they decided to do. To achieve that there had to be a real sense of collective ownership of the discussion, of a decision. So they would chair their meetings in a very facilitating way.

JL: Were there direct connections between the Lucas Plan and ecofeminism and Greenham? How did they connect?

HW: Well, it was mainly through the people involved, I suppose. Lucas was a male workforce but there were quite a few women involved in it. There was a wonderful woman called Jane Barker, who sadly died, who was a researcher with them, who was a feminist and there was later Val Wise, and Audrey Wise, an MP, who has also died since. Audrey was a working-class socialist feminist and she was involved in the Institute for Workers' Control. She would be always very strongly insisting on women's voices being central. I remember at one Institute for Workers' Control conference there was a lot of discussion about the Hull fishermen's strike and there was this amazing woman, Lily Bilocca, who came to the platform to speak for the communities in Hull. So, the Institute for Workers' Control was quite an interesting organisation that was promoting workers' control and was responsive to feminism through Audrey and then Sheila [Rowbotham] (they published a pamphlet of Sheila's). So the Hull fishermen's, trawlermen's strike … that's a good example. There's a film about it – *The Heroes in Headscarves.*

JL: Would you say feminism directly related to your capacity to create projects and institutions, including *Red Pepper*?

HW: Yeah, I think so. I suppose feminism gives you two things in terms of wider possibilities. One is it gave you a sort of confidence, but also, secondly, it gave you a confidence that was always related to working with other women. At the beginning of *Red Pepper*, there was a group of women. Denise Searle was very important and also two young women, Harriet Hanmer and Michelle Dunne, who came to work for us. Barbara Gunnell has been and still is very supportive, and there were several others. We all worked together, in different ways. And I remember when we were struggling to raise money for *Red Pepper,* we found this cartoon by feminist cartoonist, Jacky Fleming. The cartoon was printed by Leeds Postcards and it was a witty image of a very stroppy looking woman saying 'we never give up'. So we had that sort of determination. I think also, you know, feminism makes you a bit more open to taking risks – the opposite of risk-averse – willing to be, um, slightly mad! So we were. It was a bit mad, you know, going for this money and then taking the risk of doing it. And it's always been quite women-led; indeed, recently it has become more so, with younger women, Jenny Nelson, Siobhán McGuirk and Rachel Lawrence.

   And so, feminism was an important spirit in *Red Pepper,* and we were strengthened by the wider support from Sheila and Lynne and other feminists of different generations. We didn't feel we were doing it all on our own. I think if you're innovating and taking risks the mutual support of other women is vitally important. It involves a real solidarity that's personal as well as political. There have been and still are some very good men involved too, very supportive men. But I think also feminism helps you recognise that deep social transformation isn't going to be about overnight change. And a magazine is about creating a different culture, a support for what people are doing to bring about change, refuse the dominant reality, in their daily life, I think is important that we weren't – and still aren't – just oriented towards Westminster and Labour politics, and that we were extra-parliamentary in quite a deep sense, of meaning change in society.

In *Red Pepper* we have a strong feminist emphasis that's been a result, not so much of me but of younger feminists, and that's just meant an alertness to every possible form of subordination and ways of being treated as secondary. Ensuring women's voices, ensuring women write, supporting women writers. There's more of an alertness to this now: we always make sure that we actually have a proper balance of women writers. And also there's quite a strong BAME emphasis, an anti-racist, anti-imperialist emphasis which maybe wasn't always such a self-conscious feature of 1970s feminism, though it was there. It is, correctly, now to the fore. For example, right now, post-election, there seems a really impressive number of young Asian women involved in politics and as MPs. There's quite a few and they're really strong, and strong politically. I think there are more women MPs now in the Labour Party than men.

JL: Yes there are. One of the few good results of the election.

HW: Yeah, we can search for these crumbs!

JL: My final question: you have said that one of the key features of the GLC was that it went beyond sectarianism and engaged with a wide range of groups regardless of their politics. Is there a lesson here for the Labour Party and other left institutions? (This is perhaps something of a rhetorical question!)

HW: Yes. I think in general the GLC – and I have to credit Ken Livingstone for some of this – never asked for your party card as a condition of collaboration. I wasn't in the Labour Party when I was working for the GLC (nor when I collaborated with Tony Benn in organising the Socialist Conferences in Chesterfield). I don't think Sheila was either, but, you know, nobody asked us, 'So are you in the Labour Party?' That was an openness. Most of the people in the Industry of Employment Branch and in the Popular Planning Unit were not in the Labour Party. Some were in the Communist Party, or the Green Party, or not in any party; and that was important. Also, our support for projects – because we had clear criteria for the grants we gave – wasn't based on party-political criteria, they concerned equal opportunities, egalitarian politics, belief in power from below, encouraging the capacity to develop power from below. In a way we were a kind of critical reaction to the state and to party politics – hence the idea which guided us of working 'in and against the state', where the state included the Labour Party. We were working with the particularly radical bit of the Labour Party.

That open, non-tribal, unsectarian spirit is vitally needed on the left just now as we try to rebuild the left on a more effectively transformative basis. The standoff between the Greens and the Labour Party is really debilitating. At this general election, the Greens did well in their own terms; they virtually doubled their vote. If there had been some collaboration – decided on a local basis – it probably would have led to a few more Labour MPs and maybe one or two more Greens as well. One just thinks, 'Why can't we collaborate when there's so much in common'. I think the question of collaboration with the Lib Dems is different, especially after the reactionary role they played in the coalition with the Tories, on student fees, on the NHS and on austerity in general – failing completely to use their bargaining power. And in this election the stance that the Lib Dems took towards Labour and especially towards Jeremy Corbyn was outrageous. In Kensington, where I canvassed for Labour, they lied about their candidate's chances of defeating the Tories and effectively handed the seat to the Tories.

There have to be common political values as a basis for working together. Sectarianism, to me, is always about party interest coming before shared goals and transformative vision. I don't know how you put that lesson into practice, but I think it probably has to start at a local level. You can't easily knock Green and Labour leadership heads together as leaderships tend to put safeguarding their party first. We have to start from where the issues are bubbling up and struggles taking place around which the parties could unite.

NOTES

1 This interview was first published as 'Municipalism and feminism then and now: Jo Littler talks to Hilary Wainwright' in *Soundings: A Journal of Politics and Culture*, Issue 74, 2020, pp10-25.

2 Hilary Wainwright, *A New Politics From the Left*, Polity, 2018, p13.

3 Bertie Russell, 'Fearless Cities municipalism', www.opendemocracy. net/en/can-europe-make-it/fearless-cities-municipalism-experiments-in-autogestion, 21 February 2019.

4 Transnational Institute, *The Future is Public,* www.tni.org/en/publica-tion/the-future-is-public, 2019.

5 Maureen Mackintosh and Hilary Wainwright, *A Taste of Power: The Politics of Local Economies*, Verso, 1987. For Chapter 1 see The GLC Story website: www.glcstory.co.uk/wp-content/uploads/2016/11/A-Taste-of-Power-intro.pdf.

Gender, race, class, ecology and peace

Vron Ware is a writer, photographer and former academic, currently a visiting Professor in the Department of Gender Studies at LSE. Before teaching at Greenwich, Yale and Kingston, she worked in a number of NGOs and campaigning organisations, including the anti-fascist and anti-racist magazine *Searchlight*; Friends of the Earth; and the Women's Design Service, which pioneered feminist perspectives on urban planning and environmental design. Her publications include *Women and the National Front* (Searchlight, 1978); *At Women's Convenience,* with Sue Cavanagh (Women's Design Service, 1990)*; Beyond the Pale: White Women, Racism and History* (Verso, 1992); *Out of Whiteness: Color, Politics and Culture,* with Les Back (University of Chicago, 2002); *Who Cares About Britishness?* (Arcadia, 2007)*; Military Migrants: Fighting for YOUR country* (Palgrave, 2012) and *Return of a Native: Learning from the Land* (Repeater, 2022). Her documentary photographs from 1977-1983 have been used in TV documentaries and dramas, featured in exhibitions at Tate Britain, Middlesbrough Institute of Modern Art, Goldsmiths University and Atlas Gallery. This interview took place in May 2019.[1]

Jo Littler: In the first chapter of *Beyond the Pale: White Women, Racism and History* (1992) you list different strands of politics: 'gender, race, class, ecology and peace'. I thought that it was interesting and quite unusual to see them listed like that. They're also all themes that run throughout your work. Can you talk about how?

Vron Ware: It's funny you should start with that. I had forgotten, until recently, that the opening of *Beyond the Pale* is a critique of the Tory Party Political broadcast in which a man's voice reassures viewers that the Conservatives (led by Margaret Thatcher) would be the ones to save us from environmental catastrophe. The point was that the 'us' being saved was represented by a very white baby being clutched by its very white parents. It's tempting to assume that environmental politics was not on the agenda back in the 1980s. But it was, of course, and well before that too.

In 1982 I was part of a new magazine called *Emergency* started by a number of us involved in different social movements, operating outside the Labour Party. So, for example, we published a number of very interesting critiques of ecological thought, writers like Robin Jenkins, Rosalie Bertell, Joel Kovel, André Gorz, Murray Bookchin and Rudolf Bahro. So that was really important, but before that, I had lived in Birmingham for a few years, working for *Searchlight*, the anti-racist, anti-fascist magazine. There was a wonderful place called the Peace Centre, a bookshop where all kinds of protest and solidarity groups would meet, including anti-racists and anti-fascists. It was normal for those things to be happening in the same place and you'd see the same people involved in many things at once. But as the 1980s went on, politics became more fragmented, and there wasn't such a coherent movement against racism, for example.

In the late 1980s, early 1990s, I had a job in a feminist resource centre specialising in the *built* environment, picking up on the work that a new generation of feminist architects and planners were doing. We wrote guidelines about changing measurements of doorways or thinking more holistically (I suppose you would say 'intersectionally' now) about how different categories of people used public space, transport and buildings. But among some of my co-workers, there was resistance to the idea that there was any connection between gender issues (i.e. women's lives) and anything to do with either peace or the living environment. In fact there was a real aversion to the idea that feminism had a particular role to play in anti-militarist or environmentalist politics. I suspect this was largely a reaction against people saying things like: 'As a mother, I care about my children's future'. Which of course, many did say, and still do.

JL: That was the Women's Design Service, wasn't it?[2]

VW: Yes. It was a dream job for a while, especially with two small kids. Just before that, I had worked briefly at Friends of the Earth, in 1986, and was delighted to be moving into environmental campaigning after being unemployed/freelance for a while. I had effectively been fired as editor of *Searchlight* – which had also been a dream job but for very different reasons – when I was eight months pregnant, and it took me a while to figure out what to do next. FoE was an overnight education in the state of environmental politics at the campaigning end, and it was pretty dire. Here the presiding method was Science, Authority and Rational Argument, mostly delivered by the white, male proponents who jealously guarded their domains. As Information Officer, my job was to herd volunteers, cut out relevant articles in the newspapers (with scissors) and file them, and deal with media inquiries. I was expected to work a sixty-hour week, new baby or not, and to fit meekly into the office hierarchy as I learned the ropes. I made some good friends but also learned that being a serious environmentalist with a science background gave you the right to sneer at anything that called itself 'green' or which tried to integrate a political analysis of capitalism, patriarchy, white supremacy or militarism. Looking back, I understand now why it was that way because their aim was to influence government policy but in the 1980s I didn't find it a congenial place to work.

I was lucky to move to WDS after that because at least it was a feminist workspace, and at that time I was also just finishing off *Beyond the Pale*. I learned an enormous amount about urban planning and architecture. I also have fond memories because, during the *Emergency* years, we had had many discussions about the end of work, and the possibility of sabotage as a form of workers' resistance. WDS was very free and easy when I started, in the sense that there was no one standing over us and we just got on with it, but at some point in the early 1990s we were forced to employ an office manager and fill out timesheets, which was very unwelcome. Counting the hours I spent at work made me realise how much time I spent thinking about the job when I was not officially working. Sometimes I would include thinking time, or even commuting time, when I was filling out my timesheets. As long as you did what you were supposed to do, and took it seriously, that was what mattered.

There was one moment when I was writing about white women and imperialism in the late nineteenth century for *Beyond the Pale*, while at WDS I was researching ideas about social hygiene in the Victorian era as I was trying to trace the origins of public toilets for women. I managed to write something for our handbook on designing toilets (*At Women's Convenience*) that combined all or at least most of those themes. I found out, for example, that there was an organisation called the Ladies Association for the Diffusion of Sanitary Knowledge, which was the foundation of what became Social Work. It was supported by Charles Kingsley, who was a complicated figure: an advocate of Christian socialism but also a believer in the superiority of 'Anglo-Saxons'.

Around that time – this was the early 1990s – I was writing about the idea of green consumerism too – there's a section in the last chapter of *BTP* where I critique the Body Shop, which was one of the first businesses to promote the idea of 'green capitalism'.

JL: And then you went to work in academia …

VW: Yes, I got a job at the University of Greenwich in the School of Humanities, which at that time was developing links with the planning department. It was exciting to bring ideas about society and culture into an urban planning degree. Humanities was coming to an end as a popular multi-disciplinary degree so we were renaming all the individual components. I was working with the Environmental Studies strand so I said, 'Why don't we call it Cultural Geography?' So we called it Cultural Geography, which turned out to be a great idea. As a traditional discipline with roots in colonial expansion, geography was under attack so there was a lot of scope for creating a new curriculum, promoted by interventions like David Harvey's *The Condition of Postmodernity* (1989). I learned a lot from starting to teach at this point; it was the education I felt I had been lacking. It was really quite intense having to write weekly lectures on the history of urban design, for example, but completely fascinating too. The best things were the field trips to other cities, including Lille in northern France as the Channel Tunnel was opening around that time. I learned so much from my colleagues about how to think about cities historically by looking at planning and architecture.

The first course I had to teach was called 'Landscape and Society'. I found myself in an area that I hadn't given too much thought to in the past, or had taken for granted. The previous person gave me her course outline, which began with the political economy of Anglo-Saxon landownership – not something I knew anything about. But I remember the first class where I got the students to divide into landowners and ramblers. And then to switch. That was really fun. I'd never taught in a university before so I was terribly nervous. I wore a very short pink skirt for some reason.

JL: Interesting choice. And what did they have to do?

VW: Well the landowners were supposed to be angry about the fact that ramblers were walking on their land. The ramblers had to explain why they had the right to be there. It was a topical subject at the time so there was quite a lot of media discussion about it.

This is when I first read Carolyn Merchant's work, and came across the idea that Nature was thought of as intrinsically female and therefore needing to be controlled. I had to learn Enlightenment thought in terms of defining Nature. So that was really useful. And then during that time I became interested in the road protest movement and interviewed people in Walthamstow where they were campaigning against the M11 extension. The Newbury Bypass was running very near to where my parents lived so I got involved in some of those protests too in 1995.

JL: You wrote about that in *Who Cares About Britishness?* (2007), didn't you?

VW: Yes, briefly. I always wondered about the extent to which people thought about race and gender in their organising, or in the ways they represented their political demands.

JL: How do those dynamics of environmentalism and racialisation work now? It's often said in the UK that 'the environmental movement is so white', or that XR is too white.

VW: Yes, I have been following that discussion very closely for a long time. In the late 1990s and early 2000s the champions of rural Britain were definitely Conservative, up in arms about the right to hunt foxes and that sort of thing. That lobby is still very much there, but it's been overtaken by climate activists and conservationists who have very different politics and priorities. Last September [2018] Chris Packham organised a walk through central London to protest against the fact that British wildlife is seriously threatened. It was a horrible rainy day and everyone gathered in Hyde Park. I was partly there out of curiosity to see how many people came; and partly out of sympathy.

There were a few hundred, many from outside London, and lots of umbrellas. Chris Packham came on to the stage and the first thing he said was, 'I look out here and I see you're all white, basically, and that's not good enough for us. The environmental movement has failed to engage with a more diverse range of people and we have to do better'. Later on he introduced Billy Bragg by talking about how he first saw him at the Anti-Nazi Carnival in 1978. I felt like hugging him because he was saying, bottom line, 'We are anti-racist/anti-fascist and that's how it's going to be'. He had assembled a ministry of experts who had previously compiled a draft manifesto, so everyone was introduced as the Minister for This, Minister for That – and one of the first ones was the Minister for Diversity in Nature and Conservation. This was a young woman called Mya-Rose Craig, who spoke quite explicitly about the fact that many young visibly minority ethnic [VME] people feel they don't belong in the countryside and are worried that if they go there they will face hostility and hate crime.

Things have moved on quite a bit since then. Shortly after that, there were the first school strikes and then the first mass Extinction Rebellion event in London. As I said, I try to follow all these discussions about race but also monitor the connections between peace and anti-militarism campaigning too. There has been a rapid convergence between anti-militarists and climate change activists, and I think that's one of the most exciting things.

JL: You've written a lot about gender and as you've already said you were editor of the anti-fascist magazine Searchlight in the early

1980s. How is the way the right is gendered in the UK different now? What's changed?

VW: I've often fantasised about rewriting a pamphlet I wrote in 1978 called *Women and the National Front*, which analysed not just how fascist publications and propaganda tried to *appeal* to women, but how they used ideas about whiteness, and particularly white femininity, to play on people's fears. It was how their racism was *expressed*: the idea, for example, that white women were particularly under threat from immigrants – something they were reworking from Powell. The difference between then and now is that I was mainly looking at the National Front and British Movement in Britain. Most of the literature on gender and fascism at that time, such as there was, came from studies of Nazi Germany. Now you'd have to address the alt-right as well as the far right, and look at the spectrum on a global or at least transnational scale.

So just to take one example, things that were true in 1978, like 'there are no women in any positions of authority' in far-right organisations, are simply not the case today. Some of the successful far-right parties across Europe and elsewhere are actually led by white women, some of whom are openly lesbian. It might *seem* that their politics are more sophisticated in terms of gender and equality, but you'd have to look at specific issues, like attitudes to abortion or the question of rape and sexual violence, where the overt racist or white supremacist message is more or less the same.

There's one section of my original pamphlet that analysed the NF's views on 'womanhood' and the obsession with what they saw as the natural order of a white supremacist society. All the classic themes are there: a profound hatred of feminism, which they saw as the proof of how decadent western civilisation had become; an emphasis on militaristic versions of masculinity; an endorsement of eugenics as the rationale for who should be allowed to 'breed'.

One of the National Front's favourite slogans in the 1970s and 1980s was 'race-mixing is treason', which represented the classic yearning for purity fundamental to all forms of racial nationalism. At that time, they were stoking fears against immigrants and settlers from the New Commonwealth ... Now it's the idea that the growth of Muslim communities will lead to the extinction of the white race.

Of course there's a really big literature to draw on now too. I would want to connect the ways in which feminism itself can be instrumentalised by the far right, which Sara Farris has analysed as femonationalism. Then do you remember Femen and their naked protests in 2013? I found some of that imagery incredibly powerful: a woman half-naked, with 'Fascism Rest in Hell' scrawled across her breasts in red paint, being hauled away by loads of armed police. I was really moved by scenes like that. Yet there are elements of a very female voice against certain forms of patriarchy, fascism and fundamentalism, which can spill over into a critique of religion in a way that can fit with an Islamophobic agenda (without any sign that Femen themselves were being pulled into that).

JL: How are you developing these threads of 'gender, race, class, ecology and peace' now?

VW: I find I'm doing lots of different things at once, thinking more and more about the connections between anti-racism, anti-militarism and eco-socialism. My priority is to rewrite a manuscript I finished in 2004, based on the area where I grew up in northwest Hampshire. The original plan was to look at this small place in its wider historical, social, cultural context; and to draw out the ways in which it's been transformed by globalisation. I was also trying to write against that strand of English nationalism that depicts rural England as the victim of endless injuries, manifested particularly by immigration and cultural changes happening in the big cities. I finished the first version of the book in the early 2000s but it was hard to find a publisher; it was before the genre of nature and place writing had really opened up.

I wrote the first version while we were based in the US, and living through 9/11 and the Iraq War. By that time I had become a lot more involved in anti-war politics, and was engaging with Cynthia Enloe's work on militarisation. So I put that project to one side and turned my attention to militarism and military institutions for a while. Now I realise that the topic of war and the impact of war had been there in a lot of my writing and thinking from quite early on.

So in response to your first question about how themes come in and out, sometimes we are not even aware of them. When particular situations or political shifts provide the impetus to understand the intersections better, then they suddenly come into focus.

In 2018-19 I got a Leverhulme fellowship to go back to this body of material about the English countryside. The first version of the project was confined to the second half of the twentieth century – broadly 1939-2000 – but what I've realised since then is that I'm looking at a process that goes back much, much further. It involves colonial expansion, the opening of new markets; the industrial revolution, the way in which agriculture was changed by capitalism, and of course the expulsion of the rural population from the land, both because of urbanisation and also because so much of the common land was enclosed and it became impossible to make a living. So in this version, although I use examples from a particular area, it's absolutely not a 'local history'.

I think what I'm really trying to do is argue for a kind of literacy about how we understand words like 'rural' or 'countryside. Or to put it another way, I am trying to think ecologically, in a way that sees interconnections between social, economic and cultural changes registered in this particular area, but which are emblematic of deeper transformations. I've been influenced a lot by Patrick Wright's work, and his suggestion that you need to get to know a locality over a number of years before it starts to reveal the layers of power and history that have shaped it.

After a while I realised that there was a crossroads that I kept coming back to in my head. So instead of taking a village – the place where I was born – as the unit of transformation, I decided to stand there at the crossroads as a point of orientation. So now there are no distractions about who lives in the village or what kind of village it is, but I can still draw on my local knowledge and connections. I would add that it's quite difficult to write about a place you know very well, especially if it's connected to your own past. I don't want this new book to be a social history of that particular place, but thinking from one spot does help to anchor the underlying arguments and narrative.

So, just to take one example, there's an old-fashioned signpost at this intersection, which points in four directions to two towns, four tiny villages and two larger ones. There's a lot to say about how these places are connected, whether through being in the same parish, county or any other administrative unit. Then there are particular stories about the smallest of places which actually tell you an enormous amount about what's been going on in the countryside. In 2009, one of the small villages named on the signpost was bought by the Swedish owners of the H&M fast fashion empire. This made me think about the connections – or continuities – between the landowners of the late eighteenth and early nineteenth centuries who made their money through commerce and styled themselves as country squires, and the billionaires who have been investing in British farmland since the 1990s.

To give another example – there's a massive new mansion within half a mile of the crossroads which is fairly typical of many developments round there. It's designed to look like an eighteenth-century country house – even calls itself a manor, which is historically inaccurate – and was bought for £5.5 million just the other day. The developers got permission to build it in an Area of Outstanding National Beauty because it was on the site of an old farmstead.

JL: Does this book have a title?

VW: Well, the title was originally *Where Was I?*, because when you are talking about historical processes and the ways they are registered in everyday life, you can start to digress. And I do like digressions. I think they can be very productive, but you have to control them. This is an attempt to hold it together, because otherwise it could really ramble off, like a country lane in fact. But at the moment, the title has been changed to *Return of a Native* because I also play with ideas of alienation and belonging. This is not just in relation to my own connection to the area but it's also a way of addressing the exclusivity and impenetrability of the English countryside, and its place in the discourse of English nationalism. I borrow quite a lot of Thomas Hardy's descriptions as well because I love the way he makes the landscape into a historical character with moods and feelings.

So it's partly about the legibility of the landscape, which is the product of human activity – influenced by geology, ecology and climate – and relations of power that you can trace back over many centuries. This crossroads is quite a lonely spot – there's just one house there. I happened to have interviewed someone twenty years ago who had her first job as a domestic worker there when she was about fourteen or fifteen. That opens up the issue of women's work and the shift from domestic labour to secretarial work and so forth – but also the fact that electricity and running water only came there in the second half of the twentieth century, which is later than you might think.

It's amazing what you can find out from one vantage point when you start digging. I discovered that two of the fields bordering the crossroads were once part of a huge area of common land where people had the right to forage and graze their cattle. Today they are just fields as they were ploughed up during World War Two for food production, and then sold off. But in 1818 a rich Scottish family, who owned several manors nearby, enclosed most of this common area for their own use. Then I discovered that this particular family had made their money from owning a sugar plantation in St Kitts and received over £2000 compensation in 1835.

The fact that I had never heard of them growing up in the area was useful, as I thought I knew something about local history. It helped me understand the way that parish boundaries work. I had to look at books about ancient church history, and the history of poor law relief, where I discovered that parish boundaries operated like an internal border system, with rights and obligations attached to your birthplace that could not easily be transferred. The weird thing is that I have been trying meet people who live nearby – farmers particularly – some of whom have been in the area all their lives, and I came to realise that we hadn't come across each other's families before simply because we lived in different parishes, separated by an invisible line. As a child, your whole orientation to the community was governed by the church, the village hall, who organised the village fete, that sort of thing. It wasn't just me – I met someone who had grown up a couple of miles from us, who had no idea that my father had planted a wood in the 1980s, which now belongs to the Woodland Trust. As a professional agricultural conservation consultant, she seemed quite offended not to know about it as it rather undermined her expertise. She literally lives in the next village, but in a different parish.

Since then I've had some fascinating conversations with friends who grew up in the Caribbean. In Barbados, apparently, you can tell which parish someone comes from by their accent. The parish system was just transplanted as a form of local administration.

But underlying all these issues is the question of what's going to happen next. It's clear that the introduction of decent broadband has already made a big difference to people in rural areas. It makes it easier to run a business from home, for example, which then means that more people are 'escaping to the country', which has an effect on property prices, not to mention traffic and social life. The book is taking longer than I'd hoped as there is a lot to learn, not least about what's happening to farming at the moment. Then there's the question of how to make it readable.

JL: I wanted to ask you about your writing style. I've noticed that you write about mistakes you have made, which I really like and which is actually quite unusual. You write about when people have attacked you, and when you've changed your mind on things. And you mix together different writing styles. Was this difficult in an academic, sociological context, for example – or was it something that you've always found enough space for, by working across different disciplines and areas?

VW: I began writing as a journalist, and that teaches you to writes concisely, and I also learned how to edit other people's work as well, quite ruthlessly. *Beyond the Pale* was difficult to write because it combined a lot of different kinds of material. I never thought about it in terms of a particular discipline as I didn't have an academic job at that point. It took me ten years to write, with two kids and different kinds of jobs that I was lucky to get and unlucky to lose, and a lot of time to reflect on things I'd already written and time to try things out. And then there was the deep engagement with feminists of my generation or a bit older, you know, like bell hooks, June Jordan, Adrienne Rich, essayists who wrote from the heart about difficult political things and who moved seamlessly between more abstract, theoretical issues and personal experience without needlessly putting themselves at the centre. I think I learned to write from listening and talking to them and reading their work and it was this that helped me to develop my own voice. But academic writing was something else.

When I finished *Beyond the Pale*, a feminist history journal in the States asked me to write an article summarising the argument. I had no idea how to go about it and felt very intimidated at first – as if I had to use a different voice simply because it was an academic publication. So I wrote a short version and it was fine apparently, and I realised that it's more important to have something to say than dress it up in a particular kind of language. But also I was giving talks in universities long before I worked for one. That could also be quite intimidating, especially in places like UC Santa Cruz with people like Donna Haraway in the audience. It's the grilling afterwards where people try to catch you out. Mind you, talking about whiteness in those days was usually met by stony silence. I got used to that after a while too.

JL: So did you do your PhD after working at *Searchlight*?

VW: I got my PhD through publication in 1999, after submitting my book and two or three essays to Cambridge, where I had been an undergraduate. I had to have a viva, which, considering the book had been out for several years, was a bit strange. It was so rigorous that I was in quite a rage afterwards. Academic writing has become quite stifling now, I think – probably because of the insane pressure to publish journal articles. I haven't written that many to be honest. I once had a review where they said: 'This is not an article, it's an essay', and they needed 'a greater sense of what research the author has actually done'. It was a thinking piece about the politics of resentment that has turned out to be rather prescient.

JL: What about the visual and your own visual production, how does that fit in?

VW: I became a photographer while I was working at *Searchlight* and it quickly became something that was inseparable from my writing … I find I often describe photographs: not necessarily my own, but ones I've come across that say something specific. I've taken so many pictures of the wretched crossroads as well. I don't know what it is I am trying to capture. It just looks like a signpost against the backdrop of fields. But I did paint one of the fields the other day and I think that's going to be the cover. It's a way of connecting to the project: a way of expressing something about that spot, reminding myself that I was there. In the old days when I used to teach geography, I used to show my students a slide of a ploughed field and say, 'You think that's just a field don't you? But really it's a factory for producing a crop for profit, not food for eating'. I seem to be still stuck on the same image – I'm obsessed by the history of fertiliser at the moment.

And I think an image makes a subject more interesting. For *Military Migrants*, I took some amazing pictures of people I met, just to remember what they look like – but I wasn't allowed to publish them. The kind of photography I do is in a way quite personal, so I can go somewhere like Lee Valley and take the same picture every time, but what's important for me is the moment of taking it, or feeling joy at seeing the light on water, or naked branches against the sky. It's being there, at that time, and then holding onto it as a visual memory, or record.

JL: And you've been doing some Brexit paintings?

VW: Yes. Art's been very important on and off, for a very long time. Photography is a way of doing something visual that I can do quite easily along with other things. Painting is more demanding I find, and it can really interrupt my writing. Recently I've been painting quite intensely and moving more towards abstraction, which I've not done before. I had a very creative aunt who gave me an empty book to write down my ideas and poems. It was such a lovely thing for a kid! Because it made you feel that what you write is worthwhile, that it's a natural thing to do. I can still remember what it looked like. I was thinking the other day how important that was at the time and it probably contributed to my wanting to be a writer in fact.

JL: Going back to my earlier question about combining different threads, have you found ways to integrate your visual work with your writing?

VW: One of the things I've worked on fairly consistently for the last few years is the politics of memorialisation and the cultural heritage of war, especially World War One. In 2013 I was invited by some Swedish feminists to collaborate on a project looking at how military deaths in Afghanistan were treated in several different European countries. I chose to do the chapter on new monuments, and that got me thinking about war memorials, for the first time. I learned from my daughter, who is an art historian, that it's really important to ask: how did it come to be in that location, who paid for it, who designed it?

I was just starting to put together a feminist walking tour of war-related monuments in central London when the Millicent Fawcett memorial was installed in Parliament Square. What a wasted opportunity! When you look at the way that she was complicit with the policy of holding civilians in concentration camps in the Anglo-Boer/South African war, you have to ask: what kind of feminism is this? We're all supposed to worship at the feet of Millicent Fawcett as the most amazing suffragist campaigner, whose success was not only registered in 1918 (with the vote), but also subsequently in equal rights for girls and women, to this day. But stories are always more complicated than that – people's lives are more complicated.

I mean this was an opportunity to say, 'Fawcett led a complex life too, she was a liberal and she was also an imperialist'. When you go back and look at her role as head of the Ladies Commission in 1899-1901, it's clear she wanted to be in with the war planners, saying, 'The camps are ok in principle – you just need to organise them better'. Whereas there were many other amazing women who said, 'No, war is barbaric, it's not going to solve anything and we are not going to be part of it'.

JL: So what kind of progressive intersectional memorial would you like to see?

VW: Well, that's the thing, isn't it? It would have to be more abstract, not figurative, and not based around a person, for one thing. Statues of single individuals are bound to be problematic when they are expected to represent a movement. There are other aspects of the relationship between militarism and the struggle for women's suffrage that complicate things too. For example, by 1918 governments were afraid because of what was happening in Russia, and in Germany too, and they thought if they gave the suffragists a few crumbs, they would be quiet and settle down, as many of them weren't particularly radical, and were patriots, like Fawcett, who had given their support to the war effort in 1914. I mean, feminist historians have written about these dynamics for years, it's nothing new. But the memorial to Fawcett, and the tokenistic pictures of assorted activists around the plinth – this was a missed opportunity. To be honest I found it astonishing that there wasn't more criticism at the time.

For a while this made me want to go back and update *Beyond the Pale* for the twenty-first century. There's so much about war and militarism in there that I hadn't made anything of, but of course there's a lot that could be added. I ended up writing something about the politics of war and peace in relation to feminism in the context of imperialism. Actually what I'd really like to do at some point is a project around the idea of peace and security, asking the question: how might we see our futures differently? Trying to think more towards that horizon, *for* that horizon, rather than always being against.

There's an initiative called *Rethinking Security*, which came out of the thinking of a number of key peace activists and analysts and writers: people like Paul Rogers, who often writes for *Open Democracy* about emerging technologies of violence as well as the causes and interconnections. In 2014 they produced this document called the Ammerdown Manifesto, which sets out an alternative paradigm of global security. Building on the UN definition of security meaning freedom from want, freedom from fear and hunger, their vision encompassed a much wider set of issues that produced insecurity: resource scarcity, climate change, different kinds of violence, political repression and so on. Military force is relegated to being only one tool to use in particular, well-defined circumstances, as a last resort. I've used the document in teaching as it helps to provide an alternative vision of a world beyond war, and it has a sort of magical effect on students. I remember a moment at the end of a course about war and militarisation, when one of the students said, 'But why don't they teach us this in primary school?' I found that very compelling.

JL: 'Peace' is often evoked as quite a blank category.

VW: Yes, the word peace is quite bland; it can sometimes simply mean the absence of fighting. The post-war period that our generation grew up in was one of peace or so we thought, not being aware of all the small wars that were going on in the background, let alone the Cold War.

When I was at the Women's Design Service, the first thing I did was write a report on women's safety on housing estates. It connected with my work on the racist media discourse around the spectre of white women being threatened by young Black men. It was quite an interesting move to go from an anti-racist, feminist political analysis to a more practical argument around design and safety. I interviewed a number of women residents about what was making them feel safe or unsafe; and of course it was everything from street lighting to whether the entrance to a tower block was locked, whether there was a concierge, whether that made a difference or not, whether they wore a uniform, whether the council came to do repairs or not. And I was telling someone about this just the other day, and then realised that, actually, that was a microcosm of thinking with people about how they understood the idea of security: asking what might make you feel safe about where you live, or thinking about the environment your kids were growing up in. I'd like to do a more interactive thing, where people could reflect on these questions, both alone and together with others. That would be a really fantastic thing to do. Because then you could see how these questions can be approached from multiple perspectives and political priorities, and it's a question of working together so they don't conflict; what might make you feel more safe might make me feel more threatened. Or, if you took something for granted, you might realise that you haven't really thought this through from a different point of view.

JL: And finally, how do you position your work in relation to the waves of feminism?

VW: When *Beyond the Pale* was re-issued in 2015, a young woman said to me, 'But how did you find out about all these historical women?!' And I was like, 'Well, we went to libraries, we spent a lot of time looking for them!' Then I remember when the 'third wave' happened, and my students at Yale at the time said, 'We don't want Adrienne Rich, we want third wave writers', and at first I thought, what do they do, who are they, and why do we have to have waves? But now I do think that generational shifts are really important. I'm always interested to know how people synthesise things and what younger writers are bringing that's new, and I do believe it's important to anchor your political analysis in shared formative moments. I think these things really do shape you, and your perspective. And there's enormous value in hearing from people who were politicised at different phases of a movement. But it has to be two-way. There seems to be more interest in the early days of the women's movement now, but the danger is that individuals who made significant interventions get left out of the narrative as it shrinks over time. It's inevitable that this happens, but you have to remember that the process of writing a movement's history is also deeply political.

Stuart Hall used to say, 'Imagine how the world looked to this person, whoever it is you are reading, when they were twenty-one' – which would be the age of most undergraduates now – 'and then think about what the world looks like to you. What are your priorities, what are you scared of, what do you think are the dominant issues at the moment?' That seemed to me a very creative way of thinking about age difference, as well as locating ourselves – and the authors and theorists who we like – in particular historical circumstances. If you mix people from different generations, it can be really generative. Let's be upfront about where we are coming from, and not write people off because of the generation they are supposed to belong to. We all have to work to try and understand the conditions that we face today.

NOTES

1 This interview was first published as '"Gender, race, class, ecology and peace": Jo Littler talks to Vron Ware' in *Soundings: A Journal of Politics and Culture*, Issue 75, 2020, pp144-160.

2 An organisation originally set up with local authority funding to improve the built environment for women, which involved, for example, lobbying for gender neutral baby-changing facilities in public toilets. See www.wds.org.uk and Women's Design Service, *At Women's Convenience: Handbook on the Design of Women's Public Toilets*, 1990.

We haven't got here just on our own. It's a conversation

Carol Tulloch is an author, curator, maker and academic, and Professor of Dress, Diaspora and Transnationalism at the University of the Arts, London. She grew up in Doncaster in the North of England and studied BA Fashion and Textile Design at Ravensbourne College Design and Communication, and MA History of Design at the Royal College of Art and Victoria and Albert Museum. She is known for her innovative work on heritage, personal archives, style narratives and auto/biography, and her books include *Black Style* (2004) and *The Birth of Cool: Style Narratives of the African Diaspora* (2016). She has curated and co-curated a wide range of exhibitions, including *Grow Up! Advice and the Teenage Girl* (The Women's Library, 2002); *The March of the Women: Suffragettes and the State* (National Archives, 2003); *Picture This: Representations of Black People in Product Promotion* (Archives and Museum of Black Heritage, 2002); *Black British Style* (V&A, 2004); and *Rock Against Racism* (Autograph, 2015). In this interview, conducted online in summer 2021, she talks to Jo Littler about her work and the contexts and cultures it emerged from.[1]

Jo Littler: You use material culture as a way in to telling larger social and cultural stories –pulling on their threads, and considering their meaning and significance in a sensitive and capacious fashion. How did you come to adopt this kind of approach?

Carol Tulloch: I've always been drawn to objects and clothes. I'm not quite sure how that came about … maybe going shopping with my mum and my dad as a kiddie. My dad used to back horses at the bookies, and he put some money on for me at the Grand National and I'd choose my horse. Once when I was under ten my horse won, so I got some money, and so I knew exactly what I wanted to spend it on: a tweedy blue coat with a hood with fur round it that I'd seen in a shop called Busy Bees. Now I can remember my relationship with my dad through that coat: I can see us walking down the road to the shop. The other thing that made me realise I was obsessed with clothes was when a Sikh man from Sheffield used to come round and sell things door to door. I used to get really excited 'cos I always knew he was going to bring something amazing. Once he brought this amazing pair of jeans with deep turnups. I must have been about six or seven and *I got the jeans!* So there's certain images and memories.

I remember in the early 1960s television was all so new and we had a TV and we watched a programme called *77 Sunset Strip*. The main character was a private eye played by Efrem Zimbalist Jr (and at that time in America, to have not changed your name to a more Americanised name was quite radical). His friend, Cookie, used to continually comb his quiff. I remember the action of him combing his hair, and then putting the comb in his pocket, and being just *enthralled* by that. Another memory is being by my mum's side and seeing a skirt or a dress with beautiful embroidery. My mum used to buy things and then send them back to the family in Jamaica. I remember her folding it up and putting it in a suitcase or a box. I've always remembered the colours – the reds, yellows and whites.

So a lot of it is to do with connections to my background and growing up. It was also because of dreaming about fashion design, then training as a fashion designer, and working with material and tools for making – I am obsessed with them! I got into contextual studies at Epsom School of Art and Design where I did my BTEC.[2] Then when I went to Ravensbourne College for Design and Communication and did the contextual studies course there between 1985-1988, somehow it all clicked: understanding how and why I use clothes as a way of making myself visible, of claiming my sense of self. I couldn't articulate that before.

My mum was quite religious after my dad died, and I really couldn't go to nightclubs or anything like that. I really wanted to be part of the Black consciousness movement that was happening for us in the 1970s and that had started in the 1960s. I would do it by experimenting with head wraps, copying things I saw on *Top of the Pops* or on Black girls in London when I came down for holidays. I began to understand how clothes can communicate those ideas. Then doing the RCA/V&A History of Design MA course I understood how you can do a biography of an object, or figure out what an object can communicate to people.[3] Like us now, really: bringing back memories, but also showing *evidence*. That's my curating.

I always used to think my curating wasn't 'political', it was just me trying to get across another truth, other than the historical colonial, imperialist 'truth' about Black people, particularly by connecting with my familial heritage, and people in Jamaica; by connecting and telling another counter-narrative. Objects can help me do that. I didn't have the academic language to communicate what I was trying to say before I really got into contextual studies and writing, and realising what I was doing was critical practice or critical thinking. Objects could communicate what I was thinking. Sometimes all you need to see was an Afro comb, which said so much for me. But then I needed to spell that out for others. So I wrote an article about the Afro comb,[4] researched its history, and found all these patents for Afro combs that emerged in the States during the 1960s and 1970s.

So an aesthetic of presence and evidence is how it works. When I curated the *Black British Style* exhibition with Shaun Cole at the V&A in 2004 it was object-led and included quotes from lenders. When we put the objects onto the mannequins we realised the very first outfit – a 1960s suit by Julian Bridgeman – didn't have a shirt or tie. Then I remembered my dad's tie ... he died in 1971, so it was from around the right time. That said so much: being able to state that he bought it in England, and in Doncaster, in the 1960s. Another example is my work on taste and the champagne cocktail glass. In the 1960s my parents had a champagne cocktail glass that they did not use ironically; but they used it as part of their sense of taste, and as part of the act of kindness and well-being in having friends round. That cocktail glass was bought in Doncaster, so it wasn't aimed at the Black community. But their purchase of it, and taking it into their home, this Jamaican home, added a different meaning; and the way they used it added different meanings from say somebody white from Doncaster (and a lot of people around us were white working class). But it's the same object.[5]

JL: How did growing up in the north of England shape your work?

CT: I am so proud to be Northern, I can't tell you, and I'm so proud to be from Doncaster. The neighbour who lived next door to us was Mrs Taylor, who was white, and then the family next to her was a Black family, and after that all the rest were all white. Me and Mrs Taylor always got on and she taught my mum how to make pancakes and my mum showed her how to do jerk chicken. I remember her coming round one evening, and she came for my dad, and said that she had taken her husband his dinner and he wasn't responding. My dad went round; he'd died, and he had to get the doctor. But she came for my dad, a Black man – or for our family anyway – rather than the white families that were the next door along. Do you know what I mean? And this is the 1960s.

There was a close Black community because the majority of the men who moved to Doncaster came from Birmingham. My uncle CB told me that they came to England when they were young and were given the choice of conscription or working down the mines, so a lot of them worked as miners. He and my dad chose the mines. House parties developed because there was a colour bar system, so you couldn't go into clubs and pubs. That continued and so we were always going to Nottingham, Birmingham, London, Bradford, to things, and then people from those cities would come to us. So there was that sense of community. But also, from infant school to junior school particularly, all my friends were mixed together. There would be the kids from the Barnardo's orphanage, and the lovely Scottish family who ran it. They came down on their way to school and picked me up, then we'd pick up someone else – including another guy who was Scottish who would always wear those very belted gabardine macs with a schoolboy cap – and we would walk together. There were Romanis who would come to school on a seasonal basis. Sometimes people went back to places: a boy called Shanda Varga went back to Czechoslovakia and my best friend, at the time, Carol, returned to Jamaica with her family. So I was seeing all these things – people, migrants, and returning – quite early on. But in that mix of different groups ... the one thing that connected us all was the working classness, sharing foods, eating gugelhupf, all of that.

I always remember someone at school saying, 'Our world is within the school gates. Outside that world, how adults think is not how *we think*.'[6] I did feel really safe within the school. I was also the first Black girl to go to Danum Grammar School. That was tough because I had to wear the same uniform I'd worn at my previous school because my dad died that year and my mum said she just couldn't afford the new uniform, so I had to wait to get the free one. That was painful. So on one level there was this great connection ... and then on another level there wasn't. My mum went into school with me for the introduction to new pupils and she wanted to sit right at the front because she said she didn't want to miss anything and to get it, to understand it, so we sat at the front and the hall was packed, absolutely packed, so much so ... people were standing down the side of the aisles ... And the other front row of the other side was full and ours was empty. No-one came and sat with us. My mum squeezed my hand so much she was hurting me. And then we started going around the different rooms. I remember being in the chemistry lab and I saw this girl ... she kept smiling at me. That was Christine Markham and she said she saw what happened that day, and she said that she made sure that I was going to be her friend. And I'm not kidding, I just got a card from her a couple of weeks ago, and she's saying to me, 'Carol, are you still working?' 'cos she's retired. And I went, 'yeah' [laughs]. So we're still in contact.

So even when my mum was squeezing my hand I couldn't really understand the times. I once went for an interview and someone said that 'the job has gone'. The agency couldn't understand what was going on. Then in the 1980s I was punched in the face ... things had started to change and I arrived in Doncaster from London for a weekend at home and my sister picked me up and we were walking and I just heard somebody say 'black bitch'. The next thing I knew I tried to open my eyes and I couldn't open them because there was so much blood and he had punched me in the face. It turns out he went and slashed someone else's face – Michael Burt, a family friend of ours - in the Arndale Centre in Doncaster, so I could have got that. They finally caught him because he beat up a Romani man ... I went to court, I couldn't recognise him because I actually didn't see him, but Michael did, and he got sent down. So by then I think something had shifted. But that's the foundation of me as well.

I was lucky to be brought up in the North and in Doncaster. When my dad died in the seventies, I'm not exaggerating, it was 50 per cent Black 50 per cent white at the funeral. There wasn't a West Indian club so my dad used to go to the Polish Club on a Sunday – the Polish community was very close with the Jamaican community. So it's complicated, it's not straightforward at all. I think sometimes that's why I can look at things in the round. And one last story. My cousin Karen came up from London, and a friend of mine came round. Well, my cousin was in shock, 'cos she lived in Brixton at the time with my grandparents, and she said, 'Carol, there's a white boy at the door!' And I looked – because in our house the kitchen was at the back of the house and when all the doors were open you could look right down to the front door, through the dining room and then the hallway (and we had rooms coming off that) – and I said, 'Yes, that's Chris'. Chris and I were born on the same day, we went to infant and junior school together ... he lived next door to the Browns, who were a Black family, so he was really close to them and us. And Chris had come in and said hello and things and went straight to the fridge and got something out. Well, by this time, I thought Karen was gonna have a seizure or something, and she just kept saying, *But he's white!* She could not believe it, and then she sat down and started chatting. In Doncaster there was such a mix of Black and white.

JL: Your book *The Birth of Cool* interprets cool in different ways: as a condensation of histories of African diaspora, as spiritual balance, as a jazz ensemble. How does 'cool' work in relation to gender?

CT: I decided in the end to look at individual men and women that I was drawn to and had a connection with; at how they used clothing as a way of communicating who they are and expressing their particular tastes. So it ranges from Billie Holiday and the world of jazz artists in the States, to Mrs Gloria Bennett from Jamaica, who was a dressmaker with four children who worked on the buses in Doncaster. She's on the front cover of the book. Living around my mum and all her female friends, there was a strength that I didn't fully realise until I started reading about feminism and the idea of women having the right to work, to exist beyond the home and not just be defined as a mother and a wife. The women, including my mum, balanced so much: they were mums, they cooked and baked beautifully, they could sew, but they also worked – my mum worked in a factory.[7] Then they would go to parties and dress beautifully. I can remember my mum's dressing table and face powders and lipstick and the glass containers on her dressing table. There was a woman called Mrs Brown; when my dad died, she came to our house and they all did what they do when someone dies: lots of people come around and they stay up late playing dominoes and all of that and talking and drinking. And I was *transfixed* by Mrs Brown. She had, God, how many – six children? I'd never met her before, but she held the room. She had this way of telling stories that I'd only heard men do when my dad used to take me to the cricket. And I remember her telling this story, and she had the most incredible black dress on, just a very simple shift dress. She was quite meaty but curvaceous, but she had this astrakhan coat with a fur collar. She was telling this story, and talking about a fight, so she's pretending like she was one of the guys who took off their jacket, and the way she did it – she was this really strong woman, there was such a strength … but then she looked so feminine, in the sense that her hair was beautifully done, it was straightened, and her dress was stunning, she had makeup on, but she was holding that room. I was transfixed by this woman. These women, who have all these different planes they operate on, all these different aspects of what it is to be a woman in the world. They weren't professional women – they worked in factories and things. It was that power of *holding the room*, I can't really put it any better.

That's the women. Then the men: I'm interested in the 'swagger'. On a Black man, it's a little bit more powerful because of what it means. It's tough enough being a Black woman on the street, but

being a Black man on the street, whether in Britain or the States …
I used to fear if my brother came down to visit my younger sister
and I in London because he could be picked up just for walking
on the street. It didn't matter whether you dressed well or not, it's
the skin tone that's going to get you pulled over. But there is the
courage, the way of basically saying, 'We love clothes, and we enjoy
clothes, we're *just wearing it*'. Do you know what I mean? That's
why I included the Malcolm X chapter: because there was someone
who first initially had a more criminal life and then became a
Muslim, and who was both incredibly religious and political, but
did not deny himself the act of looking good and used that as part
of his honesty and respectability.

In Malcolm X's autobiography he talks about being in prison,
and his brother comes to see him in a sweatshirt, and Malcolm's
appalled because he feels that his brother's gone a little mad because
he's dressing down. It shows how that sense of respect for yourself
involves presenting yourself well. That's something that both my
parents and the Black community around me growing up would
stress because they felt if you didn't – if you went onto the street
not looking well-dressed – then you'd just be attracting trouble,
and you'd be perpetuating the stereotypical idea that Black people
are of a 'lower class'. That's why there was some of the contention
between children and their parents when people started wearing
dreadlocks. Like between my grandparents and my uncle. Oh my
god! It was too much for them because they just felt that they were
drawing attention to themselves, and for them dreadlocks were not
about looking good, respectability and being a good citizen, if you
like. But then a lot of the older generation also started wearing
afros, which was again about Black consciousness and a re-state-
ment of Blackness.

JL: On a programme on BBC Radio Four recently they had a man
on who grew up in an Afghan refugee camp and he was saying that
for him clothing was the way to resolve his post-traumatic stress –
he said, 'That's how I dealt with it, by dressing sharp'. It made me
think about how in *The Birth of Cool* you talk about how dress can
be a way to resolve contradictions.

CT: Yes! It's quite interesting because I do it now. I bought a yellow jumper during lockdown and there's days when I say, 'I just need my yellow jumper today, it's the only thing that's going to get me through the day!' Another time, I was in hospital, and there was six of us in the ward – all women – and then another woman came in. The first couple of nights she had the curtain closed but there would suddenly be this amazing smell of perfume. It turns out that she had only a few months left to live and the thing that kept her going was putting a little make up on. She put lipstick on every day and then she'd squirt perfume on herself just before she went to sleep at night. And we actually couldn't wait till she squirted that perfume because the whole ward smelled *gorgeous*. She said that she wasn't afraid of dying – she had come to terms with death – but was worried about the impact it would have on her sister. Then *my* sister came in, Elaine, who worked for Jasper Conran. And this lovely woman, who was white, came over afterwards and said, 'Your sister just looked *amazing* in those clothes', and was asking about those clothes … This woman didn't have long to live. And her face! Elaine gave us such joy that day. So, yeah, sometimes people see clothing as a trivial thing, but it's not. Like that guy in the refugee camp. In a chapter in a book,[8] I write about how, for somebody like Mrs Anella James who'd just moved over from Jamaica in the early 1960s to Ilford, Essex, into a new space for her where she'd not established a home yet, what was left was *the way she dressed*. She had herself photographed in a particular outfit that she'd made for a wedding. So her body and her clothes and the way she styled herself was her home.

JL: You've curated and co-curated a wide and pioneering range of exhibitions about gender and racialisation, including *Picture This!*, on representations of Black people in product promotion (AMBH), *Black British Style* at the V&A, *Grow Up! Advice and the Teenage Girl* at the Women's Library, *The March of the Women* on suffragettes at the National Archive, and *Rock Against Racism* at Rivington Place.

CT: I gave a talk recently for the 'Race, Rights and Sovereignty' series at Glasgow School of Art and I thought, what do I want to talk about? And I called it: 'Curate, reflect, write, write, curate, reflect, curate, write, reflect'. The title went on and on because I was saying: they all go hand in hand, the curating and the writing and then the reflecting. As I said earlier, objects help me to communicate things that are difficult to say. Sometimes an object can do a lot of it for you. I've not been that comfortable with blockbuster exhibitions. For a lot of people *Black British Style*, in terms of the actual space, was small, but for me was like, 'Oh my God, I'm so *out there* in the world!' I do want to curate but I'd be really happy if only two people came. When I did *Advice and the Teenage Girl*, which I was invited to do at the Women's Library, there was a massive double page spread in *The Observer*. It was too much! I just went to bed. And I remember Caroline Evans[9] saying, 'Carol, there are people out there who would kill for a quarter page, why are you different?' But right then, I felt too much *out there*. Then when I wrote 'Picture This! The Black Curator' for you and Roshi in *The Politics of Heritage: The Legacies of 'Race'*, that was me coming to terms with things that had happened at that time and all the exhibitions I had done; and asking myself if I wanted to be seen as a 'Black curator', and what that means.[10]

It was on the strength of those exhibitions that the Women's Library asked me to curate *Advice and the Girl*. I loved doing that exhibition because I was bringing in all the things that I've done around the Archives and Museum of Black Heritage[11] as well as *Street Style*. I wanted to say, 'Okay, if we're looking at teenagers, we're gonna have a mix of teenagers, but we do it in a way that is natural'. Do you get what I mean? Rather than, you know, your Black teenagers over there ... and other teenagers there. So, for example, I included a magazine from the Royal National Institute of Blind People. The cover was so beautiful, it had an embossed face, but they'd coloured it. And I remember, somebody from a newspaper, whose name I will not mention (but let's just say it wasn't the *Guardian*), was so excited about the exhibition, and then I showed her this item and she said, 'What do you want me to do with that?' And I thought wow, wow, because that's normally what they would say about Black people.

Black British Style at the V&A was a turning point. I enjoyed doing it, but it put me off doing exhibitions for a while because the pressure of expectation and the negotiation of what could be

included was a bit much. But because of that exhibition Donald
Smith, the Director of Chelsea Space, said, 'Carol, you've got the
Chelsea Space Gallery to do whatever you want to do in it'. No one's
ever said that to me before or since! I knew I wanted to look at Syd
Shelton's photographs on anti-racism that he put away around 1986
and never really showed again. So I took his photos to Donald to
curate *A Riot of Our Own* and then, with Mark Sealy, *Rock Against
Racism*, an exhibition at Autograph.

I'm writing a piece now for Alison Slater's book *Memories of
Dress* in which I look back at the exhibition I did called *Handmade
Tales: Women and Domestic Craft in Britain, 1840 – 2010*.
Reflecting on that exhibition, I realised that I'd become a custodian of a lot of people's memories. A lot of them were personal
objects and I got the lender to write captions that I would edit.
So there was a lot of personal detail woven throughout the exhibition; and then layers of memories *within* the exhibition; and
then my memory of the exhibition – all these different layers of
memory. I thought the editors might think it was a bit barking
mad but it gave me the opportunity to think – within today's
lockdown context – about domestic crafts and what those women
were doing. Madeline Ginsburg,[12] who passed away last year,
lent me a Jewish sampler with a psalm written in Hebrew on it,
which was translated into English on the same sampler. It was
from 1840, so that was our earliest piece, and it was given to
Madeline by her mother-in-law, so it was a family object. I loved
doing that exhibition. I had pearly queen dresses; and embroidery
from Ireland; and a rug from the Punjab that a woman had made
for a trousseau. It was such a wide range. Then this lovely woman
came in, I'd given a tour around it, and it was a Black woman ...
I'll never forget, she'd got her hair shaved really short and she'd
put her arms out and she said, 'This is me!' And what was lovely is
that it wasn't about just Blackness alone; it was about women who
make things in domestic space. And she put out her arms and
said, 'This is me!', and I went, 'Yeah!' [laughs] And it was worth
it, the whole exhibition, just for that.

JL: You've often taken your academic work out into public spaces
– both establishment spaces of 'high culture' and more 'everyday'

places. Why do you do that kind of public outreach work and what are its challenges?

CT: *Nails, Weaves and Naturals* was brilliant and so successful. It was a one-day event on hair and nails at the V&A, with a photographic display of Black British hairstyles dating back to the late nineteenth century, which lasted for a little longer. Over a thousand people came and around 95 per cent were Black; they came for that event and got themselves photographed. Then we took the photographic display to the *Afro Hair and Beauty Show* at Alexandra Palace. It was amazing, as the display was in the main walkway, like mini billboards where people came in, and you could see people walking in and then doing a double take and coming across to have a look. It was interesting to see responses in that space. The organisers invited us to put it on there as they just thought it would work. Because *Nails, Weaves and Naturals* was so successful, the management at the Archives and Museum of Black Heritage wanted me to redo the exhibition there at the gallery in Brixton. I didn't want to repeat it because it had been done so I thought, 'OK, let's focus on the tools that make the hair'. What we were presenting at the V&A and Alexandra Palace was the finished product. Here I decided to focus on the tools and the hairdressers and the spaces where the hair would be created. So I gathered a collection of tools, and a smaller collection of the photographs, and put them in hairdressers. It wasn't easy. It was a bit convoluted, but it was so brilliant. It was up to the hairdressers if they wanted to keep the photographs. Then in January 2016, Alison Maloney devised a project called *Cabinet Stories*[13] and invited six curators to contribute with their own theme. Each week she would change the cabinet and put in the next curator's work. I was the first one and mine was on flat cloth caps. Alison wanted to show *Cabinet Stories* in non-gallery spaces and so it was shown at Holloway Women's Prison just before they closed it down. It involved a mix of objects: actual flat cloth caps, nineteenth-century photographs, *carte de visites*, a record sleeve. Each curator did a workshop around their display; mine was getting the women to stitch onto a segment of a flat cloth cap. They could either keep it or hand them in, then we'd create a flat cloth cap out of it.

There were warnings that the women might not turn up on time but my God, they were there so early, they were chomping at the bit outside. They were really lovely, and we weren't allowed to know their names, only numbers. I took bits of stitching that I do myself: I took in the quilt that I started the night my mum died, just to show them the stitching on that, and the kind of things that have influenced me. I said, 'Look, I'm not a professional textile artist or anything, it's just something I like to do on the side'. But I showed them how to do couching and cross stitch and experimental stitching … using those two stitches. And there were two young women from the Philippines who were absolutely brilliant and worked together as a team. They wanted me to show them how I did the cross stitch and they made a whole cap in the workshop time, all hand-stitched with embroidery. Then there was this one woman who looked incredibly stressed, and she was saying that she was going to leave, but then she produced a piece of stitching that Alison and I were crying at because it was so incredible. Somehow her face didn't have any features at the time when she looked so stressed, but when she got into the stitching … you knew, she just wasn't going to go anywhere. And then she handed in her piece and she walked away and then she walked back and she said, 'Can I see it one more time?' And it was so beautiful what she'd produced, I'm not just saying it … it was so beautiful. And then I saw her face and she had blue eyes. She looked younger and she was beaming, and it was at that point, as she'd turned away, Alison and I started crying, saying, 'Oh my God, today was unbelievable, unbelievable!'

JL: A therapy session.

CT: I know, it was a therapy session! It made that day for me, it was incredible. The other thing I've done more recently during Covid is set up a group called *Making Time*. I sent an email to six colleagues because I was just not finding time to *not* do academic work and I went, 'You know what, Tuesdays 5:30 p.m. – 6:30 p.m. I am stopping and I am stitching, doing, making something'. I said, 'Look, if you want to join, if you just want to sit there, if you want to stitch, anything, cook, whatever'. We'd just meet for an hour online. The first one was on 10 November 2020 and we're still going. It's been phenomenal. We're a mix of more established academics and new researchers and administrators, and some are now using what we talk about in their teaching. It's expanded my thinking on things. Some people have been baking or making bread, and I painted the drawer that a local man made for me because the drawer of a second-hand table I'd brought was missing. I have a new studio, so in one of those sessions I was just folding up my things and taking them up and putting them in my cupboard. Caryn Simonson said, 'It's like an art piece, it's like a performance'. And all of us say, 'There's work *before* Tuesday, and there's work *after* Tuesday'. I've not missed any sessions because, you know, I organise it. But some of them who had other things on and missed sessions, they say their week feels out of kilter when they've missed a session, which is very interesting.

JL: At your inaugural professorial lecture at Chelsea a few years ago you ended by talking about gender and grime and showing the video for Skepta's 'Shutdown'. What interests you about gender and young people's clothes and lives at the moment?

CT: I remember Alesha Dixon saying, at the end of her lip sync of 'Shutdown' on the TV programme *Lip Sync Battle UK*, 'This is the only time I could do this'. She was going back to her roots in hip hop, in Black music, as a rapper.[14] When I saw Skepta's video it was all in code: the all-white and all-black tracksuits, about belonging and unity. What did it mean for a large group of young male and female people of colour, performing in in the Barbican Estate? As Skepta said, '"Shutdown" was a triumphant return of the repressed'.

The fear of the Black gang is about a group of Black men being together. But my dad and his mates used to be a group when they'd walk to the Town Fields in Doncaster to play cricket. And my brother and all his mates would walk along the streets, and if my mum got off the bus, they'd more than likely be so supportive, help carry her bags – do you know what I mean? I wanted to use such images to ask, 'What is a gang?', and to look at the broader meaning of gangs, and groups of people together, whether young or old, regardless of age. So many times I've said to students, 'OK gang', because we're this group, together. The parents or grandparents of the Skepta generation would have got the same sort of treatment, of being feared, but they would have been older – more like in their twenties. So we need to look again at the term 'gang'. The 'gang' is so often presented as only about violence.

JL: You've said you're more of a womanist than a feminist. Can you say why?

CT: I do remember my mum using a similar word. If you were trying to be more adult before your time, my mum would say, 'You're too womanish, you know!' or 'You're just trying to be too expressive'. I knew what she meant, in a sense. But it's the Alice Walker definition of womanist that she initially aimed at Black women, and what that means. I think with 'womanist', Alice Walker is basically saying, 'Fight for the rights of what and how a woman can be and what she wants to do, but if you want to look stunning and wear clothes and wear make-up, you don't have to compromise'. I first read *In Search of Our Mothers' Gardens: Womanist Prose*, in 1993: Alice Walker's determined fight to be who you want, who you need to be, regardless of the obstacles that emerge, that are constructed to halt that progression. Womanism is a part of feminism for Alice Walker, and her use of 'womanist' connected me with my mother and paternal grandmother who were being womanist, although they did not have a name for it.

Since then there have been standout, empowering texts for me: *White, Male and Middle Class: Explorations in Feminism and History* by Catherine Hall (notably the introduction) and Paul Gilroy's *The Black Atlantic* were key texts for my MA in History of Design dissertation, research that is the foundation of where I am today; and *Black British Feminism* edited by Heidi Safia Mirza helped me develop my thinking on what it means to be a Black woman who challenges social, political and cultural obstacles, as did Chimamanda Ngozi Adichie's *We Should All Be Feminists*.[15] In 2003 I curated the exhibition *The March of the Women: Suffragettes and the State* at the National Archives, Kew, in London, which was my support for women's rights, regardless of class, ethnicity and 'race'. But it was the invitation to contribute an essay to the Tate exhibition catalogue *Lubaina Himid* in 2021 that framed another shift for me in this context of womanism and feminism. Lubaina shared with contributors the last line of Mary Oliver's poem *The Summer Day*: 'Tell me, what is it you plan to do with your one wild and precious life?' If ever there was an unflinching question as a call to action, to pause, really think, 'What do I want? How am I going to pursue this? There is no time to delay. Let nothing stop you'. For a Black woman in her sixth decade to be moved by such a strengthening statement is profound. It has led to me putting my head above the parapet a little more.

JL: You were photographed for *Phenomenal Women: Portraits of UK Black Female Professors*, an exhibition that appeared outdoors on the Southbank in 2020. How was that?

CT: Oh my God! I couldn't believe it when the email came through. I had my photograph taken at Chelsea College of Arts and there was a launch in the City of London. We hadn't gone fully into lockdown but it was beginning. People were not shaking hands. I remember there were a couple of people I met in the lift and we all got on really well. The room was so beautiful. And these were all professors! It kind of took your breath away. I was really nervous because I wore trainers as I thought it was a regular opening, and it was a little bit more formal. I'd worn a really nice coat-dress but I'd worn my trainers, so I got upstairs and I thought, I should have dressed up more, with some decent boots on or something. There was this lovely woman, Professor Marcia Wilson, who's at UEL, who said, 'Carol, you have earned the right to wear whatever you want to an opening!' (and she's not even working in dress). I said, 'You're right!' There was this other woman and we got on really well and we sat together.[16] I said 'What are you in?' Turns out she was an engineer and in space technology and had worked with NASA, and she said, 'What are you in?' and I said, 'I look at dress and style ...' [laughs] I kept thinking, 'I shouldn't be here'.

A lovely part of the event was that they interviewed three professors[17] about their experiences. One was in dentistry.[18] She talked about how she'd got children and didn't want to move, but if they weren't moving her on, she would change jobs. She said, 'You have to have breaks and time and space to reflect and to do your research because that's the reason why you entered academia in the first place. You've got to have that space'. She said, 'You can now get a lot of information out much more quickly ... how do you do that, and not just make it all about journal articles?' They talked about learning how to do that, how to still produce the journal articles alongside doing valuable things that would not be recognised as REF-able and such. Another said, 'Take breaks, and choose your battles, because they will impact on your wellbeing'. The third said that she was put on a committee and they'd shown her a budget sheet and she couldn't understand any of it, so she went and did a business degree to understand how it works. So she emphasised getting yourself prepared and knowing what you're talking about. She wasn't talking just about being Black but also about being a woman within academia and how you're treated within those spaces. So that was quite interesting. Before that I'd felt imposter syndrome, but after the interviews I felt much more at home. Then they unveiled the photographs. That was incredible! I still can't take in that it happened ... there were a lot of people whose work I'd read there, but not spoken to ... and I just kept meeting all these amazing women. There was an atmosphere – I can't tell you – that was just ... lovely! Everybody was chatting and swapping details. It was really nice. But it did come out of the blue.

JL: That reminds me of how you're always spectacularly good at crediting everyone else who's contributed to ideas and projects.

CT: [laughs] Honestly, I sometimes read people's things and I go, 'I know exactly where they've got that from and they haven't credited that person'. It makes me so annoyed. You know, we haven't got here just on our own! It's a conversation. I try to remember those things. The textiles course at Chelsea have a new newsletter and they asked members of staff to talk about a book that meant something to them. I chose James Baldwin's novel *Giovanni's Room*. At Ravensbourne, when I was asking for books to do with Black history during writing my BA dissertation, a librarian gave me this book to read and told me to come back to him when I'd read it. I adored it! I wrote for the Chelsea newsletter that what I took away from it is that's it's about difference and its complexities, but also talks about those complexities in an accessible way. It taught me that I can write in an accessible way and get those issues across without using academic terms all the time. That changed my life. It wasn't until years later I found out from Lee Wright,[19] my contextual studies lecturer at Ravensbourne, that the librarian, John McVeigh, who was gay, used to test students out by giving them books, and you passed the test by reading the books. Then you were in his good books. So I passed the test, came back in two days, and he got me all the books I wanted and then recorded things for me and all sorts. I believe he became Head Librarian at Glasgow School of Art. I've never forgotten John and that book. I just think ... we're not alone.

NOTES

1 This interview was first published as '"We haven't got here just on our own. It's a conversation": An Interview with Carol Tulloch', *European Journal of Cultural Studies*, 25: 5, 2022.

2 An educational qualification in the UK.

3 RCA/V&A: Royal College of Art; Victoria and Albert Museum, London.

4 Carol Tulloch, 'Resounding Power of the Afro Comb' in S. Cheang and G. Biddle-Perry (eds), *Hair: Styling, Culture and Fashion,* Berg: Oxford, New York, 2009, pp123-139.

5 Carol Tulloch, 'The Glamourous "Diasporic Intimacy" of Habitus: Taste, Migration and the Practice of Settlement' in M. Quinn, D. Beech, M. Lehnert, C. Tulloch, S. Wilson (eds). *The Persistence of Taste: Art, Museums and Everyday Life After Bourdieu*, Routledge: London, New York, 2018, pp257-274.

6 Jane Batram.

7 At Crompton Parkinson, Doncaster.

8 Carol Tulloch, 'There's No Place Like Home: Home Dressmaking and Creativity in the Jamaican Community in the 1940s to 1960s' in B. Burman (ed), *The Culture of Sewing: Gender, Consumption and Home Dressmaking*, Berg: Oxford, New York, 1999.

9 Emeritus Professor Caroline Evans, fashion history and theory specialist.

10 Carol Tulloch, 'Picture This: The Black Curator' in Jo Littler and Roshi Naidoo (eds), *The Politics of Heritage: The Legacies of 'Race'*, Routledge, 2004.

11 The Archives and Museum of Black Heritage, AMBH, a short-term project that was the result of a partnership between Middlesex University and the Black Cultural Archive. It was funded by the Heritage Lottery Fund.

12 Madeleine Ginsburg was a pioneering curator of dress, notably at the V&A Museum.

13 Alison Moloney, freelance curator and writer, based in London.

14 *Lip Sync Battle UK* is a television programme.

15 I met Heidi Safia Mirza for the first time at the *Phenomenal Women: Portraits of UK Black Female Professors* exhibition. Embarrassingly, I reacted as if I had met a rock star.

16 Professor Dorothy Monekosso.

17 Professor Funmi Olonisakin, Professor Cynthia Pine and Professor Tracey Reynolds.

18 Professor Cynthia Pine.

19 Dr Lee Wright was Carol's contextual studies tutor at Ravensbourne College of Design and Communication.

Beyond anti-welfarism and social media mud-slinging

Angela McRobbie is Professor Emeritus at Goldsmiths University of London. A formative figure in feminist cultural studies and theory, her books include *Feminism and Youth Culture* (1991); *The Uses of Cultural Studies* (2005); *The Aftermath of Feminism: Gender, Culture, and Social Change* (Sage, 2009); *Be Creative: Making a Living in the New Culture Industries* (Polity, 2016); *Feminism and the Politics of Resilience* (Polity, 2020); and most recently, *Fashion as Creative Economy* (Palgrave, 2022), co-authored with Dan Strutt and Carolina Bandinelli. In this interview she talks about her work in relation to social politics, the contemporary conjuncture, cultural studies, decolonisation and feminism. This interview took place in spring 2021.[1]

Jo Littler: You're recovering from 'Long Covid'. Early on in your recovery you wrote a powerful piece about your experience, arguing that in the pandemic there has surfaced 'a sense that civil society has re-discovered itself during this great absence of leadership and its indifference to suffering'.[2] What are your thoughts on pandemic culture now?

Angela McRobbie: I wrote that first blog article for Verso during the very first days of the pandemic in the UK. PPE was as basic as one could imagine: a plastic apron and a disposable mask, of the type we are all now wearing, and sometimes less than that. I was immediately fearful that I would pass on the virus to the staff treating me. About 95 per cent of the staff across all levels were Black British or British Asian, i.e. from ethnic minorities. The women cleaning the ward through the night, those coming in with food trays during the day, and those coming in to check my heart, and oxygen, and blood pressure were most probably all on low rates of pay.

They were doing absolutely vital jobs. But it struck me with piercing clarity that these low-paid jobs tending to very ill people – whether by serving them food or giving them a wash-down – rarely received the respect and recognition they deserved. And this long-hours work was amongst the most overlooked and poorly recompensed occupations, often carried out by ethnic minority women of all ages, many of whom would go home to their families to take over duties as mother and as home-schoolers in their off-duty hours. So my key thought at that time was: surely we must have a massive re-consideration of this kind of work. This, in fact, is also where I ended up in the book I had just completed, *Feminism and the Politics of Resilience*. The logic of the post-Fordist path which Britain had pursued, and which gathered pace from the mid 1990s, was to grow the service sector at the same time as it was simultaneously being casualised, outsourced and made superficially flexible to meet the 'needs' of women with maternal responsibilities. Britain has, in Europe, the largest percentage of working mothers active in the labour market. In many respects this can be seen as an achievement for the degree of economic independence this brings. But what it means in reality is that there are armies of women up and down the country – especially mothers in their forties and over – whose only option is the work available in this new, de-regulated service sector. This includes, for example, picking and packaging in fulfilment centres for companies like Sports Direct; or working in the care sector; and there is also retail, which for older women tends to mean checkout work at supermarkets. And so for mothers of several children living in poor conditions, with long journeys to work and with few in-house opportunities for upskilling (because of sub-contracting), there is what I referred to as a 'triple female incarceration effect'. First, there is the media-shaming effect, where the working-class mother without qualifications is seen as a failure, and this becomes a label which is difficult to dislodge;

then there is the fact that in the jobs that *are* available, there are few opportunities for promotion, day release or career development; and finally wider opportunities are also reduced, further education and other equivalent training are fee-based, and adult education has been starved of funds for decades.

Employers need to be compelled to offer in-house upskilling schemes, day-release schemes, and more and better vocational training. I would like to see the women working as cleaners to be able to have paid hours off to study. Everything has been worsened by the end of the 'social wage': i.e. provisions in-kind which lessen the cost for reproduction on individuals – usually women – such as after-school care, well-organised youth clubs, Saturday schools, leisure centres, libraries and community centres. And of course, with sub-contracting and agency work, the contractor has no obligations whatsoever ...

In the early days of the pandemic little was known of 'Long Covid'. At one point I realised my neck muscles were so weak I had to lift my head off the cushion if I was reclining on a chair. I had to seek out respiratory physiotherapy, which I'm still doing once a week for thirty minutes by Zoom with a one-to-one physiotherapist. There is nothing like this available on the NHS[3] and so I have been paying. It has been the single most significant thing that has helped me over this long period; but only the fortunate can afford such a vital medical resource. The NHS provides pamphlets and the British Lung Foundation does fantastic work, but as a Long Covid patient, what I most needed was a teacher at the other end of the Zoom camera taking me through different exercises every week. It's a similar story with restorative yoga, for which I found some free and some paid classes. These are care professions requiring vast amounts of training and knowledge, and an advanced economy needs to invest in these sorts of services, for Long Covid patients and beyond.

JL: Your most recent book, *Feminism and the Politics of Resilience*, theorises changing welfare cultures and shows how anti-welfarism has reduced the scope for feminist solidarity. It highlights the different subject positions women have been incited to adopt in relation to welfare: including the scapegoating of dependency, mothers being encouraged to multitask and young women instructed to 'be resilient'. The book argues against nostalgia for welfare states past and for a 'productive, reproductive and reparative' approach. Can you outline what such an approach might entail?

AMcR: In *Feminism and the Politics of Resilience* I establish a connection between the range of disciplinary techniques which have been developed, within the frames of contemporary neoliberal rationalities, in order to 'shore up' and mobilise normative femininities. This happens when gender becomes the site of more fluid and less certain positionalities. I also wanted to show how those enticements in popular culture to 'celebrate' neoliberal leadership-feminism (female success in the boardroom) are part and parcel of a wide repertoire of dividing practices. The constant invoking of female success has inscribed within it a negative interpellation effect: just as it endorses women's empowerment, so too does it punish failure. And when this kind of figuration process looks 'downwards' towards working-class women, it articulates directly with an anti-welfare ethos. The disadvantaged woman is depicted across the right-wing tabloid press and in various TV genres in abject terms. She is someone who is reliant on the state; who has made 'the wrong choices' in life; has had too many children. This is all kaleidoscoped into the frame of an unkempt and 'poor' appearance. There is so much cruelty and symbolic violence in the poverty-shaming genre of popular reality TV, and such vernacular forms are a key channel through which the undoing of the ideals of a welfare society have been conducted.

The function of the dividing activities within the feminine genres is to refute the likelihood of class solidarity. The female subject is repeatedly addressed as if to consider herself a kind of project-in-making. If the right-wing popular press such as the *Daily Mail* or *The Sun* typically foregrounds the white, welfare-dependent woman as exemplifying a whole field of social ills, there is a subtext which extends this slur so that 'she' is also implicitly Black.

Drawing on Robbie Shilliam's, and of course Gail Lewis's work, I remind readers that the post-war flowering of British welfare which permitted the so-called 'age of affluence' to emerge by means of the family or social wage was mythical when viewed from the perspective of race. The recently-arrived Windrush Black migrant population and those who came from India and Pakistan were pushed into jobs unprotected by workplace entitlements, and this exclusion from the social contract extended to housing, to education, and to the criminal justice system, as has been well documented by so many Black scholars. Therefore, when I propose a return to a welfare society that is productive, reproductive and reparative, I am envisaging a new social imaginary which delivered universal entitlements in and out of work and for future generations. Across political culture, left and right, there has been a consensus that cuts to welfare are more or less irreversible – that the word 'generous' is only used to criticise a system of 'handouts'! So my main point was to reverse, to repair, and to offer reparation to those sectors of the population that have been excluded from what were deemed 'universal' provisions. I would like to see a debate take place as to how this could be realised. The idea of reparative funds to for example Windrush populations need not be a utopian fantasy.

JL: You've spent a lot of time in Germany. What do you think are some of the key differences between the UK and Germany in terms of these cultures of feminisms and welfare?

AMcR: Most of the time that I've been working in Germany in the last three years has been dedicated to an AHRC three-city study of fashion micro-enterprises in London, Berlin and Milan. I've assembled a great team in Berlin of designers, fashion academics and policy-makers. This also connects with the welfare question because the argument that has emerged is that it is the existence of a social wage which permits small creative enterprises to function, where there is support and subsidy for rent of studio space and equipment, and a huge number of courses for upskilling and for further training. Germany is the land of free at-the-point-of-delivery vocational education. The social democratic heritage, even as it is being transformed, remains pretty intact. And since fashion is a female-led field, these provisions benefit the context of women's employment.

But inside academia I observe timidity on so many issues, and cadres of women scholars who feel they have no option but to toe the line. There is also little risk-taking with the wilder edges of academic topics: when it comes to the hiring process it's so often the safe white male scholar who gets the job. The German academy may, now and again, look to the likes of Paul Gilroy or Stuart Hall or Saidiya Hartman; and there is a new generation of Black German feminist scholars and writers, who are producing fantastic work and who are very active on Twitter, and who do seem poised to have the confrontations that are so overdue. But Black, Turkish German and ethnic minority scholars seem quite isolated; and often they have already completed their doctoral studies in the UK (at Goldsmiths, for example) or in the US. I am thinking of my own former PhD student Onur Kömürcü, and Jana Cattien who completed her work on race in the German context at SOAS, and in Germany itself there is the writing of Denise Bergold-Caldwell in Marburg and Teresa Koloma Beck at Hamburg.

JL: Your work is profoundly connected to queer theory. You've also talked (in an interview from a few years back in Cultural Studies) about your involvement in radical feminist groups at the Centre for Contemporary Cultural Studies (CCCS) and what they generated (training for non-traditional work, e.g. car maintenance, women-only discos) and curtailed ('Endless rules were also drafted about who could write about what topic' ... 'denunciations of those who liaised with men, or indeed who had given birth to boys').[4] What are the different legacies of queer and radical feminism for and in your work?

AMcR: It's all the more difficult to answer because it traverses so many decades of my career and my personal involvement in feminist politics. And it's funny because although I look back at the times in the late 1970s and through the 1980s of angry arguments between different feminist groups, as I grow older I really want to walk away from this angry way of doing politics – which of course is intensified with social media, especially via Twitter. I feel the kind of mud-slinging we are exposed to obfuscates the issues, and does not allow us the time and space to rehearse what is really going on. It often feels that there is a too rapid sense of closure around issues that would benefit from a slower, more reflective mode of debate. And while I personally am willing to speak out on this or that platform, my skills and my expertise are in the classroom or sitting round a seminar table. At the same time, in each of these locations, the public platform and the university classroom, when there are issues at stake that pertain to, for example, Black women feeling they are not being addressed in the curriculum, or not being listened to, I'm absolutely sure that it is imperative that 'white women listen', as Hazel Carby put it back in Birmingham in the early 1980s.

I think (as was the case for so many of us) reading Judith Butler's early work had such a profound impact on me. I loved the way it took hold of all those elements of feminist theory where they had, as I recall, reached a bit of an impasse. This was back in the late 1980s. Marxist-feminist theory had gone so far with domestic labour and psychoanalytical feminism had got stuck with its more or less wholesale endorsing of Lacan, which inexorably led to a sexually conservative position on family life and the need for a 'real mother' and a 'real father'. It's easy to forget how embedded these principles were within the influential field of Lacanian feminism, especially in France.

So Butler's two books came at me like a burst of thunder, and with such a force of sheer intellectual energy. They managed to achieve so many breakthroughs, paving the way to developing better understandings of normative femininity and masculinity and persisting with such intensive readings of Freud and Lacan until they were able to answer some of the most pressing questions about lesbian desire, heterosexual melancholy, the Oedipus complex and the reproduction of normative heterosexual family life, boldly contesting Lacan with the idea of the phallic lesbian.

These works impacted on me in my academic work as a sociologist since I could see that they could be used to understand the repetitive crafting through which girls come to recognise themselves as such, and the violence this entails. There was always a psychosocial element which allowed for a translation from psychoanalysis to feminist political philosophy to sociology. There was something so profound about how Butler understood queerness, not as identity, but as fluidity and irregularity; as a repeated subversion of norms which had an accumulative force, an achievement of power through so many re-significations. There is both an openness in this kind of articulation and the capacity for so many alliances, or the contingency of the chain of equivalence, as Laclau and Mouffe would put it. It is all the more ironic, then, that the seemingly deliberate mis-readings (or non-reading, in the proper sense) of Butler by particular journalists have led to such hyperbolic antagonisms.

JL: What would you like to see work that identifies as 'cultural studies' doing – are there directions that you think it should be taking that it isn't? I was struck by how at a recent event, for example, you mentioned that work would benefit from connecting more to social policy. (This also reminds me that I often wonder whether a better term for cultural studies might be 'cultural politics'.)

AMcR: Yes, you are right, I have been gesturing towards forging better links between cultural studies and the fields of social policy and criminology. This arises out of the sheer power now attributed to all things media and screen-related and to the dominating effect that popular culture has on our everyday lives. For example, if the media demonises, belittles or scapegoats single mothers reliant on some forms of welfare or the benefit system, and if these women come to be typecast according to certain codes of what is deemed to be 'failed femininity', then we need also be more informed about how these stereotypes function at ground level. For this we need to turn to feminist criminology and social policy to look at how, for example, women on benefits perceive themselves, how they internalise these media stereotypes, and find ways of refusing them or negotiating around them.

Of course, there is research that has joined these two universes, such as Bev Skeggs' wonderful work, but I think it's important to create more active dialogues with social policy for the reason that the welfare society (and its demise) is at its core. Likewise, how is it possible to work in social policy without seeing the need for media and cultural theory? Chapter 3 of *Feminism and the Politics of Resilience*, on women and welfare, was prompted by Stuart

Hall's discussion of George Osborne (the former Chancellor of the Exchequer in the UK) describing people 'sleeping off a life on benefits'. So many of those political phrases were actually composed by speechwriters drafted in from tabloid newspapers like *The Sun*.

When I made the comment about working more closely with colleagues in criminology and social policy at our recent PhD event this was also prompted by how so many of the papers presented by students traversed these two domains.[5] For example, when looking at the entrepreneurial activity of young women on Instagram (the 'Dubai influencers') and the issue of whether or not this constitutes sex work or simply lifestyle modelling, I was suggesting a shift out of the technological emphasis on digital labour in terms of algorithms and 'likes' towards the socio-legal terrain. I also thought this was a way younger feminist media and cultural scholars could themselves bring some fresh energy to challenge the mainstream of these fields. I was glad to see that this kind of cross-fertilisation was already taking place. The whole debate about sex work and indeed issues about the new sites used for porn such as OnlyFans requires close feminist academic scrutiny – especially with *Daily Mail* celebrities moving in and out of working for OnlyFans during the pandemic.

JL: We're obviously a very different moment from that of CCCS, but do you think there are any key lessons you think we can take from it for the present?

AMcR: I think most of us who were at the CCCS or who were working alongside Stuart Hall have taken their own narratives from those experiences and it has shaped how we function inside the university system. The idea of doing conjunctural research which interweaves between different levels of the society – the political, the economic and the cultural – is so ingrained as to hardly need to be stated. However, that's still a methodology which is anathema to mainstream sociology, and it has always been the marker of difference between the two fields. For many years sociologists took absolute umbrage against Stuart and those of us associated with this kind of work: we were deemed absolutely unsociological. Actually, I am most comfortable with the versions of CCCS and of cultural studies which emphasise the dialogic value of pedagogy, of being inside the teaching machine. Stuart himself was 'lit up' by the connection he always forged between research and teaching. In effect in the early days he would be writing articles like 'The Determination of the News Photograph', while also teaching many of the foundational texts on which it was based.

Of course, we can and should contest the excessive demands made on us as teachers by the neoliberal university, but the chance we have to work on and teach topics that are so much of the present and which also require that we bring to bear on those topics the tools which cultural studies has bequeathed us (structure of feeling, the theory of ideology, the politics of meaning, interpellation, performativity, the society of control, etc) is endlessly rewarding. And it is funny how there is often a circularity. Althusser's idea of interpellation is half a century old but it can suddenly bounce back right into the feminist classroom when a young Black woman student rightly poses to me questions about that hailing process. For all the ideological harm interpellation laboured to impose by means of its subjectivising process, and the naturalisation of modes of quiescent femininity it sought to secure (such as via the front page of the girls or women's magazine), at the same time it issued a violent *exclusion* from that same harmful terrain, by means of consolidating dominant whiteness and furthering processes of longstanding Black invisibilisation. There remains so much to be done here by questioning these subject positions and their psycho-spatial logics – that 'turning around' movement, as Butler describes in *The Psychic Life of Power*. This leads us of course to Fanon, and also to Sara Ahmed and Saidiya Hartman as we seek to re-write the curriculum. So many thanks to those fantastic first year BA Black female students at Goldsmiths.

NOTES

1 This interview was first published as Angela McRobbie and Jo Littler, '"Beyond anti-welfarism and feminist social media mud-slinging": An interview with Angela McRobbie' in *European Journal of Cultural Studies*, 25:1, 2021.

2 Angela McRobbie, 'Notes on Covid: Then and Now', www.verso-

books.com/blogs/4843-notes-on-covid-then-and-now, 28 August 2020.

3 The NHS is the National Health Service, the UK's publicly funded healthcare system.

4 Angela McRobbie, 'Angela McRobbie interviews herself', *Cultural Studies,* 27:5, 2013, p830.

5 Angela McRobbie, 'Reflections on *New Directions in Feminist Thought*', www.blogs.city.ac.uk/gsrc/features, 2020.

It's not about academic life.
That's what I have to tell you

Gargi Bhattacharyya is Professor of Sociology at the University of East London, UK. Gargi has written, co-authored and edited/co-edited a very wide range of books, including *Tales of Dark-Skinned Women* (Routledge, 1998); *Sexuality and Society* (Routledge, 2005); *Crisis, Austerity and Everyday Life* (Palgrave, 2015); *Race and Power: Global Racism in the twenty-first century* (Routledge, 2016); *Rethinking Racial Capitalism* (Rowman and Littlefield, 2018); and *Empire's Endgame* (Pluto, 2021). In this interview, conducted in summer 2021, Gargi talks about state patriarchy, racial capitalism, dispossession, culture wars, feminism, the England football team, environmental degradation, the state of universities and sex on smartphones.[1]

Jo Littler: In your book *Crisis, Austerity and Everyday Life* (2015) you write: 'In common I expect with many, I write about the things that bother me. It is either this or shouting on the bus, and we all know what a dangerous pastime that can be'. I liked this, and to me it sounded like a definition of the animating principle of cultural studies. So: what's bothering you now?

Gargi Bhattacharyya: I think of myself as quite a cheery person operating in a world that seems to be knocking my cheeriness every minute. I think we're living through a time of fearfulness even beyond the fearfulness that my imagination could have dreamed of: where a period in which the global economy has further cast more people into the spaces of living death, or early death, and dispossession and surplus, has been overlaid by a pandemic that has remade a war-economy-opportunity for parasites and leeches and bloodsuckers across the world. It's made those who are already barely surviving, not surviving at all, or surviving in even more constrained circumstances, experience new kinds of disparity and boundary, and different models of global apartheid. And at the same time the planet is still on fire. So although I'm inclined to chirpiness by character, it feels truly like our collective resources – our intellectual resources – are not anywhere close to what we need. That's not a good start is it? But that is what I think.

JL: In *Empire's Endgame* you say, 'let's consider the state as a patriarch and imagine what kind of man he is', and you describe him as 'neglectful, inefficient and abusive, says he's good in a fight'. What does the alternative to the state patriarch look like?

GB: The state patriarch was almost like a cartoon figure in our discussions in *Empire's Endgame*. We were writing the book between the EU referendum and the 2019 general election. It was a time when things were kicking off, but it was difficult to exactly define the project of the right. So we came up with these cartoon characters of who, and what, was animating the political landscape in a time when there was such an active withdrawal from formal politics by those wielding power. The Johnson model involves wielding power yet backing away from doing anything that looks like wielding authority at every turn, and using indirect means of cycling resources into your friends' bank accounts. How do we understand that? One of the things we said was that there's still a process – even in this neglectful, crumbling moment of British statehood, which echoes earlier patriarchal states – in that it still references ideas of sexual propriety, and still acts like it's the big dad in the family. And yet, in this family – that is *breaking up* – no-one is getting what they need. Not a single person is getting what they need.

Are we saying we need a better kind of state patriarch? No. I'm not really interested in saying, 'Oh look, there's a better and nicer dad'. We talked a lot about masculinity whilst writing *Empire's Endgame*, and I was probably the one who was least persuaded that it's centrally a gendered incarnation. I kept saying, 'Look, we're using state patriarchy because there is a long history of looking at social policy as a replacement patriarch; and it's hard to understand British welfare if you don't understand it as an imagined heteronormative family.' If you don't get that history, it's hard to understand what the dismantling of British welfare has been, because that's the narrative it was set up in. But I'm much more uncertain about how central masculinity is to this formation. I think, rather, that it is part of the theatre of its power.

JL: At the end of *Empire's Endgame* you talk about abolitionist energies, and love and caring as an alternative. That also made me think about how the England football team, in some ways, represents a better model of masculinity, one closer to what you are discussing there …

GB: The England football team, I barely think of them as men at all – they're so boyish! You're right that partly why people are so in love with them is because they represent a speaking of young male identity in ways that have been seemingly absent from public life in Britain for years – if not decades. Everyone having a huge maternal rush toward Saka on his unicorn in the pool! (I can't tell how much of that is boyishness and how much is youthfulness … I think they all cut across each other.) They offer a way of talking about how to be in the world – to articulate self and the world as always interdependent. That I think has been lovely about them. They're young people in public life who are insistently forwarding their interdependence on others – people who've cared for them, the places they've come from – that's central to their ways of being. It's very hard to present that as a battle between masculinities. That's why the Tory party is failing in comparison with them, because they've been used to saying, 'We're *this* kind of rich bloke, and you're *that* kind of not-so-rich bloke'. Well, that's not even the game here! They're just talking past that. And what people are responding to is a different kind of connectedness of self. They do talk about aspiration, but somehow it's differently articulated to a much more heightened sense of our shared vulnerability.

JL: Yes. I've been thinking a lot about how Marcus Rashford talks about his upbringing, and his geographical and social connections and context, and how in many ways this is the opposite of philanthrocapitalism, of the Bill Gates model. It's reflected in the cooperation they show on the pitch.

GB: And the showing of friendly love. I know that's part of homosocial and masculine display, but they've also widened what's allowed to be expressed. I don't know a thing about football but I know lots of things about all these young men's families and their circumstances, what it took for them to train. There has been extensive coverage of Raheem Sterling's seventeen-year-old sister taking him to training every single day on several buses even though she didn't get home until 11:00 p.m.[2] There's something to be noted about that as a mode of performative political speech in Britain right now, in the aftermath of the monstering he's had over buying houses for his mother. The way this group of young people have talked about what was required, from their poor background, for them to be able to do this, and their *mapping* of it, is something to be noted, I think. It's worth a few minutes of our attention.

JL: Yes, they are social stories which so often aren't presented, which don't appear in the *Daily Mail*, where the energies are mainly focused on either disproving those narratives of difficulty, or glossing over them very quickly to emphasise social mobility without dwelling on suffering. I read that Raheem Sterling interview too, and I wanted to know what happened to his sister, who took him training every day, as well.

GB: Yes, exactly.

JL: *Empire's Endgame* argues that the culture wars are all connected by 'the logic of a zero-sum game': whether incels blaming women for their suffering and killing them; men's rights networks blaming feminism rather than seeking equality; the eugenicist language of demographic racism pitting 'whiteness' against ethnic diversity; or the moral panic over trans [people] which claims 'there are only enough resources (emotional and moral as well as material) either for trans women or for cis women, but not both – it's them or us'. To what extent can these cultural wars be understood in terms of scrabbling for resources in the wake of neoliberal austerity?

GB: The argument we're making is not that the zero-sum is *about* the scrabbling for resources, but the point of the culture war is to transform every political issue, or not even yet political issue, into a *version* of scrabbling for resources. So, there's no actual scrabbling for resources between cis women and trans women; rather, it's concocted as a scrabbling for resources. I know that people think there are, but in the end, do you know what, if a trans woman uses a toilet cubicle, there aren't less toilet cubicles for me to use after that. The way it's framed as a 'debate' between different groups is as if we are all fighting all the time – because times have been very hard, in real ways, in material ways and in symbolic ways; and it's as if the only way we can mark our space, whether it's in the discourse or in the lived world, is through this sense that there's only so much to go round, and everything that you do that's not-quite-me is *against* me. Now that structure, that way of thinking of things, is actively concocted through the kinds of online cultures that we're living through. If you read the playbook of the online right, that's absolutely what they say: 'make everything an either/or polarity, doesn't matter what the polarity is on first, because once you have people in the polarity then they're in your way of thinking and being and feeling'.

So, once people start to think that Easter eggs are being banned, or that our fruit is being straightened, or some other absolutely fantastical thing, as long as you can make them fall into an absolute zero-sum either/or polarised vision of how the world is understood, then they become more amenable to the content that the white racist is being wiped out, that climate change is a fiction, that 'we have to kill them before they kill us'. That division is already built into the playbook of the global right's mobilisation via online cultures. It's not a surprise that this is translated into different articulations. What's more interesting, I think, is what the trigger points have been. Many people are saying, 'There's something really odd about the ways in which British feminism is so consumed by issues of transness'. There are many other kinds of really horrible, class-privileged feminist movements around the world, not just here, but what is it about

Britain – why did that issue get set off so effectively? It feels like it's calmed down a little bit now, but I might just be muting more of that space. I'm still finding that I'm surprised that, if I meet people who are aligned to feminism who are my age or older, even if they're not outright transphobes, the chances are that they'll say, 'Oh, but it's eroding the gains of feminism'. How did that happen? You speak to people from other parts of the world and they don't talk like that. I think that is part of how the culture wars work: by setting off a lot of hares and seeing which ones will run and where. That wasn't the only issue set off, but for particular, odd, local reasons, issues around trans identity seem to work in Britain. Perhaps for the US, 'critical race theory' is working better. I don't see the narrative about critical race theory getting the same purchase in this country.

JL: You write a lot about diminished political expectations, about all the huge institutional and media work which goes into lowering our expectations of public life, of mutuality. Can you outline some examples? The war over trans politics is probably one example of this.

GB: I think if I was going to tell the story of British post-war life and politics, I'd say that the post-war period sets up the welfare state as an aspirational set of contracts. That has some downsides: it says you can have these aspirations if you're *this* kind of creature, if you do *these* things, if you live your life in these tidy ways. This starts to shift with Thatcher, who says, even more explicitly, 'Some people can be aspirational, but we can't have aspiration for *everyone*'. Aspiration will be conditional on certain kinds of ways of being. Then, from Thatcher onwards – and escalating when we come to 2008 and the formal new institutionalisation of the new austerity – part of how any kind of public consensus around welfare or any social support operates is by increasingly making all of us guilty until proven innocent. Nearly all state functions become modelled as punitive, instead of via the cuddly daddy who will tell you off, who will give you all a sweetie if you'll all just come and line up. Instead, we've got the state patriarch saying, 'Well, I'm not sure any of you are my kids anyway. Can you *prove* it?' And so then we're all endlessly having to prove how we are deserving of the smallest indulgence, even the indulgence of being allowed to live our lives. That really shifts expectations. Because instead of thinking, 'I have an entitlement', it's always, 'How can I avoid punishment?' even if the punishment is only taking away some of the small supports.

And because that logic increasingly cuts across different levels – policy, interactions with state machineries from schooling to health to housing – everyone gets trained to look over their shoulder and to not ask for help because sometimes the threat of punishment is greater than the small social good that might be gained. That's a quite clever and precise technique. It was already built into the British benefit system but has been finessed in recent years. Alongside all of that we have a state which now appears in most of our lives only as either a chaotic Etonian grouping or as a violent and neglectful person. The machinery enacting our rights is becoming increasingly punitive.

So, actual state machineries have changed, not just the media story about it. Through that change in how policy is enacted, the state increasingly shows itself as inadequate and randomly violent, which means even our hope that there might be a different politics gets curtailed. I think that's had a huge impact on the centre and the centre-left of politics, which is all based around saying, 'If you just give us the machinery of the state, we will do it better'. The contract of trust in the state has been actively broken by the day-to-day practice of what it is and how it behaves in your life. The outcome is systematically diminished expectations.

JL: This reminds me of how you discussed the military in *Empire's Endgame*, when you note that, because the military is perceived as being outside the political, it becomes regarded as 'safe' (just like Trump's 'anti-politics').

GB: The authors of *Empire's Endgame* are all minoritised (some third generation), so we all see how 'back home' the military is often understood as the last trustworthy political actor. That's a Global South game: all of the places where the North was earlier have had that for decades. What's new is how explicitly that is now being played out in places like Britain and the US. The US always had a slightly different mythology around the military, but for

Britain I think that's quite new. It's certainly no more than a decade or two old. The military as a political actor was already happening around Brexit ('Who will save us? Who will do distribution? The military will!') and similarly with Covid, when the argument has been, 'Oh, the state just can't do anything', we hear, 'Don't worry, the squaddies will save us!'

JL: Yes that argument of the military as safe and saviour has become increasingly pronounced. That's depressingly right. Shifting back to gender for a moment – what feminist work would you say has been particularly useful or important for you?

GB: I was thinking about this with such a heavy heart yesterday. I have almost no interest in reflecting on academic feminism. I think academic feminism has wrecked feminism for me. I don't normally even call myself a feminist now, and I was wondering why that was, as it's so clearly part of my political formation. I just think of it as shit institutional management. I don't organise around the idea of being a feminist. I know the younger ones move between institutional spaces a bit differently, and that's all a bit different. But when I think of UK feminism in my age range and older, it feels like the spaces of material organising either collapsed, or were not only co-opted, but actively rushed into being institutionally incorporated in quite dodgy ways. A lot of the life of feminist discourse has been through academic structures which are violent and ugly and are not making anyone freer – male, female or other. I don't think feminist work has caught on from my work now, although that seems ridiculous when you *read* my work.

JL: Yes, your first books (e.g. *Tales of Dark-Skinned Women*, *Sex and Society*, *Race and Power* and *Dangerous Brown Men*) were on sexuality, its intersections with 'race', and its place in society amid late capitalism. Can you say why you worked in that area at that time and what you saw that work as doing?

GB: The first book I ever wrote, *Tales of Dark-Skinned Women*, was actually a really happy experience for me ... because I was thinking, 'I *can* write this book!' They did try and stop me. I was meant to have study leave, and my workplace said, 'How will you be able to write a book within this time? And what if you don't write the book? And what will you be "known for", because you do so many different things?' And I thought … I have this time, these few months … and I just wrote this book because it was all in my head already. Lots of people seemed to think it was my PhD, but of course it wasn't! There's no way you could get a PhD writing that.

JL: What was your PhD about?

GB: It was on aesthetic literary education in British-ruled India, and the birth of working-class education in Britain, and the ways in which literary education was used in these spaces to explore how an idea of aesthetic education might form a particular kind of disciplinary subject.

JL: Really interesting. Did you also write about how English literature was used as a mechanism for keeping colonial wives busy and spreading imperialism?

GB: It was more about what is being taught when you teach literature to people who aren't meant to be people. So how physical discipline at school was augmented by the emotional trainings of literary education and together these were ways of making different imagined docile, classed and colonised subjects. And what challenges that raises for trying to use cultural education as a liberatory vehicle, given that most anti-racist education in Britain was based around the cultural, really. With my first book I did feel like I got away with something. Lots of people told me that. You could only write that kind of book as your first book, then after that people know that you might not play by the rules and don't let you do it again. I do think there was some telling off involved. You say you're going to write a standard textbook and then this new thing emerges … but because I was young and full of beans, they didn't mind.

Tales of Dark-Skinned Women was an attempt to do *1001 Nights* meets *Das Kapital*; to show how you could think about race and gender and sexuality and narration and eroticism alongside a story about global capital, and show how those stories are always in and out of each other. It's told as a series of stories about racialised types. It suggests we might think of global capital through certain moments of race and gender, and in terms of knowledge and communication but also entertainment, titillation, sexualisation. Where is it that the racialised and gendered body can emerge? When can it speak, when can it be visible? Then the book's got a whole other subtext about meat, mad cow disease and bodily integrity.

So this first book was an attempt to say: the big analytic stories belong to us, to Black and brown girls as well. That our '1001 stories' are not only of the bedroom and the kitchen and the street, they're also about the global economy. That the story form is not only important, but possibly the central form of linking together different modes of knowledge, of telling them together as one interlinked issue. I'm interested in that. Without saying 'here is my overarching argument and it reaches this conclusion *here*', it tries to show people, emotively, the meaning of the sexualised body. *This* is what it is to be a colonial whore. This is what it's like to be the disembodied voice through which information can pass only if the body is erased. This is what it's like to be the most dispossessed labourer. This is the history in which we have cut away the segments of labour underneath. I was probably a bit too young to write it really, but I'm still pleased I gave it a go.

JL: And your other early books – *Sex and Society* and *Dangerous Brown Men*?

GB: The first three books were *Tales of Dark-Skinned Women*, then *Sex and Society* and then *Race and Power*, which I wrote with some other people. You need to remember that at this moment there were a lot of people saying, 'Oh, everything's about globalisation!' And, yes, the answer to every human question *is* globalisation, but we also need an understanding of the nature of the shifts in our global interconnections, in every element of our lives. *Sex and Society* and *Race and Power* are both attempts to say, well, something epoch-changing *is* happening, but we're not narrating it very well in terms of particular, lived structures. *Sex and Society* tries to be a book about how you might think about global economic restructuring, and sex, in a way that people might want to read. It's an attempt to rethink the challenges of living and understanding an uncertain sexual landscape, and how the economic juggernaut remakes that terrain. I think we still often imagine sex as if it's a private, personal, matter of identity. But maybe that's not the most helpful way. Instead, we can think of sex as an array of collective arrangements and experiences that are always made against and in relation to these other structures. There's something freeing about that: it stops sex being precious, in the wrong way. (It *is*, of course, precious in that it's *valuable*, but I mean precious in the sense of, 'Oh, let's not have *too* much fun!') Different things become possible because the world changes, and the world changing also makes us understand why some things become more painful, and the challenges we face together. I haven't thought about that book for a long time.

JL: I was looking at it yesterday and noting your argument about the separation of intimacy and the rest of social life, and the idea that you want to reconnect them without being too clinical, in a mainstream-sociological fashion.

GB: Yes, exactly. ('And tell me, how many times did you do this today? I've just got my clipboard here'.) Though I *am* interested in sexology. A lot of sexology assumes – a bit like seeing colour – that when you say something about a certain sexual act, the other person understands what you mean, and how it feels, in the same way. But I'm not convinced that sexual scripts or even acts are easily translatable. There's an aura we give to sexual experience in the cultures we live in so that sexuality is a space where certain things are allowed. Some things in public life get siphoned into the space of the intimate. That means there's many more layers of symbolic narration that everyone is using all the time, and you just don't really know them all with your own partner, let alone with someone you've only been using a clipboard with! So I think that's all interesting stuff – and, again, deserving of some of our attention.

It's also a public health issue, isn't it? I grew up through the beginnings of AIDS. The political discourse around being able to tell sexual stories meant something different in that moment: what needs to be said, and how, became an issue. Even after the Thatcher moment, with its message of 'you're all going to die!', it still had a ripple effect on how people want to imagine a better world, and think sexual knowledge might fit in it. That sense seemed to go away for a while in between. I wonder if the war on terror, etc made it more constrained … and now it seems to have come back a little bit with the younger ones. Don't know if you think that?

JL: Well, there has also been the increasingly intense online mediation of certain very limited sexual scripts, which has changed the landscape – as well as an impoverishment of literacy around it. The shape and boundaries of intimacies have really shifted in the digital and smartphone era. And yes, again, that seems to be changing now – there are more conversations about consent, for instance, both in schools and in media coverage. So, that's something.

GB: I do welcome some of the talk about consent. A few years ago my students were saying, 'It's so hard, you've got to get consent for everything, you'd need a form!' I was saying, 'Look, are we really saying that the person you're getting off with, you're so clueless about how they're thinking that without a form you couldn't tell if they were consenting?' That opens questions about all our sexual behaviour. But despite that, the framing of consent as the main issue so easily slips back into sex as risk, sex as danger, sex as hurt. Of course, those things are real; but without all the other components, we're not doing the job. Where is the bit about sex as laughter, sex as pleasure, sex as loss of self, or just sex as uncertainty? Sex as physical testing? On pornographic scripts, I think you're right; it's difficult, isn't it, because now you don't have to search them out. Your phone will just give them to you. 'Would you like to …?' I get asked all the time, 'Wouldn't I like to extend my penis size?' You think, 'Well, yes, I, kind of, would', but it changes people's range of experimentation with their own heads about it, I guess, doesn't it? That bit does matter.

JL: Yes. This also reminds me of Katherine Angel's recent book, *Tomorrow Sex Will Be Good Again*, where she discusses how 'consent talk' is both really important and helpful but also frames sex as dangerous and as a risk, and therefore does something potentially reductive to power dynamics that she wants to think through and pick apart – like you are here.

GB: Absolutely. Because on the one hand of course it's still the case that people who are seen to be embodied as women, especially young women, face all kinds of intrusions, violence and hurt which are mediated through sexual behaviour. On the other hand, it feels dangerous for us not to understand that some kinds of sexualised contact might not be so straightforward: for example, that people might want things that also hurt them. First, what do we do with that? Where does consent go in that? Second, all of the uncertain kinds of activity that people do as they're learning to work out what being sexual means for them – which every human being, I think, probably has to do – gets categorised early on again into 'allowed' and 'disallowed' actions. And we know how that story works. Lots of us had to grow up with it. It doesn't go anywhere nice. I feel like we need more intergenerational discussion, both ways, because you can also see that older people are again demonising the sexual behaviour of younger people. Maybe that's inevitable to some extent … every generation thinks they won't, but they do ('You lot are doing it on your phones! Oh, no!'). You think, well, younger people could explain to older people, 'This feels safe but this doesn't, and that's the distinction'. That's needed in progressive circles. Otherwise how would we imagine a world where intimacy gives us all the things we need? If you know anyone who wants to do intergenerational sex talk, I think there's also a need for that.

JL: I wonder if Justin Hancock might do some good work relating to that? He has done great work on sex education with teens as well as for older people in his work with Meg-John Barker.[3]

Moving on. The synthesis of tradition of Black Marxism and global ecofeminist political economy in *Rethinking Racial Capitalism* is very powerful. You read environmental crisis in relation to histories of racialised dispossession and the subordination of women (drawing on the work of Cedric Robinson and Maria Mies). How has your thinking on environmental issues moved on since you wrote the book?

GB: In *Rethinking Racial Capitalism* I was trying to work through the idea that there's something cataclysmic that we're living through. In every previous era of human existence, the powerful have found ways to extract as much as they can from those below them, to cast some people out of the terms of belonging, and humanness. There are different versions of that story, but it's ubiquitous. Once we come to capitalist development, this story acts as if people will eventually be incorporated. That's the fantasy of industrialisation: in the end, no-one will be a peasant anymore. The industrial juggernaut will capture everybody; or even if it doesn't quite capture everybody, it will *interpellate* everybody, so being a peasant won't mean the same thing anymore. We might be *differentially* affluent, but the machine will work. What's different for us is that the machine is on fire.

Now I think there's a question about whether what David Harvey calls 'the spatial fix' can be achieved in the same way – the idea that when you've saturated this particular market you can always go somewhere else. The world on fire makes that a much trickier kind of move. It contracts the spaces that existing capital can be in, and moves people by force, quickly and rapidly, in little dinghies around the world, just trying to survive. These factors make the previous self-regulatory tendencies within global capital much more uncertain. It also means that some populations who perhaps could be relegated to a slow death, or an in-between existence on the edges of affluent economies, now seem to have nowhere to go at all. Where's the space? Where are you going to go? You can't be 'the new market' because your village just fell in the sea. You can't be the undocumented migrant worker because the metropolis cannot absorb that number of people – or it *says* it can't. That seems to be the moment we're in. We can't imagine a new, beautifully commodified, innovative element of the economy that comes to your space because the space you're in is not even sustaining life right now. There's no innovation to be laid onto the former agricultural sector because the former agricultural sector has now become a desert. I try to write about all these things in *Rethinking Racial Capitalism*, which is why it's about reproduction and survival.

If reproduction under racial capitalism has been a way of allowing capital to remake itself along the lines of pre-existing racialised divi-

sions, and to concoct *new* racialised divisions, that's happened by
piggy-backing on social reproduction. You can pay some groups of
people less and enforce that through under-protection in law because
you have other ways of ensuring the work you do for free in that
community can be retrieved into the global economy. Maria Mies
was already talking about that in the 1970s and 1980s through her
idea about 'housewifisation': the non-waged route of exploitation.
Social and economic activities are retrieved for the global economy
without the status or agency that straightforward proletarianisation
provides. None of that works so well if the non-waged economy
becomes constrained by the world on fire. All of that system
becomes very uncertain. The reproduction of capital has relied for
a long time on not reproducing human life through the workings
of capital alone, but by colonising the spaces of social reproduction
– by relying on the possibility of *just enough* socially reproductive
work being done to sustain life. When the natural world contracts or
collapses – and the Covid pandemic might be part of that as well as
the world on fire – it's not clear that the machinery or the resources
to sustain life are there in this space outside the wage.

Then I just want to cry. I don't know the answer to that. I think
it is, perhaps, one of the most urgent political questions of our time,
about this kind of genocide by neglect, or inadvertent genocide. I
think we all can see that. You don't have to be a scholar in that area.
You can see we have already entered that moment – but what our
collective intellectual, political and ethical resources are to answer
that, I'm not sure. Well, I don't know yet, but before I die, which
I guess is not long away, that's the end project. Given that we can
understand how this bit of the story, which was just about keeping
people alive, is collapsing, then what will be a politics that lets us
survive? Of course, I want us to *thrive*, but we're even further from
survival than we were at the beginning of my life.

So, even our ability to make the demand is not yet there, because
the demands are still made within the framework of 'business as
usual'. Business as usual was just slightly better regulated genocide; now we're in freefall genocide. How can we think about the
articulation of a global or transnational demand that addresses
the climate crisis but also tackles the acceptance of highly classed
and racialised divisions of early death and immediate death, as

well as planning for what collective survival would be – which must also be an economic agreement of some kind? I know there are people doing parts of that work, but they're not in the same spaces. But there are people trying to ask those questions, which is the first step.

JL: You mean interlinking decarbonisation with anti-racism, anti-patriarchy and anti-capitalism – banning billionaires, creating co-ops, abolitionism, sharing the wealth, joining all those dots ...?

GB: I guess, maybe, to start from a different space, to think about what an anti-capitalism of survival and mutuality might be in our moment. I don't think we can start with what the super-rich are doing wrong. I think we focus on the super-rich because that's a way of managing the extreme unsettlement of having no realistic claim to make. The idea of a claim is that there's someone to make the claim to, and through whom that behaviour could be moderated. I don't know if that's right or not anymore. But, yes, I think we have to start from a different place, asking: who needs to survive? What are the barriers to survival right now? What, if any, levers of agency do we have to achieve some of those terms of survival? It would have to be cross-border and include practices of bordering, but it has to be extremely technological too, because it's a food science question as well. And when it feels like the left of the Global North is almost irrelevant, and how they speak to each other is almost irrelevant, who cares?

JL: I don't think these issues have to be mutually exclusive. In some ways the moment where there was no real traction around criticising billionaires has been breached, the scales have been tipped, because they are quite conspicuously playing with space toys while the planet burns, and so there's the potentially a lever there to highlight how that massive amount of money that they're pissing against the wall could be used to let people live. There's a way that discourse could be mobilised, and I think it's starting to get some traction. But I also take your points about not overestimating the left in the Global North, and asking hard questions about mutuality and focusing on survival.

GB: Maybe more what I fear is that a lot of the left, including the active street left who I love most and live with most – in Britain and beyond Britain – are still wedded to a politics whose core is an ethical claim. The claim about why there shouldn't be billionaires: basically, it's an ethical claim. Of course, there are ethical claims to be made for *our* side, and of course, we *should* make the ethical claims because how else do we find each other and speak to each other? The bit that I think is needed to survive is not an ethical claim, it's an operational technique, and I think we have almost no machinery to develop operational techniques – within one nation, let alone globally. That's where my irrelevance comes in. I don't think this is a matter of persuasion, I think it's a matter of invention. Does that make sense?

JL: Yes, I agree it's a dead end to make everything into a moral rather than a vital political argument about survival and justice. There are also a range of different issues here, aren't there? Of political strategy and practice, of hegemony, of inventing new forms of appeal and connection …

You've done a lot of co-writing (for example in *Race and Power, Go Home, Empire's Endgame*). Can you say something about different experiences of co-writing, how it's evolved, and why you do it?

GB: *Empire's Endgame* is the most delicious experience that I've had professionally – probably at all! They are properly like my family. Previously, I've done co-writing in the ways that most people do co-writing: we all talk to each other and write our different bits. The projects I've been involved with, we've tried for it not to be, 'You write your section, I write my section, then we'll stick them together in the middle', but still it's remained broadly tied to ideas of the authorial intent and process. With *Empire's Endgame*, right from the beginning, we were very clear that we wanted it to end up as a book where no-one, including ourselves, could remember who wrote which bit. That's what every bit of it is like. I know people don't believe us, but really, it was written like that. We'd go in a room – an office or a café or somewhere – and talk for a while about what the worst things happening in the world were, what questions they raised, write the main points on a big board or piece of flip paper; then, at a certain point in the conversation, say, 'Okay, let's start writing now'. Exam conditions! We'd try and write for a while about the thing that we'd talked about.

JL: Did you all write about the same thing?

GB: No, we could all choose whatever we wanted to write about. Whatever you needed to get out of your head at that moment – write that. That became the first draft. We had a series of meetings like that. The drafts got rewritten; we all reworked them, and cut and pasted, and added slightly more academic bits, until there was a thing that got put out into the world. As a co-written project it really feels collectively written. There's not Gargi's bit, and Sita's bit, and Adam's bit, and Luke's bit, and Kerem's bit. Every part is all of us, and every paragraph probably has a number of us in it. What I thought was most cathartic about that – and I think the rest of that family think that as well – is that we didn't really try and write the book to make an academic point. We didn't really know what we were doing at the beginning. We thought we might be writing a collective book, maybe not. We did think we were writing a homage to *The Empire Strikes Back*. There was something really sustaining about having these spaces of reflection and enquiry with comrades about things that were very, very difficult and were happening in Britain at that time. Bad times, but at least you're doing this thing together … and using our intellectual skills and training somewhat differently. Universities take all the fun out of ideas. Universities say, 'You're smart and imaginative, but I'm going to steal all the fun out of those best bits of you, and make it into this spreadsheet with two and a half outcomes'. Instead it was a way of de-individualising intellectual pursuits, like training with a friend, so that we all could run a bit faster, swim a bit further, jump a bit higher, because we were with each other. That felt very different.

Even though there *is* an output, it breaks apart that kind of preciousness of, 'I'll write something, and then I'll go and present it to people who are just waiting for the bit where they get to talk, and say, "Yes, but *my* point is really this"'. I really recommend it to everyone. I just think universities are not sustaining our intellectual souls and spirits at present, so we need to find some ways of being with each other that will do that: because it does matter to us, as individual human beings, and actually to society, that ideas are *not* nothing, that the pleasure of thinking together *can* be retained, however colonised our whole lives are; and some of the human excitement of understanding, and hoping, can be done together. That's part of our job, and universities are not up to it, frankly, so we have to make some of the space for that to happen.

JL: I completely agree! Which brings us to the next question, which is, basically, what's university done for you or not done for you? You've produced all this work, you've been an active union campaigner, and then the university has tried to cut your and other people's posts in recent years.

GB: I feel like university has made me much dumber than I was when I started. I'm sure I used to have a shiny enquiring mind when I started this game, and God knows where that's gone. Universities are odd places, aren't they? I think universities, even in this period of being smashed apart, and having ideas stomped on, and it being so difficult to stay in work – there's something about university that, even despite all of that, is a bit permissive, and anarchic, and odd. It's where the odd kids come to gather. Even the most intrusive and overreaching management can never quite reach into all of that. Although I've had an exceptionally difficult 'career' – and I put that in inverted commas – I always say to younger people, 'God, if someone like me can have even something half like a career, any of you can, obviously. There's not been a minute of my working life when my employer hasn't been trying to put me out of work, and I assume that will carry on until I crawl towards retirement, sooner or later.' Despite all that, you always meet other odd fish, and odd conversations happen, and little bits of intellectual romance, because the most awkward and misshapen people with no social boundaries can come to universities to say, 'There must be an answer somewhere!' Even a neoliberal university could bring you to those people. There's something exciting about that. It just seems harder because there's so little time for us to see each other now. I wonder if the pandemic has changed that again, and people are much more actively looking to find ways and spaces of being together, and different kinds of platforms for those kinds of fleeting connection – not necessarily to articulate some grand project (I know some people are trying to do that, but they tend not to be my people).

So there are small gains of hope everywhere: little innovations, incongruent laughter, irreverence in the face of bureaucracy. They're the best bits of universities. Frankly, it doesn't matter how many external consultants they bring in, they're not going to stop that, because you'll just have to have not a single academic or student in the university to stop it. I know some have fantasised that as well – a university without academics – but we *are* that kind of odd fish, and there's a limit to how much you can make us behave, even the ones who are not comrades. I think there's something interesting about that: about having a social institution which is really constructed to just provide a shed for all the unruly ones to live in.

JL: Lastly, can you talk about the work you've done outside, or alongside, the university? Perhaps another way of asking this question is: what kind of impact actually matters?

GB: I don't know. I've started to think that people should stop talking about the other things they do. It's all a bit crappy because everything gets recuperated by our rubbish employers. It's not their business. I would like the world to be a better place, and I try to live in it in a way that that might happen; but I don't think that's my employer's business because it's certainly not their objective. This is stuff I try and say to younger people as well. It's not just universities, but all workplaces now: working life steals your energies. It's like Sarah Jaffe's book: *work won't love you back*, but it acts as if it's the best partner you never had, yet leaves you bereft and weeping. When we live our lives, somehow we have to steal back some of our time and energies and self-esteem from a narrative that says '*You are your work*'. Part of that is thinking, 'What other things would I like to have done in my life?' I have a checklist. The things I think are worth doing are: service, so you're useful to others; adventure, so you're entertaining to yourself; imagination, so you make something new; and care, so those that need you feel like you were there. I think as long as you get some mixture of those four things in your life, as much as you can, you can die as happy as anyone can be when they're dying. It's not about academic life. That's what I have to tell you.

NOTES

1 This interview will be published as "'It's not about academic life. That's what I have to tell you": Jo Littler talks to Gargi Bhattacharyya' in *Soundings: A Journal of Politics and Culture*, Issue 82, 2002.

2 Raheem Sterling, 'It was all a dream', www.theplayerstribune.com/articles/raheem-sterling-england-it-was-all-a-dream, 22 June 2018.

3 See www.bishtraining.com; www.megjohnandjustin.com.

Feminism is a project,
not an identity

Sylvia Walby is a sociologist who has written extensively on gender inequality, patriarchy and feminism, for example in books such as *Theorizing Patriarchy* (John Wiley & Sons, 1990), *Patriarchy at Work* (Polity, 1986), *Gender Segregation at Work* (Open University Press, 1989), *Out of the Margins* (Falmer Press Ltd, 1991), *Gender Transformations* (Routledge, 1997) and *The Future of Feminism* (Polity, 2011). She was a founder of the Feminist Studies Association and the European Sociological Association. Her work theorising social change includes books such as *European Societies: Fusion or Fission* (Routledge, 1999), *Contemporary British Society* (Polity Press, 2000), *Globalization and Inequalities* (Sage, 2009) and the recent book *Crisis* (Polity, 2015). In recent years much of her work has been on violence, including *The Concept and Measurement of Violence against Women and Men* (Policy Press, 2017) and work for the UN on violence against women. She is Professor of Sociology and Director of the Violence and Society Centre at City, University of London, UK, and UNESCO Chair in Building Peaceful Societies through Research on Gender Equality. This interview took place in December 2021.[1]

Jo Littler: In *Theorizing Patriarchy* you theorised patriarchy by splitting it into six different categories: paid work, housework, sexuality, culture, violence and the state. But later you largely stopped using the word patriarchy in favour of 'gender regimes'. Why did you stop using the word, and what do you think about the current rebirth of interest in it?[2] Can 'patriarchy' be used alongside 'gender regimes'?

Sylvia Walby: The term 'gender regime' and the term 'patriarchy' refer to exactly the same concept, which is a system of gender inequality. The underlying meaning is identical. I shifted the term because people were misinterpreting me: when I was first using the term patriarchy, people misinterpreted me as being biologically essentialist, and ahistorical, and I wanted to talk about changes and varieties, and the possibility of change. People were saying that they couldn't see that in any text which referred to the concept of patriarchy. So I decided I would translate myself! And from 1997, I translated myself from patriarchy to gender regimes. I did say in the book *Gender Transformations* that I was merely translating and I meant exactly the same thing. Not everybody accepts that it *means* exactly the same thing, but that's my position. So I'm intrigued about the increased interest in the term. I'm very comfortable with that. Can it be used alongside? Yes, absolutely, they mean the same concept. There is the possibility of a non-patriarchal gender regime, but I don't know of any.

JL: You also describe feminism as a project, rather than an identity. Why?

SW: The concept of a 'project' contains the implications of change, of movement, of fluidity, of possibility. The concept of 'identity' is very fixed. I'm not comfortable with the concept of identity because of its tendency to essentialise, albeit on the level of culture rather than biology; hence I find it a relatively unproductive term compared with the advantages of using the concept of 'project'. Indeed, the concept of 'project' is better than 'movement' because it contains notions of *practices*, as well as of ideas. So, yes: project, rather than identity. I wrote about this in my book *Globalization and Inequalities*, in the chapter 'Civil Societies'. It was part of my attempt to develop the concept of civil society – using that term rather than culture or ideology – and to deliberately take civil society as a broad concept.

JL: You often pay attention to forms of feminism that might not conventionally be labelled as such (such as union activity), as well as to historical/social complexities (e.g. what happened between, or across, 'feminist waves'). Is this a Gramscian feminism? To what extent do you locate your work in that vein?

SW: Well, to start with, it's about coalitions and alliances and about the breadth of the project for gender equality. The trade union question is really important. The trade unions are one of the most important organisations in the contemporary world pushing for gender equality in the economy. And yet, because gender is not unions' *primary* concern, a very narrow definition of feminism would tend to exclude the trade unions, even though they're an important part of a coalition of civil societal forces pushing for gender equality. I think it's really important that we have the concepts to be able to capture those alliances and coalitions, and that we have the capacity to include organisations and projects for whom feminism isn't their only or lead component. In order to include the trade unions, it's necessary to use that notion of feminism as a project, and to have a proper understanding of inter-sectionality – of the relationships between different groups pushing for progress and justice.

Is it Gramscian? Gramsci's a very important writer. It's not only Gramscian, but it's inflected by Gramsci, absolutely. I think there are multiple Gramscian components. One is the interest in coalitions and large-scale issues. What's hegemonic and what's counter-hegemonic? What does it take to build a bloc, to build an alliance which is concerned not only about the things which *directly* concern that group, but also about a broader understanding of what it would take to create the broader societal transformations which improve the standing of not only that group, but other groups too? So from that school of thought, I adopt not only the concepts of 'civil society', and 'projects', and the importance of coalitions and alliances, but also the way of connecting them back to macro-societal processes – and the significance of the macro-societal level in understanding the ways that politics are organised and the possibilities for change.

JL: You have been involved in, and associated with, 'gender mainstreaming', which is an approach to policy-making that takes gender into account. For some people, such a move would probably involve

a dangerous complicity with neoliberal regimes. What's your take
on this and on why gender mainstreaming is important? How are
you involved in gender mainstreaming now?

SW: I think of gender mainstreaming as being about more than
policy. It's a way of thinking about the relationship between radical
politics and the mainstream. It's deliberately designed to think
about the tension between radical, critical, alternative ways of
thinking and the contemporary embodiment of power – especially,
but not only, in the state. And most politics is about the relationship between the two. It's neither situated in a separatist focus
upon the radical, critical space, nor is it a focus upon the existing
forms of power. It's all about the relationship between them. And so
'mainstreaming' is a movement in both directions. It's about how
feminism changes the state, but is also changed *by* that process.
Both sides change: both feminism and the mainstream will change
during that process of gender mainstreaming. So I think of it as a
dynamic. There is inherently tension there, and that tension can be
productive. There are risks, of course, that one side can consume
the other … the one that you point to is whether feminism simply
gets absorbed, is too weak to withstand the pressure to be absorbed
into the mainstream. It's possible, but it's far from inevitable. And
if feminism means other than sitting in its own private space, it's
inevitably engaged in that process of mainstreaming, which is the
relationship between critical, radical thinking and existing forms
of power. Almost all contemporary politics is engaged in mainstreaming of some kind.

JL: Can you give examples of when it's been successful?

SW: The history of feminists' engagement with violence against
women is an example. Once, women were outside the protection of
the state if they were subjected to gender-based violence. The state did
very little for them. Feminist politics built separate feminist institutions such as Rape Crisis lines and refuges for women who suffered
domestic violence. But these feminists didn't actually *stop* with the
building of these institutions, they were also trying to engage with
the state. For instance, they wanted access to public housing and for

the welfare state to deliver income support to women who left their husbands. They wanted to change the way that the criminal justice system operated so that there would be sanctions against people who'd been violent. So that's a set of politics which, even though it might have appeared as if they were only setting up separatist institutions, actually engaged very productively and over decades with challenging orthodoxies. I think the movement of violence against women, gender-based violence, domestic abuse, #MeToo, are often instances of gender mainstreaming which have been effective in changing things. Not sufficiently; but they've all been effective in securing some kind of change in that tension between the radical, critical thinking and the existing basis of power.

JL: And a more negative example …?

SW: A negative example would be how contemporary feminism, in trying to engage the state to act against men's violence against women, has inadvertently led to increased securitisation and excessive use of coercive state power, rather than the development of specialised targeted welfare to assist women, the weak and the disadvantaged (as was the earlier focus of feminism). In this form of politics there is a tension in calling upon the state in a way that potentially enhances the development of a too powerful, coercive state, as compared with the development of targeted welfare forms. Balanced reaction is important; it's important to have nuanced arguments about the extent to which a particular kind of intervention is counterproductive or not. There *should* be sophisticated political discussions, supported by research in the academy, so that we can accurately determine in which instances such a 'calling-upon' part of the state is effective or is counterproductive. I don't think it's always obvious. I don't think slogans like 'selling out' or 'complicit' are very helpful. I think these are things to be examined in detail, with assumptions of goodwill and good faith, but nonetheless to critically examine exactly what are the outcomes of particular kinds of intervention.

JL: Your approach is engaged with both theoretical and abstract complexities and with materialisms and systems of power, as displayed in, for example, your books *Globalization and Inequalities* (2009) and *Crisis* (2015). How might you update *Crisis* now?

SW: The book *Crisis* was written with a focus empirically on the financial crisis of 2008. It was written as a theoretical text, but that was its main empirical example. How do we understand the relationship between crisis and society? What did it mean for a crisis such as that to emerge? How do we understand the potential for change in positive and negative directions? Could the crisis be simply reabsorbed? Was it something which was relatively small-scale and absorbable? Could it give rise to significant change, or would it be potentially catastrophic? The book was an attempt to explore the relationship between crisis and society, using the example of the financial crisis, and to examine how large-scale change always engages with gender relations.

Even though the type of change I was looking at wasn't primarily focused upon gender, it was making an argument that you can't understand macro-level societal change unless you understand how those macro-societal processes are also gendered. It was also an attempt to engage with complexity theory: change is not simply linear, where the cause has proportionate effects. It was an argument about the importance of non-linear effects: the possibility of very major effects from relatively small changes in relatively small events. I think the concept of crisis the book developed is applicable to lots of other kinds of crisis. My example was finance, but I could have used others. I could have used the climate crisis, which is still with us. Or, now, Covid. Covid is a crisis: what are its possibilities and outcomes going to be? I think some of the theoretical developments in that book are still relevant for the analysis of Covid. There is a possibility of a cascade of changes; something which appears to be quite small can have very large effects.

JL: The book analyses how crises are 'cascading' into ever-increasing crises. Yet what about the non-linear elements – for example, might you take the Biden election as not being an intensification of that crisis …?

SW: The concept of cascade is really important. It's an analysis of society as being made up of multiple systems. Society is a system, made up of multiple systems, of two main kinds: regimes of inequality and institutional domains. The notion of the crisis 'cascading' is that it cascades through these interconnected systems. It's not that the whole society will move at once, but that, step by step, one system could change another. But there is no inevitability; and any specific system could absorb it. I used the example of the financial crisis, for example, to examine effects upon the real economy, which had effects on the state. There was no inevitability that there should be austerity. You might say the same with Covid: there's no inevitability that the closing down of the economy had to mean austerity. The government can simply print money! And if we compare the two crises, the government in this instance *has* simply printed money, whereas it didn't in the previous one.

During the previous crisis, many people said it was inevitable that the economic crisis would lead to austerity, but I didn't think that was inevitable. The current crisis shows it wasn't an inevitability. Fiscal problems for the state don't have to give rise to austerity, that's not a necessary consequence. The financial crisis, combined with austerity, causes a series of further changes. It led to an exacerbation of other existing inequalities in civil society: it led to forms of scapegoating; it led to the intensification of ethnic inequalities; it led, in part, to the Brexit vote, which itself then led to another 'cascade'. But there was no *inevitability* that the Brexit referendum was going to go the way it went, or that the interpretation of the Brexit referendum would be such a hard Brexit. It didn't *have* to mean that. So it's an attempt to run a systems level-analysis, while still containing a component of contingency.

JL: You recently wrote an article, 'The Gender of R', which argued that any attempt to reduce the transmission of Covid needs to pay attention to the gendered dynamics of care. You've also written other pieces about Covid and social theory.[3] Can you outline what you've come to focus on in your social analysis of Covid and the pandemic?

SW: In the piece in the *European Journal of Social Theory*, I argued that we should take seriously public health as a social-democratic intervention, and that pushing back on Covid required the kinds of social-democratic projects of which public health is a really important part. Public health and social democracy are closely intertwined. Theoretically, it was an attempt to address the question of whether all state actions were intrinsically authoritarian. So it was an argument against Agamben, and the mobilisation of some Foucauldian writers who were arguing in the very early days of the pandemic that all state interventions were inherently problematic.[4] Instead, I argued that we really should be theorising state interventions through the lens of social democracy and public health. In that article I argued very strongly for public health interventions to push back the extent of Covid and save lives.

The libertarian impulse has, I think, been highly problematic. We've seen an extraordinary coalition of left and right libertarians opposing the development of public health interventions. Some early theoretical work in this area inappropriately fed what has since become a strong anti-vaxxer movement. The article was also an attempt to theorise public health because it's so important and I think some social sciences had almost forgotten about it. It had become separated off to 'the health world' and was no longer central to social science. But in the last couple of years, through the lens of Covid, we've begun to rethink the place of public health, which involves not just the provision of care after somebody's sick, but strategic interventions to *prevent* people becoming sick.

My attempt to 'gender' this was by focusing on how gendered public health interventions were concerned with care and the household. I wanted to draw attention to the transmission of Covid inside households and *between* people who cared for each other. This was being neglected. We were seeing the transmission of Covid in patterns of care, care between generations, grandparents and children, intergenerational household forms of care, domiciliary care; but what became the sole focus of attention were institutionalised forms of care, especially care homes. I thought we saw a serious underestimation of the extent to which Covid would be transmitted through domestic relations of care. When the UK government talked of closing down parts of the economy, they ignored care! The voices about care were not at the table making the decisions, they were typically excluded from the conceptualisation of what it meant to 'close things down'. So we saw very little, and very late, support for forms of care which would not transmit Covid. I compared it to what was happening in China, where from early on they were setting up 'in between' hospitals. When you've got Covid you don't want to infect your nearest and dearest. Why would you tell somebody who had Covid to go home and stay with their family? Why didn't we offer people somewhere else to go? In China, they were offering alternative forms of accommodation; you could go somewhere else, and not infect your children, your partner or your grandparents. The UK's provision of resource, money and targeted welfare seriously underestimated the significance of gendered welfare interventions which were necessary to prevent Covid's spread.

Another example was people's capacity to stay away from employment if they knew that they were infected with Covid. If you didn't earn very much money, if you didn't have proper sick pay, then you didn't have much incentive to stay at home. There has therefore been a highly classed, gendered and racialised dimension to the Covid crisis, in which the failure to deliver basic resources like proper sick pay meant that we didn't interrupt Covid's transmission to the extent that we could have. In that way, I was trying to think through what a feminist political economy of Covid would look like, and to think through measures that would lead to the reduction of its transmission. Unfortunately, I think it's still relevant.

JL: Your work has been quite invested in the idea of economic growth, i.e. you have written about the concept of making economic growth more inclusive and feminist, and mobilising it as part of a social-democratic, rather than neoliberal, programme. Yet there are a fair number of other environmental/left/feminist thinkers (such as Kate Soper and Kate Raworth) working in the grain of the ecological economics tradition who definitely do have a problem with it. What do you think of that? Is there not any problem with economic growth for you?

SW: I think economic growth can take various forms. It's not inevitable that economic growth takes a neoliberal or destructive form. And it's that variation I'm really interested in. Think of the varieties of capitalism, varieties of gender regime, the varieties of economic growth. There's no inevitability that economic growth *has* to mean the destruction of the planet. There's no inevitability that economic growth *has* to mean capital accumulation or generate inequalities. For example, if we're going to go green, we need to completely restructure our energy sources. The renewable energy sector is growing, it's transforming, it's really important, and is part of the way there. Now, that's a process of economic development which involves the closing down of old industries and the growth of new ones. It means the development of wind power and of solar power. It means putting turbines in rivers. It means the increased insulation of homes. There's a series of economic activities which are necessary to reduce the amount of carbon that we emit. So that's a process of economic development – economic growth, if you like – which is necessary for the transformation of the economy in a progressive direction.

It's the same for gender equality. In order to transform society in a gender-equal direction, we need to transform the economy. We need institutionalised childcare, we need nurseries. We need to invest in the human capital associated with the training of nursery staff and teachers. We need to invest in healthcare and a variety of forms of care. All of these are forms of economic growth. I've typically summarised them as social-democratic. It depends where you sit as to how you interpret the concept of social democracy. In Britain, we can use it quite abstractly. In other parts of Europe it's so tied up with specific political parties that the term is harder to use. But in a British context, it's relatively straightforward to say that a social-democratic trajectory can entail forms of economic growth, investments in human capital rather than merely fixed capital, and transformations of the economy in a green and gender equal direction. Which means economic growth *can* be good, it all depends upon how it's constructed.

For instance, in the chapter on progress in *Globalization and Inequalities* I compared the extent to which economies grew using different proportions of carbon: how much carbon there was per dollar of GDP. Different countries have different rates of economic growth in relationship to it. So it's always been possible to imagine economic growth having different effects, and green economists have always been able to count it. So it is possible …

JL: So no time for the de-growth movement?

SW: OK, it depends what's meant by the economy here. And we might say, well, is the development of *care* part of the economy? Do you really want to stop the development of collective forms of care? I don't want to argue for that. If you are narrowing the concept of 'growth' merely to profit then we can all agree. I think the concept of growth is too important to be narrowed in such a way. I think it's really important to keep a concept of a dynamic transformation of the economy, of which growth is simply a part, and to keep the focus on the nature of the *transformation* of the economy, not just to think about whether it's growing or not and about GDP.

JL: Okay, yes, I agree with that. Let's turn to sociology. To what extent has sociology, in your experience, been a hospitable home for feminism?

SW: I think sociology has been very hospitable. It's been a site of engagement with society, it's been open to offering an important, scientific, analytical response to contemporary societal developments. I think the heart of sociology has been in an intellectual response to contemporary societal developments. Sociology's always done that – from Marx, Weber and Durkheim looking at the challenges of industrialisation and capital accumulation, to contemporary developments in society. Is it always hospitable? It's a complicated space, so you should expect to have argumentation about what kinds of space it should be. We've had discussions about the extent to which there should be a separate analysis – Women's Studies, Gender Studies, Feminist Studies – and the extent to which it is separate or integrated. Multi-disciplinary research centres have involved really important practices which have allowed for that joint development of those forms of analysis. So yes, I think sociology has been hospitable, but the interdisciplinary, multidisciplinary spaces have also been very important. There is inevitably a tension between the two, and I would like to think of that as a productive tension which keeps these debates live.

JL: So that's an answer that is mainly oriented around the theoretical tools, rather than 'lived' university experience and working cultures. What if you looked at it from that perspective?

SW: That's asking about universities, rather than sociology. Are universities hospitable environments in which women can operate? Historically, that's been extremely varied. Women were excluded from universities. It's only relatively recently that we've had women in senior position in universities, and we've seen high levels of contestation when women have attempted to take positions of leadership or authority within the university. So universities have been spaces in which the inclusion of women has been highly contested – even as universities themselves often think that they constitute the most liberal spaces in society! I think universities usually understand themselves as being more hospitable than would be warranted by the experiences of people in any minoritised group. The challenge is always to draw upon the goodwill of that self-understanding, in order to deliver effective transformation of institutional practices so that they actually live up to their ideals, rather than engaging in defensive reactions to their critics. It's a contested space. All contemporary organisations have been challenged by the transformation of gender relations in which women are increasingly entering higher levels of employment. Universities have engaged with this, as have other organisations, and it has generated varied experiences on the ground.

JL: Why did you start to work on violence?

SW: I've always worked on violence. Very early on I was interested in the development of the new forms of politics and provision in relationship to refuges, and in the media representation of rape and the way that it was portrayed in newspapers. *Sex Crime in the News* was one of my earliest publications.[5] Whilst I'm often thought of as having written particularly around political economy, that was always there. So why do I focus so strongly on it *now* is, I think, the question. I think violence is critical, theoretically underestimated, and a site of major contemporary political contestation. A lot of the left is led from either political economy or culture, and has treated violence as something to be regarded as empirically, but not theoretically, relevant. Many theorists of capital accumulation don't notice violence: they say, 'Oh yes, that's horrible', but it's not built into their accounts. Much of the development of cultural studies and the radical politics around cultural studies didn't treat the *phys-icality* of violence seriously; and insofar it was addressed, treated it as a discourse, or something newspapers wrote about, or something that you saw in media and film. And I was always interested in the *physicality*. That is, in how violence is a form of power with its own specificity, its own rhythm, modality, patterns and form of deployment and regulation. It's not reducible to other forms – to political parties, to the economy, to the polity, or culture, or civil society – it's distinctive (although, of course, related).

Theoretically, I thought it was a mistake that contemporary – by which I mean post-Second World War – social science underestimated it. But before that, violence did have a place in sociological thinking. For Weber, it was fundamental: the modern state had a monopoly of legitimate violence in a given territory. Weber's account of the state analysed its relationship to tax-raising powers and to war, as well as the power to regulate violence and civil society. Durkheim's book *Suicide* is about violence against the self. It's an argument for the significance of thinking through violence and its distinctive forms to understanding society.

So, theoretically, I thought it.was a mistake to ignore it. It *matters* as a form of power for gender inequality. And analysis led through political economy underestimated the extent to which violence shaped women's lives. There was a constant feminist political pressure to take violence more seriously that the left typically ignored; they treated it as an epiphenomenon, something which is marginal, empirically relevant, theoretically not significant for drivers of change in society.

My next point is about the significance of violence *politically*, which again, I think, is often underestimated. I think the interpretation of violence is very important for contemporary political alignments. Feminist movements concerned with violence against women have long argued for the improvement of welfare and the reduction of gender inequalities as part of their understanding of what drives violence in society. They know there's an interconnection between gender inequality and violence against women: that gender inequality has *caused* violence and was the *product* of violence; that there's a deep interconnection between inequality and violence; and that the strategic way forward was welfare –

either by specialist feminist organisations or by persuading the state to provide the general forms of welfare necessary to reduce gender inequalities and to provide the targeted forms of welfare support needed to escape the violence. Feminist movements from the 1970s onwards had a radical, social-democratic interpretation of violence, which was, politically, an important contribution to the development of counter-hegemonic thinking – indeed, what *ought* to be, hegemonic thinking in contemporary society; and the left was wrong to ignore it and to treat it as not very important.

An alternative interpretation of violence has been to see it as a form of pathology: as something which is the consequence of drugs or mental illness, and therefore is not understood as connected to inequality. That is an influential interpretation. It's also unfortunate because it tends to ignore the significance of inequality in generating violence.

A further interpretation of violence is that it's something that's so terrible that we should increase the coercive powers of the state in order to subdue it. Some of the debates around terrorism have moved in that direction: we have seen an argument for the increased coercive capacities of the state. Violence is becoming, if it has not yet already become, an important terrain of political argumentation between the major political alternatives in contemporary British, European, and indeed global society. The capacity to intervene intellectually in this area, which is – and will increasingly be – a hot political issue, is important. So I'm situating myself as a researcher in this field, generating the data, and coordinating the development of better data, so we can have a better scientific understanding of violence, which can then feed these policy and political debates, because I think this will become a critical turning point in the contemporary political conjuncture.

JL: How does this relate to what some people would call a 'fourth wave' of feminism: a renewed, often transnational, focus on violence against women and girls, everyday sexism, #MeToo, that cluster of issues?

SW: It's gone global, very effectively. Today, violence is a very important focus of transformational feminism. It's articulated in multiple ways, but I think there's a clear understanding that gender inequality drives violence, and it acts as a very important site for transnational political developments. There are different sides to it – different forms of violence have been constituted as the sites of particular campaigns. They feed on each other, and that's important – I wouldn't want to say any one of them is *the* most important. We are seeing wave after wave of these politics. #MeToo is one of the latest, another site where we see a particular way of understanding how coercion and violence come to the fore. Some of these contemporary developments have argued for the connection between physical violence and other forms of coercion. There are some very interesting intellectual and policy questions around what constitutes the boundary between these issues, and just how far the concept of violence can be and is being usefully extended. The debates around #MeToo have been important in pushing some of those issues forward.

JL: There's been a recent upsurge in feminist academic interest in violence, such as the recent books by Jacqueline Rose and Judith Butler. How does your focus relate to such work and how is it different? I know, for example, your specific different definition of violence is that it has to involve a physical, or bodily, component.

SW: I think it's important that violence is being taken seriously across all the social sciences. Everyone is picking it up within their own theoretical framework, so it's not surprising that Butler will relate it to her theory of performativity. It seems to me appropriate that different disciplines, theoretical and political frameworks would look at the question of violence through their own concepts and forms of engagement with the world. Some writers have interpreted violence through the symbolic and the cultural and I think that underestimates the specificity of violence. You need the physical, the bodily dimension. There is something distinct here.

I don't want to be biologically essentialist about it, but there is something distinct about forms of power which involve forms of physical harm: pain, death, and the threat of these harms. There are certain forms of irreversibility which are unlike other forms of power. Forms of economic power can go backwards and forwards, but once you've physically maimed a body, that movement is much less likely. In terms of history, once one group has used violence against another, it's really hard to go back. The reversibility of violence as a form of power is much less than other forms of power, such as cultural or economic. So I'm making an argument for the *specificity* of violence as a form of power, and not to underestimate that. I'm not saying that a cultural analysis of violence is inappropriate, but I argue for the significance of violence as its own distinctive form of institution. I interpret violence as a fourth 'institutional domain' – perhaps that's the crux of it.

I connect all kinds of violence. I connect, deliberately, violence between individuals, between groups, between the state and individuals, and say that they form an institutional whole. You can see it, empirically, that these forms of violence cluster. If you have a practice of violence in one area, you typically get it in another. States with a high likelihood of going to war, high rates of militarisation, are also in societies with very high rates of homicide and increased likelihood of using capital punishment. These forms of violence, even at these different levels that are highly correlated, feed each other in a way that I want to then describe as an 'institutional domain'. Social scientists have typically *fragmented* violence in their disciplines. We give interpersonal violence to the criminologists; we give inter-state war to the political scientists. We separate it into the different disciplines. I think it's important to overcome some of those disciplinary fractures in order to be able to do a proper analysis of violence; to bring those fragments together in order that we can more appropriately understand the significance of violence for society, and so we can build the kinds of policy and politics that are important for the transformation of society.

A lot of sociologists treat war as exceptional, whereas I think of it as a war system. Certain kinds of social systems generate wars. War is not exceptional if you have a war system. In some disciplines, like criminology, the tradition has been to see violence, like crime, as happening from the bottom up: 'It's the disadvantaged who do it'. I think that's wrong. Empirically, it's incorrect. Most violence is top-down; it's the powerful who do it to the weak. Feminist analyses have long argued that typically it's more powerful people who do it to the less powerful, and more typically men to women. Anti-racists argue it's more typically white violence on Black, not the other way around. Stuart Hall's work on the social scapegoating of 'the Black mugger' was a really interesting early example of that, showing how the construction of violence as if it came from below is so problematic, when most violence actually is top-down. And so, to pull all these threads together, the understanding of the construction of violence in society is an important part of the construction of contemporary politics around multiple forms of inequality, of which gender is one part, but not the only one.

NOTES

1 This interview was first published as '"Feminism is a project, not an identity": An interview with Sylvia Walby' in *Soundings: A Journal of Politics and Culture*, Issue 81, 2022, pp128-142.

2 See Rosemary Hill and Kim Allen, '"Smash the patriarchy": the changing meanings and work of "patriarchy"', *Feminist Theory*, Vol. 22, No. 2, 2021, pp165-189.

3 Sylvia Walby, 'The Covid Pandemic and Social Theory' in *European Journal of Social Theory*, Vol. 24, No. 1, 2021, pp22-43.

4 See Giorgio Agamben, 'The invention of an epidemic' in 'Coronavirus and philosophers: M. Foucault, G. Agamben, S. Benvenuto', *European Journal of Psychoanalysis*, 2020.

5 Sylvia Walby and Keith Soothill, *Sex Crime in the News*, Routledge, 1991.

We need to look at how we can build bridges and solidarity

Finn Mackay is a Senior Lecturer in Sociology at University of the West of England in Bristol and the author of *Radical Feminism: Feminist Activism in Movement* (Palgrave, 2015) and *Female Masculinities and the Gender Wars* (Bloomsbury, 2021). They have been involved in feminist activism for over twenty years, working in education, youth work and the women's sector before returning to higher education. Finn founded the London Feminist Network, revived London Reclaim the Night, and in 2010 won the Emma Humphreys Memorial Prize for their work on male violence against women and children. They are a Trustee of the British Sociological Association and the Feminist Archive, a member of the Women's Commission Women's Safety Taskforce, and an Ambassador for the Worker's Educational Association. This interview was conducted in July 2022.

Jo Littler: Your books outline the complexities and different traditions and positions within radical feminism, and a key point of your work is to reclaim or demarcate radical feminism as a project which isn't trans-exclusionary. Can you summarise what 'radical feminism' means?

Finn Mackay: Radical feminism shares the same overall aim or agenda that all feminism does: an end to sex discrimination in present society. It involves an end to sex discrimination in every area of life: in employment, culture, domestic life, representation, media … everywhere! As a branch of feminism more generally, radical feminism shares the aim of ending sex discrimination, and of ending discrimination and unfair treatment of women vis-a-vis men; but as the name suggests, radical feminism then goes further because it says that sex discrimination is not the end point, it's a step along the way towards liberation – and that *is* the end point. So ending sex discrimination is an important goal, but it's not the liberation of society from patriarchy and patriarchal governance, which, for me, radical feminism has as its more radical aim.

In my first book, *Radical Feminism,* I explain how radical feminism can be distinguished from other schools of feminism that people might be familiar with. At school and college, when people do social sciences, they tend to study what are called 'the big three': liberal feminism, socialist feminism and radical feminism. As part of this there are often a lot of myths that people are told about radical feminism. Certainly, I see that in my incoming students who are doing social sciences and who, along their learning journey, have gleaned that radical feminism is the most extreme version of feminism – one that thinks all women are better than all men, and which wants to put women in charge instead of men. And that's certainly never what radical feminism argued for in the past, or argues for now. Radical feminism can be distinguished from those other schools, I would say, by four main features. One is it that accepts the existence of patriarchy – of male supremacy – as a *fact,* rather than a theory. That's not to say that all men are in power in all institutions. The men in powerful institutions are men that tend to be from elite, powerful backgrounds, and in this country tend to be rich white men from very particular backgrounds, who have all been to the same handful of private schools and universities. There are rich women there too, but we don't see 50 per cent of them in power, and so our major institutions of power are overwhelmingly dominated by men. I think the term for that is *a patriarchy.* Some other schools of feminism would disagree, and would see that as, for example, a symptom of capitalism. Whereas radical feminists would say that patriarchy is not just an offshoot of something else, but rather a form of social governance that we live within at the moment. It's real.

Second, radical feminism promotes and creates opportunities for women-only organisation. This is very different to separatism. It promotes and creates women-only leadership, women-only spaces, and women-only organisation on the principle that the people most affected by a structural oppression should be the ones leading the social justice movement to end it. Third, radical feminists view sexualised male violence against women and children as a cornerstone of women's oppression that needs to be accounted for. And I would say that during the second wave in the late 1960s into the 1970s and early 1980s, across the Western world, it was radical feminists who really wrote the book on what male violence against women is: what it looks like, why it happens, and how it might be ended, at a time when other schools of feminism were not doing that work. They were basing that work on ground-up theorising coming from consciousness-raising groups, the early refuge movement and the early Rape Crisis movement. And then, fourth, radical feminists extended that analysis of male violence against women and gender-based violence and the significance and importance of studying that to also critique the institutions of pornography and prostitution, which remains a very contentious area within feminism, and one that different schools of feminism have quite different views upon. So I would say that those are the four things that distinguish radical feminism from the other schools. But it shares the same aim, as I think all forms of feminism do, of looking to end blatant sex discrimination against women. We're all working towards that, in every area of life.

JL: You identify as a radical feminist and you also discuss how that tradition sprung from socialist feminist, anti-racist and anti-war traditions. Reading your work it seems very clearly coming from a left perspective to me, and increasingly so in its critique of conservativism; and yet I also noticed that your earlier book featured endorsements from right-wing feminists such Nimco Ali. Could you talk about how you relate to left politics and the socialist feminist tradition?

FM: Yes, Nimco Ali endorsed my first book, which is quite odd now that she's a godmother to Carrie and Boris Johnson's child and an advisor to the Conservative Government. I would hasten to add that when she gave that endorsement I knew her through community and grassroots organising against female genital mutilation in London and Bristol. She was working with young people on that, that's how I knew her. That was quite a long time ago and at that time she wasn't an advisor to the government. I wouldn't ask her to endorse anything now!

How does my feminism relate to left politics and socialist feminism? Well, I identify as a socialist. Not as a socialist feminist because of the issues I've already outlined, as I think socialist feminism historically hasn't paid enough attention to male violence against women, which is an area that I've just been involved in so much, working on policy and activism. So that's very important to me. But I've always worked alongside socialist feminists. I always find those women to be very hard-working comrades who are always on the frontline of the most current and important struggles, many of whom I return to for comment and analysis on current issues – especially if I'm not sure exactly what I think about certain current events. So yes, I'm a socialist, I've always been on the left, and I've always been involved in left wing-organising in terms of activism and protesting. Since I was a teenager I've been involved in the women's peace movement – I left home to live in a women's peace camp. But during that time we were also involved in campaigning against the Criminal Justice Act, for example, which was the right thing to do, as it was a crackdown on people's right to protest as well as the free rave movement, on new age travellers and just on alternative lifestyles.

My parents are socialists. My dad gave me his copy of *The Ragged Trousered Philanthropist* when I was a teenager and said it was one of his favourite books. He was a joiner and a builder from a very rural working-class background. It's increasingly important to me. I've taken my son on Kill The Bill demonstrations and protests against the actions of this current government. I'm a member of the Labour Party: I'm a Corbynista and proud to say so, although at the moment I haven't renewed my subscription just yet. Part of me believes that passionate, left-wing people should not leave the party because that's what right-wing members of the party want; and another part of me just can't bear to carry on paying my membership subs at the moment when Labour is so right wing. I recently got a letter from the Labour Party urging me to continue paying and in that letter they said, 'Oh, please be assured that that we are rebuilding the party, and you can pay your subs knowing that.' I found that really offensive. I thought ... rebuild it from what? From over half a million members, from being the largest democratic socialist organisation in Europe? 'Rebuild it'... it was already built! And now you're busy smashing it.

I met Jeremy Corbyn a few times when I was involved in CND, as he's the Vice President. I've always been a trade unionist, from my first proper job in local government. When I was a youth worker I was a member of Unison, and I'm now a member of UCU. Collective left-wing organising and solidarity along structural issues is the most important thing to me. Although my latest book focuses on quite a specific issue, that's because I see it as part of the broader culture wars, and as part of efforts to divide people – to continue down a road of ever-increasing, vicious, right-wing conservativism that would be happy to continue to try and turn this country into a nation of oligarchs. I think the more we can all work together to preserve the democratic structures we have, and to build better ones upon them, the better.

JL: I agree. How would you define 'the gender wars'?

FM: Well, I don't like militaristic language, and the term itself, 'the gender wars' is militaristic. It suggests that there are these two warring camps that have clear sides. I don't think the term itself is helpful. But then again, it's also become a shorthand, and most people recognise it as a commonly-used term, so now it's in mainstream culture. And what people think it refers to – and certainly what the media presents it as – is a battle that is theoretical, but also about policy and legal issues, between women, and women who are feminists on the one hand, and trans women on the other hand. I think that's what most people see 'the gender wars' as; and that's certainly egged on by famous names like the author J. K. Rowling writing her statements on sex and gender, the pronouncements of MPs and the pronouncement of ministers, and what they focus on is women's objections to trans rights and trans inclusion. So I think that's what it's seen as in popular culture: as a war, as competing ideas, laws, policies and rights between women and between trans people.

I think the gender wars are part of the broader culture wars, which is an attack on the small steps of progress that social justice movements have made over the years. I think the culture wars are part of larger fractures and shifts as old elites who are dying out are trying to maintain power. As we go through a period of economic chaos and even more economic and environmental and social uncertainty these culture wars are increasing. People are increasingly drawn to them because, in this period of instability, they are being sold an idea of a rose-tinted past which was more stable, one that we can all look back on, which often hinges around an idealistic idea of the heterosexual nuclear family, where 'men were men' and 'women were women'. It presents the idea that everything is so chaotic now, but at least in this mythical past people knew where they stood: they had dedicated roles, children were raised well, you left your door open, communities were safe and people looked out for each other. There's a universality, unfortunately, about the culture wars, and that's why it's so powerful, as it signifies so many things. People who are against immigration are well into a lot of the narratives from the culture wars: people that don't want more migration into this country, people that are racist, people that don't support divorce, people that are against abortion, people that are homophobic, people that don't want trans rights … it attracts a lot of people all under that one banner of culture wars. I think attacks on trans people's rights are one component to that. It's a backlash against the small steps of progress that have been made – an attempt to re-solidify and future-proof power by elites.

JL: You write of how you are situated in an interesting or nuanced way in relation to the gender wars – a position that crosses dividing lines – how the unique position of your queer, butch, female masculinity means you are an 'insider-outsider'. Can you explain that and outline that for us here?

FM: Ever since I was young I've been involved in activist organising. When I went to university and did my undergraduate degree I was in the Lesbian and Gay society, as it was called, and we organised for LGBT officers and Pride events and inclusion events. When I lived in Leeds I was involved in the early organisation of

Pride there. So I've always been involved in LGBT activist groups, and obviously in LGBT communities and social spaces. Since I was a teenager I've also been in feminist spaces and feminist activist spaces, and I've very much been involved in in feminist organising, in terms of my work and career in the women's sector as well. And what I know, and what anybody in either of those communities knows, is that they overlap. They are all mixed together. There aren't dividing lines between them, you know: there are people working in the women's sector who are LGBTQ. Likewise, there are feminists working in LGBTQ organisations and activism: all of these things overlap, because people have multiple identities and multiple parts of themselves. And so that's another reason why I wanted to write the book about what was happening in in the gender wars: because I know that they aren't two discrete and warring camps. I know that they overlap, and I know that not least because I've been involved in both myself at the same time.

I've also been involved in creating social spaces for butch and femme lesbians, transgender and trans-masculine identified people. And you know those communities don't feature so much in the gender wars, because the focus and the scrutiny is very much on trans women. Whenever trans men, or trans masculine people, or butch lesbians, or masculine women get mentioned, it's often in quite an infantilising way. They are constructed as convenient victims. Gender war narratives will say that people are 'being trans-ed', they're being brainwashed; that there's some sort of attempt to 'steal those people away' to a trans identity. And these borders between female masculinity and butch lesbian masculinity, the question of what is a transgender identity or trans male identity – well, we've been having those debates ourselves within our communities for years, for as long as I can remember, and for as long as I've been in them, and we managed to have those debates and disagreements and arguments with each other. But what's happened now with the gender wars is that people from the outside, who are often *not* from those communities themselves – and, in fact, in many cases are heterosexual women – people are now on the outside looking in and scrutinising and pathologising communities that I've been part of, are using issues that we ourselves have addressed and discussed, and then have weaponised them to attack trans women. So that's another reason why I feel have a stake in this. Another reason is that, on the other hand, I did not like to see feminist theory – and particularly radical feminist theory, a lot of which I subscribe to – again being used to attack another minority group, to attack trans women.

JL: And as part of talking about your position, you talk about different positions you've held at different times in your life – tomboy, butch lesbian, thinking about identifying as trans and not having surgery, rejecting then embracing 'queer', becoming queer butch. It's a very moving and frank – and also a very three-dimensional – account of intersectionality, and of assemblages of gender, in their wider social context. Why was it important to you to write about your personal history in this book, and was it difficult?

FM: It didn't come easily to me, I have to say. Although people who might have seen me talk at big events might think that I'm quite full of myself, or quite happy to talk about myself or to be the centre of attention, for me the issues are the most important. I usually don't see why I should have to, in effect, 'send myself' into them. I also object to these narratives we see in our culture, so often, which is that you *have* to have personal experience of something before you can care about it. I think that narrative is very widespread. You'll see people doing something for charity because they or a loved one have been personally affected by it; or you'll see people saying oh, since a friend or whoever has been sexually assaulted or in an abusive relationship, now I'm really passionate about campaigning against it. I think that's actually something that we need to get over as a society. We shouldn't have to wait until any of us have personal experience of some sort of injustice or tragedy before we can see that the injustice and the tragedy is wrong and that we should try to do something about it. So that's why I don't usually like to centre myself in things. Instead, I usually like to say, 'Right, here are the issues. We should *all* care about these issues'.

But with this book I didn't want to be seen as a tourist. I didn't want to be seen as just jumping into this debate, into the fray, just to start talking about the gender wars because it's so 'current' at the moment. I didn't to be seen as opportunistic, although I knew that people would accuse me of that anyway. They do on social media – I get plenty of, 'Oh, now you've changed your career to write about the gender wars because that's the current trend, because trans is trendy. You're a careerist, a sell-out who used to write about male violence against women and children'. I know some people will do that anyway. But I suppose, for all the people that I know in the transgender and queer and trans communities, and for my own involvement in that, I wanted to put on the record that I do have a stake here. I'm not a tourist, I'm not jumping on a bandwagon, I've long been involved in these communities. I've long cared about them, and I myself have wrestled with differences of identity, identity terminologies, of where I best fit. I have experienced hostilities against me personally as well because of how I present, and because of my identity and who I am; so it didn't come easily at all. The last thing I wanted is for people to think that I was centring myself or making it all about me; but on the other hand, I very strongly didn't want to be seen as jumping on a bandwagon. I wanted people to know this wasn't disingenuous, I do have a stake here. I'm writing about this with integrity, I am upset with a politics I subscribe to being used to bash another community who I also stand with.

JL: Your new book provides a vivid sense of the complex histories of feminism, showing how, for example, both trans-exclusion and inclusion was part of the second wave. It critically unpacks where 'gender critical' feminism comes from and its range of perspectives, as well as conflicts within queer and radical traditions and spaces. I really like the discussion of 'feminist faultlines', as you call them, which provide a prehistory to the present. For instance, you discuss and contextualise how a spiritual, 'woman-loving', cultural feminism, which scapegoated butch lesbians and queers as representing the patriarchy, emerged. Do you think we need a much better and wider understanding of these historical feminist faultiness and their difficult legacies?

FM: We can dream! I'm sure everybody from their own particular social justice movement would wish that mainstream culture had a better idea of their histories and political underpinnings and were taken seriously as political and theoretical movements. That would be great, but I don't think it will happen because mass media has got a very shallow understanding of feminism. It tends to focus on consumer choice as representative of feminism, when, of course, it isn't at all. Consumer choice has got nothing to do with feminism, although feminism could certainly have a critique of that. But that's the dominant media narrative of how people engage with feminism. Or the media use feminism to pit women against other women in some sort of catfight – that's another thing they love to do.

I know from going out and doing public events – book festivals, speaking events, book groups, workplace talks, or whatever – that in mainstream culture, most people are not really sure what feminism even is, or what feminism as a movement even means, what it wants, what it's trying to get, who a feminist is, or what it means to be one. I think that's deliberate as well because I think feminism as a radical movement to change the current system does present a threat to the status quo. Feminism has been wilfully misrepresented, reduced and demeaned as some shallow but tenuous entity. It's for that reason that we've been able to be sold these lies, that feminism is having a tote bag that says 'feminist' on it, or Theresa May wearing a T-shirt that says, 'This is what a feminist looks like'. It's a sign of the times that people are not only willing to accept those things but will buy into them. So I can't really see the wider culture getting to grips with those histories.

I also think history books, textbooks and political commentators often hugely overlook the cultural influence of the second wave women's liberation movement. If you look at the 1970s and how changes were beginning in terms of people's lifestyles – people experimenting with communal living, with polyamorous relationships as a political act, with raising children communally, with raising children against consumer culture and trying to do things differently – all that that was a lifestyle movement informed by politics. There were consciousness-raising groups and women's groups in every little village, town and city across the country. It had a huge impact on relationships and culture, on relationships between men and women, and on what those could look like. I think that was partly why the 1980s then came along with all the individualistic movements that we're familiar with. There really was a huge backlash against that freeing, and quite radical, influence that women's liberation represented.

Today, with the gender wars, I don't think people are going to go back and look into this history, and that was partly why I wanted to write the book. I wanted it to be as simple and as clear as possible to provide people with a potted history and to say to people, look, it's not as clear-cut and as simple and binary as you might think, or as you're being told. What you see in mainstream media, remember there is a history to this, so don't just accept the media's largely reductive account of feminism and gender politics. Again, this is what I get asked at events: well, what exactly does feminism say about about trans people? Is feminism always transphobic? Do you have to be transphobic to be a feminist? These are the sort of questions that I get. So I wrote the book with that in mind. It's not an abstract theoretical academic book; I wanted to try and explain and contextualise for people where the current gender wars have come from. I hope that people reading the book will be given a bit of that background, and know that these narratives comes from somewhere; that it has a history for different reasons; and that the women who have a politics and ideology of trans exclusion – although I don't agree with them or go along with them – also have a theoretical history and a background. And, of course, that we shouldn't reduce everything within the gender wars to a 'TERF versus trans women' battle. It discusses all the really significant, legacy-building trans women that were involved at key moments in the second wave. There were trans women in lesbian feminist communes, in women's publishing houses, in women's music production, in women's organising conferences, in bands; women like Sandy Stone and Beth Elliot. Trans women were there and involved in the women's movement. Again, that gets erased when we just simplify everything to this whole 'TERFs against trans women' narrative.

JL: So much gender critical feminism argues that queer/gender analysis is 'anti-materialist'. On the contrary, you write that 'the question has never been whether biology is real, because of course it is; the question is what does it mean, where does it matter and what should it mean in the future'. I agree, and I like this formulation. Can you say more on this? For instance, are you arguing for a better materialism, a more capacious understanding of how bodies are sexed and gendered in history and society …?

FM: One thing that that queer activists, the queer movement and trans people get accused of is of ignoring or denying biology. That charge being put against trans people who have transitioned is especially ridiculous because, as if people who have taken steps to bring their biological features into line with their identity, to shape their bodies into ways that are most liveable for them, as if they wouldn't be aware of the materiality of the body! Of course they're aware of the materiality of the body. And then there's accusations, you know, that queer activists want to pretend that that sex doesn't matter, or pretend that sex doesn't exist. I don't think actually anybody is saying that.

Then there is a lot of actual misinformation: a while ago there were major stories in the mainstream press saying that Brighton and Sussex NHS trust would no longer use terms like 'mother', 'pregnant mother' or 'breastfeeding' – that they were only using terms like 'uterus haver', or 'chest feeder', and 'pregnant person'. This turned out to be an absolute fabrication. What Brighton Trust was doing was working with people to produce a booklet for midwives who might be working with queer and trans families in order to provide a glossary of terms they might need to know, preferred words that they might want to use, a bit of background about the trans community and trans rights – specifically for working with trans families, not anybody else.

If you believed everything that you read in the press, you would think that there was quite a lot of negative things happening. You'd think language was being taken away, that most services being were renamed or changed, when, in fact, what is actually happening is people who were historically excluded and who never even had a name, never even had a term, who were fought against and treated like apparent freaks, are now being included – that's all. That's what is happening. People who were historically excluded are now being given names and being included. That doesn't take away from groups and identities that have always been included, and always had names and widely understood, recognised labels in there.

But such stories are behind this idea that the queer movement wants to 'erase sex' and other terms. I don't think that's true. That's not what I see. In fact, if you look at queer writing, it's always involved deconstruction, but it's not been about pretending that these material features are not there. Judith Butler is often attacked. Butler's first book was *Gender Trouble*; in the second, *Bodies That Matter*, they had to point out some of the misreadings of that earlier work: that most babies are born with external genitalia and assumed reproductive systems that, in general, will fall into two main categories that we sex as male or female. At the moment bodies have sex differences, and that matters in terms of how we have relationships, how we have sexual relationships, how we might want to become parents, how we might want to carry or birth children, if that's possible. It matters for our health needs. Of course all that matters, and nobody's denying that; but on top of these features of the body we have a very conservative gender system which then seeks to construct people in the image of the two available binary genders, masculinity or femininity. I think it's that which queer theory has most critiqued and argued should be taken apart because that's built on sex differences of the body. But then you look back to radical feminist writing of the 1960s and 1970s which said, well, sex should cease to matter as a cultural marker: there are differences between bodies, but having one particular sex characteristic shouldn't invoke or confer power. These features of the body could be neutral in terms of politics and status. The body, of course, is never neutral in terms of its needs and protections and healthcare and care. So all this is to ask questions about why, *politically*, does sex mean something and why, culturally, does it mean so much. I think what we see at the moment is very reactionary, conservative sex and gender movement, one that really wants to reinstate this idea of women and men as a separate species. To me, that is the very foundation of patriarchy and is anti-feminist.

JL: Another thing I like about your book is that it's both capacious and generous yet doesn't lapse into a liberal middle ground position – it's clear about the extreme violence done to trans people whilst it also unpacks the complexities of a wide range of different feminist positions. I also liked how you try to learn from past examples to suggest what could have been done better: for example, how the Michigan Women's festival could have been more inclusive. Would it be accurate to say you are concerned with developing an approach which is about learning and reconciliation? Is that your peace background coming through …?

FM: Yes, and I suppose that relates to where I cut my political teeth – in never-ending circle meetings trying to make decisions by consensus! I can, for example, remember endless discussions into the night about single incidents, like: was a woman throwing a cold mug of tea over an American soldier at the gate of a military base, so that it went through the holes in the chain link fence and onto his uniform, an act of violence? Should we all agree that we *don't* do that because he didn't know the tea was cold – he didn't know that he wasn't going to be splashed with boiling hot water, he might have been fearful about that and so could have reacted more strongly, with more violence … you can see, it can go on and on and on! So yes, maybe that experience is coming out.

I have also known so many occasions where it really doesn't have to be an issue – where women's groups and women's activism and women's organizing has included trans women, and that has not been to the detriment of anything; in fact, it's *good* for women's groups and women's organizations to build solidarity and to work with other women. We know that the women's movement has excluded lots of different women at different times, and isn't immune to racism and classism, like the rest of society. So activism should be a leveller. It should be a zone in which we can occupy a critical more open and questioning space, never escaping the wider society that we're in, but trying to create a more questioning, free space, a space where we mix with lots of other people and meet with people from backgrounds that we're not in the least familiar with. That's where I end up at in the book: that we need to look at how we can build bridges and build solidarity.

JL: You have spoken elsewhere of knowing people who hold very different positions (for instance you talk about knowing and joking with Julie Bindel whilst you both hold wildly different perspectives), which will resonate for anyone who has been around feminist activism or politics for a while.[1] You also say in *Female Masculinities* that the vast majority of people aren't sure what they think about the gender wars, and that you aren't even sure what you think about everything, e.g. children, medication and the age of transition. So do you think it's important to talk across divides, and to register both nuance and uncertainty? Are you trying to build better understandings across what you call this 'brutally polarised' divide with its 'rush to litigation'?[2]

FM: Yes, absolutely, because I think if we don't all talk about it in the particular groups and circles that were in, then what we all have is people talking *for* us; and, at the moment, those very loud voices do tend to be from highly conservative sex and gender positions. It's been a long time coming, of course, but we've seen the recent move in America to curtail women's rights to abortion with the overturning of Roe v. Wade. That happened very quickly, but of course religious conservative groups and right-wing groups have been working for that for decades. We can't be complacent because that decades-long work then comes to fruition, and when it does, it can happen very suddenly. Institutions that were seen as untouchable can be ripped apart literally overnight. I think that, especially right now, we need to be looking at all that we share together, and we need to be very suspect of sex and gender-conservative voices who will speak for us. There are so many groups out there who want to tell us what we should think of trans people: that they're all deviant, that it's some sort of perverted movement to corrupt children and to gain access to women's spaces in order to abuse them – we're being fed that narrative all the time. It's a broader anti-gay and homophobic message as well; it would see us back to some sort of Section 28 situation, which we can already see happening in this country. There are sex education curriculums being taken to court, being attacked, being taken to judicial review because people don't like the fact that they are LGBT-inclusive. We have MPs and ministers reassuring people that children won't learn about 'the gay lifestyle' too young. This is a real backward step, and it's happened because the people in the middle, that are respectful and that mix with lots of different people, and don't want to offend anybody, and just want to get on with their own lives and for everyone else to have the right to get on with theirs, have felt frightened and disempowered to talk to each other about it. Into that void has come vicious and visceral sex and gender-conservative right-wing voices. And if we don't take that narrative back, a fast train to Gilead is what we're on, which is what I said in the book – and, in many ways, we're several stations along.

JL: The book argues that the greater enemy of both camps in 'the gender wars' is the religious conservative right and male violence, that this is what needs to be focused on. I completely agree. To some extent the gender wars are being encouraged to detract from this – it's quite explicitly the agenda of right-wing politicians in many countries, including the UK. How can we reconnect resistance?

FM: I think that's a really interesting question for social justice movements at the moment. Having been involved in direct action and peace activism as well as campaigns specifically around the Criminal Justice Act, I now see the Police Crime Sentencing and Courts Bill coming, and the attacks on the right to protest; and whilst I know that we can protest and that there is resistance in the Kill The Bill movement and demonstrations, it does all feel quite fragmented. Over the years, the new Labour government as well as the Conservatives have taken away the structures that enabled people to do things differently and enabled them to protest and resist. It's harder now to claim unemployment benefit or welfare; it's harder to find short-term housing; because of CCTV everywhere it's harder to flypost; there's no such thing as short-term squatted housing anymore; people are not able to set up communes and co-ops. The machinations of activism have been made more and more difficult or impossible against the backdrop of neoliberal brainwashing. That has really had an impact, and means that although we're seeing now a familiar 1980s/1990s-style attack from the government on people's freedoms, we're perhaps not seeing a 1980s-style uprising against it. Where are our massive poll tax riots, where is our mass resistance? The mechanics that enabled them have been taken away.

However, what we've seen again during the pandemic was the rise of mutual aid movements and of community organising. I think that attacks on the right to protest actually have facilitated this: the fact that protest was banned forced people into adopting 1980s-style DIY activism. During Covid I saw call-outs for demonstrations which would say, 'Called by nobody, organise yourselves! Some of us will be meeting here at this point, do whatever you want!' I recognised that DIY style from the 1990s, and people have been forced back into it by necessity through it becoming illegal to protest at all. All those long-winded systems that people got used to were taken away – getting a form, getting permission to have a road closure, getting permission to use a piece of public land, working with the police – all that went out the window. Instead, we saw a more spontaneous kind of DIY activism; information would go around on social media – 'people are all gathering here to say that we're angry about this' – and then people would go down there, but as it wasn't organised by anybody, nobody could be fined for doing so. I think that's really interesting. I hope that the current attacks on the ways people can protest will force people into more DIY, community, ground-up resistance and organising.

However, I don't think that the Tories are stupid; I think they know that people will resist. And they're building more prisons! They're quite happy to bring more people into the criminal justice system. But that's why I think it has to be mass protest and resistance; and I think maybe these developments of the mutual aid movements are rebuilding how people organise and make those networks together, for their mutual aid. Well, I hope so anyway.

JL: It's interesting to think how that might connect with abolitionist feminism.

FM: Exactly, yes, in that it's more spontaneous, it's grassroots. You know, there's pros and cons with all of that, but all resistance is good.

JL: Finally, you've been involved with a range of feminist activism and work: women's peace camp, founding member of EVAW, founder of London Feminist Network and reviver of Reclaim the Night marches. How has the traffic between activism and academia shaped both your writing and your activism?

FM: I don't really think of myself as an academic because I'm in a post-1992 university where the bulk of my work is teaching – we don't really have research time. So I mainly think of myself as a lecturer or a teacher. When I was very involved in activism I was frustrated with a lot of feminist academic texts that I thought were very dense, overly wordy, and overly theoretical because although I often found them interesting, they didn't address the concerns of activist groups or provide things that activist groups might need. When I was very involved in activism people really wanted grand overarching theories like women produced during the second wave – because it's one thing to know what you're against, but we also need to know what are we *for*. What would a different world look like? It's become a cliché, but actually such a question is really important to activists because being an activist involves asking structural questions: what do we want and what would it look like? What would doing this differently look like? These are strategic questions and they involve trying to build our own political strategy. Again, and wilfully, government and mainstream media narratives often demean and dismiss this, and treat such large questioning as something frivolous or indulgent precisely to stop us building it up.

So I was frustrated that academia didn't provide that. I still am actually, even now; all the time I see how ideas and trends are being shaped by the main journals in the English language, and by how you get a 'big name' on one topic and then they're the ones that are always cited on that topic, forever. It's bizarre, it's quite narrow. Academia is its own game and culture, isn't it? Within that game, you're not encouraged to do what people were allowed to get away with in the second wave, in the 1970s. I think if Kate Millet, for example, tried to write *Sexual Politics* now, let alone Shulamith Firestone's work – there's no way any of that would get published as a piece of academic work because it's grand theory, it's women's own views and ideas and visions about how things should change, and that's not seen as rigorous, or having appropriate referencing, or as being 'proper' academia. So sometimes I'm quite frustrated with that, and I've been told on several occasions that my work is too journalistic, too popular, too crossover, not academic enough. But I take heart from the fact that also people go out of their way to contact me, or to find my work email and say that my books or writing has helped them to understand the particular current issue or has helped them finally know what particular terms mean. That's what I think academia should be about: using concepts and ideas to contextualise current events that matter to everybody.

NOTES

1 Gaby Hinscliff, 'Finn Mackay: the writer hoping to help end the gender wars', the *Guardian*, www.theguardian.com/lifeandstyle/2021/oct/05/finn-mackay-the-writer-hoping-to-help-end-the-gender-wars, 5 October 2021.

2 Finn Mackay, *Female Masculinities and the Gender Wars: The Politics of Sex*, Bloomsbury, 2021, p96.

This is a collective history that belongs to all of us

Sophia Siddiqui writes and lectures on anti-racist feminism. Born in 1994, she grew up in Manchester and now works at the Institute of Race Relations in London, UK, where she co-ordinates the production of IRR News and is Deputy Editor of the journal *Race & Class*. Sophia's theoretical analysis of reproduction and gender in European racism is outlined in her 2021 article, 'Racing the nation: towards a theory of reproductive racism'. [1] She has written several articles for *gal-dem* and has given a wide range of talks, including to charities, NGOs, community groups and university students, and at the political festival *The World Transformed*. This interview took place in July 2022.

Jo Littler: In your recent article 'Racing the nation' you develop a theory of 'reproductive racism' to explain contemporary racism and right-wing politics, in which some women (i.e. mainly white Europeans) are positioned as breeders, encouraged by pro-natal anti-abortion policies, whereas others (mainly migrant women, or those from former Soviet bloc countries) are positioned as either threats or cheap sources of care. You suggest this is pivotal to understanding how society is being restructured around exclusion. This seems exactly right to me. Can you discuss how this theory emerged?

Sophia Siddiqui: The article emerged from looking very closely at what was happening across Europe, and particularly at how the far right was mobilising through anti-feminist measures – through attacks on gender studies courses, attacks on domestic violence legislation and rollbacks on abortion rights. I wanted to make sense of this moment, analyse what was happening and consider what we can do to combat it. But I quickly saw that it didn't just involve attacks on women's rights, it involved attacks on LGBTQ rights, and trans people's rights too, and it sat alongside an anti-migrant and Islamophobic agenda. I was beginning to see that gender and sexual politics is absolutely key now to how the far right operates ... this is a very unexplored subject, one that some far-right researchers don't even touch the surface of, and one that can be neglected by feminist researchers too. I wanted to address this gap, and speak to anti-racists, anti-fascists and feminists at the same time.

I realised I needed to show how these different aspects were all working together. Reproduction, both the biological reproduction of children but also 'social reproduction' – the work of maintaining and up-keeping society through 'reproductive labour' – is key here. One of the main contradictions the article draws out is how the reproductive labour of migrant women is essential to maintaining the capitalist system, as the care work needed to sustain families is increasingly outsourced onto their shoulders. But in every conceivable way, migrant women remain cordoned off from the body politic through immigration regimes that exclude them and push them out to the edges of society. And these immigration regimes often prevent them from being with and caring for their own families, who they have to leave behind in their countries of origin to care for the families of more affluent others. We can't look at these issues in silos; we need to see them together, particularly in the context of the multiple crises of care and of capitalism.

That was how the term 'reproductive racism' emerged, by drawing together all these different contradictions ... this was my first article on the subject, but I see it as part of a body of work that I will develop further, and I hope other researchers and activists take the analysis further too.

JL: It's really useful. It relates to Sara Farris's work on 'femonationalism' too in some ways.[2]

SS: Yes, Sara Farris's work on how the far right co-opts feminism and uses 'the name of women's rights' to push very repressive agendas is so important and was crucial in helping me to understand these dynamics.

JL: You also emphasise how we need to move beyond solely using a language of intersectionality, and to ask: when is this language useful, and when isn't it? In that article you write that whilst it is 'important for providing the language to articulate how different axes of oppression exist and overlap beyond single-issue politics, the theory falls short of providing the tools to show us why these oppressions exist and how they are reproduced in a late capitalism marked by multiple crises in neoliberalism and in democracy itself.'[3]

SS: I think the language of intersectionality is useful in many ways. As a theory that shows how overlapping systems of oppression interact in the life of an individual, it is crucial; and it is hugely helpful in getting people to understand how race, gender, sexuality and different forms of oppression intersect. But I think there are limits to the term, which relate to the legal framework in which Crenshaw coined it. Intersectionality does not reckon with or challenge the wider system of capitalism in which these oppressions are reproduced and sustained. That is where I feel like the theory can be stretched. We need to push it further, to help us understand how race, class and gender are produced and relational to each other, not separate entities that only intersect in an individual's life, but actually are co-dependent on each other to create an overall system.

JL: Yes, so we need to understand intersectional dynamics in relation to the historical conjuncture, and the different dynamics of capitalism happening at that moment ...

SS: That's right. Something that I find really interesting is how, if you look at the history of Black feminism going back to the 1970s and 1980s – even before the term 'intersectionality' itself was coined – women have always been looking for ways to articulate how race, class and gender intersect. It goes by the name of intersectionality now, but as far back as 1949, Claudia Jones was using the term 'triple oppression'. So intersectionality is not a discrete term, but it should be seen in conversation with the longue durée of women attempting to name their experiences.

JL: Your work also shows how racism and anti-LGBT policies and narratives in Hungary, Poland and beyond are intimately interconnected. Do you think there needs to be a wider understanding of this? How do you think campaigning against it is progressing, and can progress further?

SS: This is a subject that's really important to me. I think it's often neglected. Much more attention needs to be paid to the fact that rights for LGBT people are being rolled back in many places across the world. We've seen attacks on trans rights in Hungary, for instance, where a law was passed that made it impossible for trans people to legally change their gender. This politics went hand-in-hand with attacks on the queer community as a whole. And I want to really show how attacks on trans and LGBT rights, attacks on feminists, attacks on migrants and refugees are all profoundly interlinked. What drives these attacks is the desire to erode the right to self-determination and bodily autonomy and more work needs to be done on this subject. I think it's one of the most urgent issues of our time, really. And in terms of campaigning, I think we need more solidarity between, for instance, trans people, the queer community and feminists, because often the issues that we're fighting against – rollbacks on reproductive rights, gender-based violence, attacks on LGBT rights, or nativist politics – impact all of us. A real priority of my work is to show how these issues are interlinked and therefore our solidarity must be too.

JL: You work for the Institute of Race Relations, which has just celebrated its fiftieth anniversary as a UK anti-racist educational charity and 'think tank'. What's your experience of working for the IRR, and the challenges of doing that work in this climate?

SS: I came to the Institute of Race Relations just over four years ago now, and the time has flown by. It's been an absolutely amazing experience. By working here, I have gained a political education from my colleagues who have been key anti-racist and anti-fascist activists. In many ways it's a very unique and special workplace. We make the time to *read*, to learn from each other and from communities around us to inform our struggle for racial justice. It has been wonderful! I have learnt so much from my colleagues – Liz Fekete, Jenny Bourne, Hazel Waters, Anya Edmond-Pettitt, Liam Shrivastava, Jessica Perera and Frances Webber (and I met the founder A. Sivanandan before he passed away).

I work closely with Jenny and Hazel, the joint editors of the journal *Race & Class*, which is our quarterly journal on racism, empire and globalisation. Being able to read submissions and to work closely and collaboratively with authors around the world has been wonderful. I also co-ordinate our fortnightly news service, IRR News, and conduct my own research on anti-racist feminism. That's one of the reasons why I really love this job: because there's lots of different roles, and we all work in a very collaborative and collective way, always helping each other to grow personally and politically, and to think about how we can take the IRR's work into the future too.

As you mentioned, the IRR is celebrating our fiftieth anniversary this year. We're doing lots of exciting interventions throughout the year, both to tell the history of the IRR and its very unique origin story,[4] but also to be very 'forward-facing' in these critical times, when anti-racism is under threat. At a time of increased authoritarianism, racism is becoming more pronounced. Meanwhile, our government is denying the existence of institutional racism. These are some of the key challenges we face. But at the same time, we're seeing an incredible anti-racist movement coming to the fore. A key part of the work of the IRR is always learning from activists and amplifying their voices and making sure we're always guided by their work. So it's a very creative and collaborative process and it's really exciting to be involved with the Institute at this time.

JL: Can you tell us something about your background and how it shaped your anti-racist feminist politics?

SS: Lots of different things shaped my politics growing up. I've learnt a lot from my family in Manchester and Pakistan, from my grandmothers, parents, aunts and siblings, many of whom have always been involved with community work. One of the key moments for me was during my final year of university when I was able to visit Palestine as part of an educational program called FFIPP. It was a six-week trip that aimed to show students from around the world what life is like in the West Bank, so that when we returned home we could confidently engage with activism with a knowledge of what is happening on the ground. In the West Bank we were able to travel around, to see what an occupation looks like, and to hear from people on the ground – to learn from everyday people's resistance. We went to visit the Freedom Theatre in Jenin; they use theatre as a form of resistance. We went to different refugee camps, where I spoke to lots of people, and was sobered to realise just how *permanent* refugee camps are when there's no prospect of a return.

That was one of the most formative experiences of my life ... that was the point when I made a commitment to dedicating myself to struggling against injustice in some small way. From then on, I've been involved with a range of anti-racist campaigns and groups. I know I've been very lucky to be able to work at the Institute of Race Relations, which helped everything really come together for me.

JL: You have said that as 'our current moment often feels like a moment of crisis – state racism permeates all aspects of life for many, the rhetoric of the far-right has become normalised by the mainstream, solidarity can feel tenuous in the face of a neoliberalism that atomises and divides', we might look to past examples of anti-racist feminism instead. What examples do you look to?

SS: Learning about an anti-racist feminist history in the UK has been pivotal to my understanding of racism in this country, but it's also given me a huge amount of inspiration and made me feel connected to a larger community. Someone who has been really key in my journey is Amrit Wilson, who wrote *Finding a Voice* (Daraja Press, 2018), about the experiences of South Asian Women in Britain in the 1970s and 1980s. Reading her work and discovering that, actually, this is a collective history that belongs to all of us, was really empowering for me. Often as a young activist, you can feel like you're discovering, or resisting, things for the first time. But from people like Amrit, as well as my colleagues at the IRR, I learned that state violence in all its forms has been resisted by communities for years. For instance, there is as a long legacy of women resisting immigration regimes in this country that we can learn from and draw on. One of the key moments for me was learning about resistance against the so-called 'virginity testing' that South Asian women were subject to in Britain in the 1970s, where women were frequently medically examined on arrival in the country to check they 'really were' virgins and hence bona fide fiancées who should be allowed into the country. It was Awaz, the first Asian women's collective, and OWAAD, the Organization of Women of African and Asian Descent, who came together and organised a really powerful picket at Heathrow Airport, where the community came together to demand an end to this inhumane practice and, eventually, it was stopped. Learning about the history of state violence, but also the histories of resistance, was really important for me. I'm also very interested in thinking about these historical moments in the context of the present day, when sexual abuse continues to be a part of immigration regimes.

There's a wealth of groups and campaigns that I find really inspiring, particularly OWAAD, as well as groups that were involved with OWAAD such as the United Black Women's Action Group (UBWAG), which was based in the Campsbourne Estate in Haringey. UBWAG did a lot of work for the community around education and policing. They went on to become part of the campaign against the Sus law, a section of the 1824 Vagrancy Act which was used to prosecute young Black men before any offence had been committed. Another example is the Grunwick Strike of 1976-8, of course, where a wide cross-section of society came together to support the workers at a northwest London photography processing factory who, led by Jayaben Desai, were striking over sweatshop pay and conditions. I think all these histories of resistance are important to look at in context today because often we're fighting the same or similar struggles. What can we learn from these histories, what can they teach us, how can they help us in the present day? That's what I'm really interested in.

JL: You have written of how both the reissue of Amrit Wilson's book *Finding a Voice* and the reissue of Beverly Bryan, Stella Dadzie and Suzanne Scafe's *Heart of the Race* have been 'catalysts for the following generations'.[5]

SS: Yes. It's really interesting seeing the very creative ways that young people are using these histories to respond to present day issues. There have been oral history projects, podcasts and radio shows that draw on this history and bring it right up to the present. For instance, a grassroots oral history project in East London called 'Fighting Sus!' excavated the history and impact of the Sus law, and drew continuities from this history to present day policing. They created a zine, poetry and learning resources for an anti-racist curriculum.[6] On a broader level, it's exciting to see activism coming more to the fore now, often built on the same principles articulated in these books.

JL: Can you given some specific examples?

SS: We're seeing a return of community resistance. The feminist direct action group Sisters Uncut have done incredible work for many years around sexual violence and the violence of austerity. In response to the killing of Sarah Everard, they launched CopWatch intervention and training groups across the country that give communities the skills to intervene. Another example is Kids of Colour in Manchester, a youth group in Manchester that creates a space for young people to challenge racism.

JL: A lot of this activity is fuelled by the new interest in and enthusiasm for abolitionist feminism …

SS: Yeah, definitely. Abolition – which, for me, is about building as much as it is about undoing structures of violence – has very much come to the fore now. But the principles of abolition have been here for a really long time, they just didn't use the term 'abolition'.

And actually, if we go back to Amrit Wilson's book, or *Heart of the Race*, you can see the same principles of abolitionism in the *words* of those books as well. Awaz was calling for an end to immigration controls, OWAAD was calling for an end to police brutality, and both groups were involved in building community-led alternatives to give people the tools to create their own structures of community care, and to deal with harm and violence. They may not have used the term 'abolition', but they were putting into practice the principles of abolition today – of abolishing structures of violence, but also building alternatives. So I see a continuity between the past and the present here.

JL: Are you directly involved in any campaigns yourself?

SS: Over the years I've been involved with refugee and migrant solidarity campaigns, doing behind the scenes case work for people in detention centres facing deportation. It is difficult work. I'm continually in awe of activists who are at the coalface doing this work on a daily basis. That work is so crucial and so important.

JL: Yes, there are lot unsung heroes out there doing everyday crucial case work.

SS: Yeah, completely. Just in the past few months, I've been so inspired by the work of activists who are literally putting their bodies on the line: lying down in front of immigration vans attempting to deport people and saying, 'No, this isn't happening'. We've seen inspiring scenes in Peckham, Dalston, Manchester and Glasgow. Communities are coming out and saying, 'No, you can't deport our neighbours and our friends'. That's solidarity in practice. It's really brave.

JL: What do you think the challenges are of doing anti-racist feminist activism in the current climate?

SS: Broadly speaking, there's a push to the right, which means that feminists and anti-racists have been demonised and targeted.

We've also got bills such as the Policing, Crime, Sentencing and Courts Act and the Nationality and Borders Act – all these different types of legislation that are making the work of activists harder, particularly with the way that protests are being criminalised. These are some of the key challenges. I also think the difficulties of forging unity is a key issue for feminists today. Trying to forge a meaningful solidarity that brings us together is the hard work of activism, particularly if there are splits within the movement.

JL: What about transnational connections? You talked about going to Palestine, which is a very transnational experience of solidarity. Do you see good examples of feminist transnational activism happening now that you're involved with, inspired by or connected to?

SS: That's a really good question. Transnational solidarity is so important. One example that stands out for me happened a few years ago in Verona in response to the ultra-conservative World Congress of Families, which brought a global network of anti-abortion, anti-LGBT and anti-feminist activists to the region. In response, feminists from around the world travelled there to put on an incredible protest, helping to create a resistance movement to combat the messaging that was being put out there. That's one vivid example of transnational feminists coming together, and such work is so important right now because attacks on reproductive rights and LGBT rights are happening on a transnational level, and we really need to be learning from each other to understand what's going on in different geographical contexts.

Whilst the IRR is a UK-based educational charity, we have lots of very strong connections with different groups and organisations around the world, both through our editorial board and our council. In the US we're close to Barbara Ransby, who's part of the *Movement for Black Lives*, and is coming to speak in an IRR50 conference we're putting on in October, along with human rights lawyer and abolitionist activist Derecka Purnell. There's the *Africa World Now* podcast which we work with, which is based in America with a global perspective. We also have connections with groups across Europe, such as *Reach Out* in Berlin who monitor racial violence and the *Never Again* association in Poland. These are just a few examples, but we're always trying to build more on those connections and to find ways to support each other.

JL: What kind of actors do you think are inspiring the generation younger than you at the moment?

SS: The abolitionist movement is really inspiring for a lot of people right now. This is partly because abolitionists are saying that we're not going to look at things in silos as separate issues, but that actually we need to think about these issues *together*. We need to try get to the root causes of violence to understand all the different types and forms of violence that are in that are impacting communities. This holistic approach is really crucial. The abolitionist movement isn't just looking at policing, but is looking at immigration, domestic violence, education, mental health provision. In particular, the anti-racist education movement in the UK, when it links to abolition, has been really powerful. In the past year, for instance, we've seen large mobilisations following revelations about Child Q, the young girl who was strip-searched by police at her school.[7] I think that was pivotal. It mobilised a lot of young people and got them involved in activism.

JL: What feminist work would you like to see more of in *Race & Class*?

SS: *Race & Class* covers racism, empire and globalisation, and really the journal is a home for scholar-activists – those are the kind of people who usually write for us. So it covers a huge amount of topics. I'm always excited to see feminist scholarship coming into the journal as well, and you can't separate issues of race and class from gender.

We've published lots of different work over the past years, but one piece that really stands out for me was an article about the experiences of women in detention centres, based on interviews, by Victoria Canning.[8] Going ahead, I really want to see even more cutting-edge global feminist research. I want to read more on the experiences of colonialism and imperialism across the world, and the particular experiences of indigenous women, for instance, in Latin America, where extractive processes are destroying the land. What impact does that have on communities, and how are these processes used to fuel capitalism on a larger scale? It's a problem we've seen in lots of different places, such as Kashmir, where a lot of foreign companies are going into the region and destroying livelihoods and leaving communities shattered.

JL: So you'd like to see more work on how extractivism and environmentalism are connected to race, class and gender?

SS: Definitely. These are huge issues that are absolutely urgent in the present day, so yeah, we need to do more work on that.

JL: And what are you working on in your feminist work at present?

SS: One of the key areas I'm looking at is the 'great replacement theory': the far right's conspiracy theory, which rests on the notion of populations being replaced by immigrants who are coming in, reproducing and changing the demographics of a country. This is an urgent issue because this theory has been one of the central motivations driving mass shooters in recent years, but we've also seen mainstream politicians draw on the conspiracy theory and normalise it. I'm looking at this from a feminist perspective, particularly as the great replacement theory, as well as targeting immigrants, is also targeting women who choose, for instance, to not have children, as well as demonising Muslim women's fertility.

JL: Yes, there's a lot to talk about right now in relation to what you call reproductive racism, isn't there … like how discourses on population are often so nationalistic and blinkered. Anxieties about a single country's falling birth rate often don't take into account either environmental issues or the obvious solution to a falling national birth rate that could be provided through immigration.

That leaves the door open for these extreme, right-wing perinatal policies that we are seeing.

SS: Definitely! And the way migrants and refugees are viewed as a threat to the nation is so embedded in the mainstream, without any context on why people are forced to move in the first place – often due to reasons that the Global North is complicit in, such as war or climate catastrophe. Another aspect of my work that I've been hoping to start soon is mapping out what a reproductive justice movement looks like in the UK. A lot of my work has been inspired by the US movement, and how they see reproductive rights as part of a broader web of issues in relation to racism, class, environmentalism and criminalisation. I'm interested in figuring out what this looks like from a UK perspective, and amplifying the groups on the ground are doing this important work.

JL: That's interesting and links together so many issues. If you expand that lens of reproduction to include issues around childcare and care, there are a lot of contemporary campaigns it connects to, aren't there? Whether schoolkids and food poverty, the unaffordability of nurseries and social care, or access to healthcare. It also makes me think, for instance, of the recent Level Up campaign, lobbying that no pregnant women should be held in prison.

SS: Yes, and that work is so important because often the voices of people who are imprisoned or in detention are often not at the centre of feminist analysis. But I think it's crucial that when we're talking about reproductive justice, the most vulnerable and the most marginalised voices should be centred.

JL: You do educational outreach work, including talking to my students about anti-racist feminist history. How would you like to see those histories becoming more widely known?

SS: It's been a privilege to do that work, I love engaging with young people and telling them about these histories. I remember how much of a 'lightbulb' moment it was for me to find out about anti-racist feminist campaigns, so talking to young people and seeing what they think about these issues has been such a good experience. I've spoken to a range of groups, including homelessness and mental health charities and mutual aid groups. It shows that there's a thirst for this sort of knowledge. It also shows how important it is to make these histories more accessible as well, whether that's through film, or podcasts, or artwork. I'm really hoping we'll see more of that, particularly as younger people increasingly engage with these histories.

JL: There's a bit of a boom in anti-racist history in the UK at the moment since BLM ...

SS: Yes. When I was growing up, anything that engaged with racism felt very US-centric. Whereas more recently, a lot of important work has been emerging which has shown people that actually we have our own very specific anti-racist history and tradition that we can learn from here in the UK. That's been great.

I think the Covid-19 pandemic has also helped to sharpen these histories a little bit because people are starting to see the resonances between community organising today and what was happening in the past. An upsurge of mutual aid organisations and forms of community activism sprung up when the pandemic hit, including community food banks; sex workers' collective hardship funds; and groups who were distributing masks when where there was no PPE.

Another aspect of my work has looked at the continuity between Black self-help groups which emerged from the 1960s onwards, which still aren't often spoken about really very much – like, for instance, the supplementary schools movement, women's movements, community bookshops and police monitoring organisations. This is a hugely rich history that's often marginalised. But during the pandemic, as mutual aid became more important, people started drawing from these more radical histories as well. I wrote an article for IRR News about mutual aid and the tradition of Black self-help to illustrate these connections and to invite groups to think about links between the past and the present.[9] Then I did a talk on this issue with a few different community groups who came together to discuss mutual aid. There were quite varied perspectives; some people hadn't really thought about this long history of resistance, but others had.

There have also been a few art exhibitions that have been amazing in recent years, such as Stafford Scott's 2021 exhibition *War Inna Babylon* at the ICA on UK anti-racist history.[10] This showed the history of many of these grassroots groups that were springing up. Then there's the 'Grunwick at 40' events organised by Sujata Aurora.[11] She co-created a really beautiful mural that commemorates the Grunwick strike with the local community in northwest London. That's another example of the creative ways that these histories are being made more visible. What I really like about murals is how they change the public space – someone who has no idea about this history could might walk past the mural and it could suddenly spark their interest. I do think there's a lot more exciting projects to be done to make this history more accessible, particularly through film, which is such a powerful medium to tell these stories.

JL: And what film would you like to see being made?

SS: I would love to see a film made about OWAAD, especially drawing on interviews with people who've been involved with the campaign, getting them to tell their story.

NOTES

1   Sophia Siddiqui, 'Racing the nation: towards a theory of reproductive racism' in *Race & Class*, Vol. 63, No. 2, 2021.
2   Sara Farris, *In the name of women's rights: The rise of femonationalism*, Duke University Press, 2017.
3   Siddiqui 2021, *op. cit.,* p20.
4   To find out about the transformation of the IRR in 1972, led by its staff, radical academics and Black activists, read A. Sivanandan, 'Race and resistance: the IRR story', *Race & Class*, Vol. 50, No. 2, pp1-30.
5   Sophia Siddiqui, 'Anti-racist feminism: engaging with the past' in *Race & Class*, Vol. 61, No. 2, pp96-104.
6   www.fightingsus.org.uk.
7   Caroline Davies, 'Child Q: four Met police officers facing investigation over strip search', www.theguardian.com/uk-news/2022/jun/15/

child-q-four-met-police-officers-facing-investigation-over-strip-search, 15 June 2022.

8   Victoria Canning, 'Degradation by Design: Women and Asylum policy in Northern Europe', *Race &Class*, Vol. 61, No. 1, 2019, pp46-63.

9   Sophia Siddiqui, 'We starved but we shared', www.irr.org.uk/article/we-starved-but-we-shared, 7 May 2020.

10 www.ica.art/exhibitions/war-inna-babylon.

11 www.grunwick40.wordpress.com.

Acknowledgements

Just as with the interview project itself, I am bound to miss lots of people out through the impossible task of acknowledging all the sources of help and contribution. Nevertheless!

First and foremost, many thanks to all my interviewees for their time, attention and patience. I am very grateful.

The majority of these interviews were published in *Soundings: A Journal of Politics and Culture*, and I am extremely grateful to all the editorial collective, past and present, for their unfailing encouragement of all these interviews. Particularly large thanks go to Sally Davison, whose well-honed editorial eye vastly improved many of these texts. Thanks also to Ali Rattansi, Catherine Rottenberg and Dave Featherstone for suggesting questions for Nancy Fraser, Wendy Brown and Hilary Wainwright respectively; and to Alison Winch for co-organising the two roundtable events with me which connect to this project.

Aside from Soundings, two interviews were published in *European Journal of Cultural Studies*. Many thanks to my co-editors there for their enthusiasm for the pieces, and to Jilly Kay for further astute editing suggestions. Thanks to Sage and Lawrence Wishart for permission to reproduce the articles.

The transcriptions that I didn't do were conducted by Gabriel Bristow and Hannah Curran-Troop: many thanks to both for doing a great job and for all the insightful comments along the way. I am grateful to both the Sociology Department and the Gender and Sexualities Research Centre at City, University of London for help with funding those transcriptions, as well as for providing me with some wonderful colleagues.

Thanks to all the team at Lawrence Wishart for endless patience/ effectively containing their frustration as I deferred the deadline once again, as well as for their very helpful constructive engagement with the book.

I am very grateful to Roshi Naidoo, Catherine Rottenberg, Sylvia Walby and Jumanah Younis for their helpful, challenging and encouraging feedback on the introduction.

Thanks to the various support structures that keep me afloat, including; The Coven, Friday Club Reunited, the Care Collective, all my E17/E10 walking and talking companions, my extended family and friends and several of my interviewees. You know who you are.

And finally, big thanks to Estelle du Boulay, Emma-Jane Berridge, Ros Gill, Roshi Naidoo, Jeremy Gilbert, Robin and Isla.

Index